t
14.11.07

Thanks to Linda and the girls.
Thanks to Fred, Mum, Ollie and Paddy.

Devolution and Identity

Edited by

JOHN WILSON and KARYN STAPLETON
University of Ulster, Jordanstown, Northern Ireland

ASHGATE

Published by
Ashgate Publishing Limited
Gower House
Croft Road
Aldershot
Hampshire GU11 3HR
England

Ashgate Publishing Company
Suite 420
101 Cherry Street
Burlington, VT 05401-4405
USA

Ashgate website: http://www.ashgate.com

British Library Cataloguing in Publication Data
Devolution and identity
   1.Ethnicity - Great Britain 2.Decentralization in
   government - Great Britain 3.Ethnicity - Northern Ireland
   4.Unionism (Irish politics) 5.Nationalism - Wales
   6.Nationalism - Scotland 7.Great Britain - Politics and
   government - 1945- 8.Northern Ireland - Politics and
   government 9.Wales - Politics and government 10.Scotland -
   Politics and government
   I.Wilson, John II.Stapleton, Karyn
   305.8'00941

Library of Congress Cataloging-in-Publication Data
Devolution and identity / edited by John Wilson and Karyn Stapleton.
     p. cm.
   Includes bibliographical references and index.
   ISBN-13: 978-0-7546-4479-8
   ISBN-10: 0-7546-4479-0
   1. Regionalism--Great Britain. 2. Nationalism--Great Britain. 3. Decentralization in government--Great Britain. 4. European Union--Great Britain. I. Wilson, John. II. Stapleton, Karyn.

   JN297.R44D48 2006
   320.941--dc22

2006021136

ISBN-13: 978 0 7546 4479 8
ISBN-10: 0 7546 4479 0

Printed and bound in Great Britain by MPG Books Ltd. Bodmin, Cornwall.

Contents

Notes on Contributors

Jackie Abell is a Social Psychologist at Lancaster University. Her current research interests include the examination of nationhood in political and media debates, the construction of local and national community and belonging, and football support.

Arthur Aughey is Professor of Politics at the University of Ulster. He has published widely on Northern Ireland politics, British Conservatism and constitutional change in the United Kingdom. Recent publications include *Nationalism Devolution and the Challenge to the United Kingdom State* and *Northern Ireland Politics: After the Belfast Agreement*. He has examined the diverse elements of the contemporary English Question in R. Hazell (ed.) *The English Question* and his own book *The Politics of Englishness* will be published by MUP in 2007. He is also writing jointly with John Oakland, a major text on *Irish Civilisation*, to be published in 2008.

Carol-Ann Barnes is a Doctoral Student at the University of Ulster. Her research interest lies in memory studies with specific reference to commemorative practice as a hybrid of professional history and popular memory. She is currently researching state sponsored commemorations in Northern Ireland in the early 1950s.

Hywel Bishop is Research Assistant on a 5-year programme on 'Language and Global Communication' at Cardiff University, funded by the Leverhulme Trust. His research interests are in semiotics and discourse analysis, cultural theory, and media and political discourses, especially those relating to issues of migration, labour and resistance movements.

Dominic Bryan is Director of the Institute of Irish Studies at Queen's University, Belfast, Chair of Democratic Dialogue, Ireland's first Think-Tank, and has worked with the Northern Ireland Human Rights Commission and the Community Relations Council. Dominic is an anthropologist researching political rituals, public space and identity in Northern Ireland. His book *Orange Parades: The Politics of Ritual Tradition and Control* used theories of rituals to examine parades organised by the Orange Order in Ireland. Dominic also works on issues around public order policing, human rights, ethnic politics and sectarianism and has done comparative work in South Africa and the US.

Susan Condor is a Social Psychologist at Lancaster University. Her research focuses on everyday understandings of the social and political world. Specific interests include the role of historiography in constructions of social identity and political legitimacy; national consciousness and everyday political philosophy in England; and constructions of the public in political rhetoric.

Nikolas Coupland is Professor and Research Director of the Cardiff University Centre for Language and Communication Research. He co-edits the *Journal of Sociolinguistics* and the book series, *Oxford Studies in Sociolinguistics*. He is currently directing a 5-year project on 'Welsh Language and Welsh Identity under Globalisation' as part of a larger programme funded by the Leverhulme Trust, titled 'Language and Global Communication'.

Richard Fitzgerald gained his degree and PhD from Bangor University, and has lectured at Cardiff University and Brunel University. He is currently Lecturer in Communication and Language at the University of Queensland, Australia. He has published widely in the areas of media interaction; most notably radio discourse, and the application and development of the methodologies of Membership Categorisation Analysis, Conversation Analysis, and Discourse Analysis for exploring the organisation of cultural knowledge oriented to in talk.

William Housley is a Lecturer in Sociology at Cardiff School of Social Sciences and Deputy Director of the Research and Graduate School in the Social Sciences, Cardiff University. He has published numerous articles on interaction in organisations, political communication and cultural identity. He is the co-author (with Paul Atkinson) of *Interactionism* (2003) part of the BSA 'New Horizons in Sociology' millenial series, co-editor (with Stephen Hester) of *Language, Interaction and National Identity* (2001) and author of *Interaction in Multidisciplinary Teams* (2002). He is currently working on the role of culture in the regeneration of post-industrial communities, citizen participation within post-devolution Wales and new frontiers in interactionist analysis and theory.

David Irwin is Head of the Department of Humanities at ITT Dublin. His research interests focus on Michel Foucault's discourse of power and its applications and relevance to the study of geo-political identity. In particular, his recent papers have focused on Foucaultian interpretations of (the Irish political party) Fianna Fáil's neo-republican discourse of civil society.

Sharon Millar is Associate Professor at the Institute of Language and Communication, University of Southern Denmark in Odense. Her research interests include normative mechanisms in language, metalinguistic awareness, the discursive construction of identity, and computer-mediated communication. She is currently involved in projects on the nature of lingua franca English in corporate email communication in Danish companies; and the dynamics of multilingualism in the European Union.

Gerry Philipsen (PhD, Northwestern University, 1972) is Professor of Communication at the University of Washington. He teaches courses there in cultural codes of communication, communication and conflict, and communication in small groups. He is the author of *Speaking Culturally: Explorations in Social*

Communication and several versions of an empirically grounded theory of communication known as Speech Codes Theory, among other publications. Presently he is working on multiple case studies of the speaking of the discourse of difference in the contemporary US and on disciplinary naming practices in the history of the Communication Studies discipline in the US.

Carmel Roulston is Senior Lecturer in Politics and Head of School of Economics and Politics at the University of Ulster. She is a member of the Management Committee of the Women into Politics Project and an Associate of the University of Ulster/ United Nations University International Conflict Research Centre. She has edited (with Celia Davies) *Gender, Democracy and Inclusion in Northern Ireland*. Her major research interest is women in conflict resolution and post-conflict transitions. She has participated in workshops and courses on various aspects of women's roles in conflict and peace processes for, among others, International Alert, the International Centre for Ethnic Studies in Sri Lanka and the University of Ivanovo, Russia. In 2005, she presented papers on Gender and Post-Conflict in Transitional Societies in a short course on *Women's Leadership in Transitional and Post-Conflict Societies* organised by the United Nations University Institute in Amman.

Karyn Stapleton is Research Associate in Discourse Analysis at the University of Ulster. Her main research interest is in Discourse and Identity; and especially in how (socio-)cultural, psychological, and political issues are negotiated and displayed in talk. Most of her recent work has focused on Northern Ireland, and she has a particular interest in Northern Irish Protestant/unionist identities. Her recent publications include papers on gender and nationality; communities of practice; Ulster Scots; and community understandings of devolution in Northern Ireland.

John Wilson is Professor of Communication and Director of the Institute of Ulster Scots Studies at the University of Ulster. His research focuses on the construction of linguistic meaning in varieties of everyday talk, drawing mainly on the fields of Pragmatics, Discourse Analysis, and Sociolinguistics. He is author of *On the Boundaries of Conversation* (1989) and *Politically Speaking* (1990), and he has published papers on a wide range of topics in a variety of major journals. He is presently editing (with Sharon Miller) 'Narrating Europe'; a volume that focuses on everyday talk in a variety of European contexts, and preparing a book on the pragmatics of Presidential language. He is an elected member of the Consultation Board of the International Pragmatic Association, and a member of the Chartered Institute of Public Relations.

Introduction

John Wilson and Karyn Stapleton

Nation-State, Devolution and Identity

Most of us in Northern and Western Europe take the democratic form of national government for granted. We believe the nation-state to be some kind of older historical and normative programme of political organisation. The reality is, however, that the nation-state emerges only directly in the second half of the eighteenth century, being fused out of a range of different processes. Habermas (1987) argues that a major factor here was a shift of communicative structures from a bourgeois public sphere of discussion, which laid the foundation of European democracy, to a populist nationalism. In this process 'the state' becomes aligned with the 'nation'. The state is defined as a sovereign or legal form of state power, while the nation (or the people) refers to a community bound by a common heritage language and culture. In the nation-state the form of government is seen as organised for the benefit of the 'nation', that is the people. As Habermas (2001: 113) puts it:

> Only a national consciousness, crystallised around the notion of a common ancestry, language, and history, only the consciousness of belonging to 'the same' people makes subjects into citizens of a single political community – into members who can feel responsible for one another.

It is this vision of national unity that allows the operation of state power since it becomes seen as a natural component of the sovereignty of the nation itself. And so for many years in the United Kingdom (UK) it has been possible to meld the potentially independent cultures of Wales, Scotland, and Northern Ireland (and at one period the whole of the Island of Ireland) around a unified form of identity, Britishness.

Despite the success of the nation state within Europe there are signs that this historical form of political organisation may be coming under pressure (see Ohmae, 1995). The emergent Eastern states of post communism have been born, often through extreme bloodshed, of a belief not in the nation-state, but rather in the 'nation'. What has been sought are ethnic alliances, founded on some form of historical and cultural legacy, as opposed to a pragmatic political unit which might bind various allegiances under one flag for the perceived benefit of all. Equally, many of the post-colonial states of Africa now struggle within an environment of multiethnic claims to power, with limited opportunities in terms of political, legal or economic power to coalesce around a single vision. And within the borders of the classic nation-states of Europe, and to some extent the USA, a multinational and pluralistic context challenges the *raison d'être* not only of a single concept of Britishness, but of other sub-national concepts such as Scottishness or Welshness.

In this context the programme of devolution set out by the Labour government in 1997 raises a range of interesting issues for both the present and future processes of government within the UK. The potentially far reaching consequences of the move to devolution can be seen in the funding allocated by the Economic and Social Research Council to research addressing the nature and outcomes of devolution. Browsing the list of projects[1] where £4.17 million has been invested, it is interesting to note that they focus, in the main, on questions that generally exclude the 'populace', or more directly, the devolved citizen. The focus is on law, economics, political theory and so on. However, if we return to the quote from Habermas above, the point made is that whatever the political or economic case one might have made for the nation-state, it would not have been enough on its own. The trick was to get the people to see such advantage within a concept of nationalism; that this advantage was for the people, i.e. the 'nation'.

Perhaps surprisingly, the views and opinions of 'the people' involved in the process of devolution have often been taken for granted. The Scots know who they are, the Welsh know who they are, the Northern Irish know who they are; consequently, the devolved 'peoples' are definitionally straightforward. But why should that be the case? Devolution is not a cessation of all power from the centre with the establishment of new states; rather, it is the redistribution of selected responsibilities, with core state power residing in the national, that is, the British, parliament. This alone creates a form of dual identification, Scottish and British, Welsh and British, and Northern Irish and British. However, there is no concept of Northern Irishness that is on a par with Scottishness and Welshness. Indeed, for many Northern Irish unionists, the goal is to remain British; they do not need a second identity. Paradoxically, in the Government of Ireland Act of 1920, they were given the first devolved government of the UK for this very purpose, that is, to ensure that the region of Northern Ireland remained British.

One very real issue for devolution, then, which has not been given significant attention, is what does it mean for the construction and reconstruction of forms of national and sub-national identity? Further, how do devolved peoples cope with a restructuring of the concepts of nation and state? And in a globalised, multicultural context, what is the value of a devolved identity? Indeed, is there even a need for such devolution, given that certain nationalistic claims have always included the devolved regions? These, among others, are the kinds of issues we wish to tackle in this volume. In doing so, we want to draw attention away from the macro contexts of law, economics, and general politics, to the everyday construction of meaning and identity in the complex of options available to the modern citizen. Starting from this general perspective, the chapters deal with a variety of topics; ranging from language policy to the use of symbolic space to individual constructions of identity within the devolved regions. We will return to these topics in more detail below. First, however, we will consider more explicitly the nature and context of devolution in the UK.

---

[1]   http://www.devolution.ac.uk/Research_Projects2.htm.

Devolution and Identity in the United Kingdom

In 1997, the Labour Government began a process of constitutional devolution, which would see the delegation of powers from the central government (Westminster) to regional or national institutions across the UK. Bogdanor (1999) sees devolution as comprising three main aspects: 1. the transfer of power to a subordinate elected body; 2. the transfer of power on a geographical basis; 3. the transfer of functions at present exercised by Parliament. In line with this initiative, and following referenda in Scotland, Wales and Northern Ireland[2] in 1997–1998, devolved administrations were set up in these regions. The Scottish Parliament, the National Assembly for Wales, and the Northern Ireland Assembly were formally established in 1999.[3] The different institutions have varying powers (Sandford, 2002), although certain key issues such as taxation and defence generally remain within the control of the central government.[4]

Devolution necessarily alters the political and constitutional landscape with different financial and governance and legal structures implemented across the regions (see Hazell, 2003). However, as indicated above, what is less clear is the impact of such constitutional transformations on issues of personal and group identity within and across the respective regions. Opinion is divided as to whether the introduction of devolution signals the beginning of the break up of the UK (see Curtice and Seyd, 2001, Mitchell, 2000, Paterson, 2002, Robbins, 2001). Theoretically, the notion of separate parliaments/assemblies might be expected to intensify feelings of (ethno-)national distinctiveness and/or nationalism, which could ultimately lead to a disintegration of the Union. On the other hand, devolution could work to bolster the Union by providing a space within which different political aspirations can be articulated (Hazell, 2003). Examples of this are explored in the present volume. For example, Condor and Abell (Chapter 2) discuss differing orientations to regional and national governance in Scotland and England, and how these constructions relate to personal identity. In Chapter 3, Coupland and Bishop examine the way in which the Welsh language movement is constructed around issues of 'community' and 'identity' in post-devolution Wales. In a different vein, Irwin (Chapter 10) looks at the British National Party, and concepts of exclusive nationalism within the devolved context.

Whatever the ultimate outcomes, the concept and process of devolution clearly have implications for issues of citizenship, nationality and national identity within the UK. Indeed, in this respect, the working out of devolution can be seen to encapsulate a number of processes which are increasingly and universally salient; e.g. globalism, localism, (ethno-)nationalism, exclusion and identity rights. As discussed above, we have recently witnessed the emergence of new forms of government and political

---

[2]   Because devolution in Northern Ireland was entwined with the Belfast (peace) Agreement, which entailed changes to the Republic of Ireland's constitution, a referendum on the Agreement was also held in the Republic.

[3]   The Greater London Assembly was also established in 1999, and a number of further regional assemblies are planned throughout England.

[4]   The Scottish Parliament, alone among the new institutions, has minor tax-raising powers.

administration; and the consequent 'diminishing' of the nation-state as a marker of civic/ethnic boundaries (see Cable, 1994). In this context, the conventional model of bounded and integral nation-states is challenged by the dual forces of globalisation and deterritorialisation, on the one hand, and regionalism and devolution of government powers, on the other. These forces function in a dialectic, however, such that national alignments and demarcations are simultaneously eroded and strengthened, in different ways (see e.g. Bauman, 1998, Jenkins and Sofos, 1996). This process may be seen, for example, in Chapter 7 of this volume, in which Barnes and Aughey discuss the construction of 'fantasy echoes' of Britishness and the attempt to create sameness and identity with the past, within a changing contemporary context.

The growth of supranational administrations such as the European Union (EU), then, diminishes the political power of individual nation-states, while simultaneously fostering a diversity of regional identities and national collectives (Jenkins and Sofos, 1996). In fact, as a number of commentators have pointed out, the very nature of globalisation/supranationalism can itself prompt a search for identity, and hence, the (re)emergence and strengthening of tribal-type ethnic bonds (see Giddens, 1991, Ignatieff, 1994). Moreover, in contexts such as the EU (and the UK), constitutional commitments to cultural diversity mean that these cultures can be granted varying status and rights within the (supra)national order. This facilitates the assertion of cultural minority rights in a way that was not possible within the traditional order of the nation-state, and further, foregrounds the issue of identity rights and recognition for minority groupings *within* national/regional boundaries (Benhabib, 2002, Stapleton and Wilson, 2004a).

In the UK context, post-devolution, we can see the global/local dialectic at work in the forces of progressive regional autonomy alongside increasingly centralised civic structures. A number of writers have observed that this dialectic opens up a complex of new identity possibilities (see e.g. McCall, 2002a, McCrone, 2002). At the very least, UK citizens have the dual identities of (ethno-)nationality (English, Scottish, Welsh or Northern Irish)[5] and a common state-based 'British' identity.[6] Moreover, because devolution intensifies the distinction between national/territorial and state structures, we might expect a consequent decoupling of cultural and civic identities. As mentioned above, much debate surrounds the extent to which the British state is being undermined, or diluted, by the devolution process (e.g. Curtice and Seyd, 2001), and such issues are clearly bound up with concepts and perceptions of identity and citizenship within the UK. Some writers, such as McCall (2002a), claim that devolution potentially bolsters 'exclusivist "ethno-national" identities ... at the expense of a "civic" British identity' (McCall, 2002a: 158). This theory is supported by some recently available research which suggests that, in its first few years, devolution

---

[5]   The Northern Irish identity is less straightforward as an ethno-national category within the UK context, since many of its (nationalist) citizens reject any association with the UK, preferring instead to describe themselves simply as 'Irish'.

[6]   Of course this conceptualisation does not engage with the further complexities of ethnicity/race within these categories (For a useful discussion of these issues, see McCrone, 2002).

has *not* strengthened feelings of Britishness, but has somewhat strengthened national identities in England, Scotland and Wales (Jeffery, 2004). On the other hand, this same research, collated by Jeffery, highlights the usage of multiple identities among UK citizens, and shows little evidence for an actual rejection or deterioration of Britishness as an identity category (see also Rosie *et al.*, 2004).

Devolution does not only have implications for (ethno-)national and civic identities. Ideological shifts and institutional/administrative changes are likely to influence (in different ways) the positioning of minority identity groupings, both indigenous and migrant, within the different jurisdictions (see e.g. McCrone, 2002, Stapleton and Wilson, 2004a). Some identity developments of this sort are publicly articulated and are visibly and formally linked to constitutional change. For example, in this volume, Roulston (Chapter 8) discusses the ways in which women's political representation has developed across the UK regions pre- and post-devolution, while Bryan (Chapter 6) looks at the struggle over symbolic emblems (in particular national flags) in post-devolution Northern Ireland. On the other hand, some identity processes, which are less explicitly linked to changes in formal political structures, may nonetheless be considered as emergent within this socio-political context. For example, Wilson and Stapleton (Chapter 1) discuss the current prominence of, and debate over, the Ulster Scots identity in Northern Ireland in relation to issues such as institutional support afforded under the Belfast Agreement[7], and the identity questions posed by progressive devolution across the UK. It is also worth noting that the particularities of regional/national contexts will shape experiences of devolution, and hence the extent to which newly available identity frameworks are embraced or rejected (Wilson and Stapleton, 2006).

The Present Volume: Aims and Overview

As stated at the outset, this volume addresses issues and questions of 'lived identity' under devolution. This approach should be distinguished from, on the one hand, macro-level analyses of the political, economic, legal and societal aspects of devolution (e.g. Bogdanor, 2001, Hazell, 2003, Pilkington, 2002) and, on the other, quantitative, or survey-based, studies of devolution and identity (e.g. Curtice and Heath, 2000, Jeffery, 2004). Here, we are centrally concerned with the ways in which identities are shaped and negotiated within the changing socio-political landscape(s). The volume as a whole is situated within a broadly qualitative framework, in which we see cultural, social, political and discursive structures as simultaneously constructing and being constructed by individual and group subjectivities (for a general treatment of these issues, see Barker and Galasinski, 2001). Hence all of the chapters focus, in different ways, on the newly available structures and spaces for identity realignment and/or on the negotiation and articulation of identities within these structures and spaces.

---

7   Throughout the volume, this is referred to as, variously, the Belfast Agreement, the Good Friday Agreement, the Peace Agreement, the Multi-Party Agreement or, simply, the Agreement'.

The volume draws together a range of different social science and humanities perspectives on these issues, with contributors from fields such as Politics, Linguistics, Psychology, and Communication. Crucially, given the emergent nature of this topic, we have *not* attempted to impose a particular, or 'unitary', research agenda/paradigm on the chapters; the authors were asked to address the core questions and issues relatively independently from within their own theoretical and methodological frameworks. Similarly, we have not tried to foreclose on particular findings or to draw 'overall' or definitive conclusions from the analyses (such as, for example, the extent to which devolution has strengthened or weakened attachment to particular identity categories – answers to which would almost inevitably be inconclusive and context-dependent). Rather, our primary aim, in compiling this volume, was to generate different perspectives and approaches to the lived experience of devolution; thereby providing new insights and understandings, while, at the same time, raising further questions and potential research synergies, within an open-ended format. This approach is further consolidated in the *Epilogue*, in which Gerry Philipsen reflects, from an American perspective, on the diversity of issues raised in the collection, which, in themselves, cause him to consider fresh queries, reflections and avenues for research.

The volume contains theoretical and empirical analyses from across the devolved regions of the UK. However, just as they do not address a unitary set of questions, the chapters do not follow a 'neat' inter-regional comparative framework. Rather, as suggested above, they address a range of emergent thematics (e.g. language, marketing, art, gender, parliamentary debates), which are heightened, or thrown into relief, by the devolution process. Indeed we believe that it is important *not* to regionalise these themes in any definitive manner, as any given outworking of an issue has a general and shared significance across the regions, while simultaneously reflecting the particularities of the context within which it takes place. Nonetheless, a number of the contributions show interesting cross-referring themes and areas of interface. Hence, while we have not formally divided the book into sections, we have facilitated these natural interfaces by grouping the chapters into three clusters, loosely organised as: (a) language and discourse; (b) the symbolic and artefactual; and (c) specific social projects.

Language and Discourse

This cluster comprises *Chapters 1–3*. In each of the chapters, outlined in more detail below, there is a central concern with language/discourse and how this is deployed in the realignment of 'devolved' identities and subjectivities. In *Chapters 1* and *3*, the focus is on the ways in which social actors construct and negotiate their own identities, and indeed that of their wider cultural/national groups, with an emphasis on everyday sense-making and on the construction and delineation of particular identity categories. *Chapter 2*, on the other hand, discusses how language and language-related issues are themselves being conceptually and discursively reformulated in relation to broader alignments of national, cultural and minority identities.

In *Chapter 1*, John Wilson and Karyn Stapleton discuss the growth of Ulster Scots as an identity category among Protestants/unionists in Northern Ireland. They consider the ways in which devolution both motivates and facilitates the expression of this identity. Then, drawing on empirical discursive data, they examine the configuration of Ulster Scots as a personal identity category, as well as its relationship to conceptions of Britishness (and other ethno-national categories) in the post-devolution context. This analysis highlights two issues central to any consideration of devolution and identity: changing relationships between Britishness and regional/(ethno-)national identities and the emergence and articulation of 'new' and/or minority identities, in the post-devolution context.

In *Chapter 2*, Nikolas Coupland and Hywel Bishop consider how the post-devolution period in Wales has seen the National Assembly for Wales take several significant new funding initiatives regarding what tends to be called 'the language' (Welsh), linked to new policies relating to 'heartland communities' (those where the Welsh language is deemed to be, still, a 'living, community language'). The chapter focuses on the political and para-political discourses that make up the ideological climate in which language and community are debated. The authors develop critical analyses of key passages from governmental and non-governmental sources, with the aim of providing a 'road map' through the complex politics of language and community in post-devolution Wales, set against wider sociolinguistic assumptions about these concepts.

Susan Condor and Jackie Abell (*Chapter 3*) discuss the concept of 'vernacular identity construction' in post-devolution Scotland and England. They reject the social scientific tendency to treat 'national identity' as an analysts' resource, but rather consider the ways in which ordinary social actors themselves construe nationness as a psychological matter of 'identity'. Using interview accounts produced by comparable samples in Scotland and England, they note the tendency for speakers in the two countries to adopt qualitatively different orientations to their nationality as a matter of identity. They note the correspondence of these lay understandings with formal academic theories of national identity developed by writers in Scotland and in England. From their analysis, they also highlight the need to be wary of attempts to equate the constructs of 'national identity' either with attitudes towards the Union, or with the construct of 'imagined community'.

The Symbolic and Artefactual

Returning to the notion that identities are structured and articulated within broader cultural and socio-political realms, we have grouped *Chapters 4–7* together on the basis that they all deal with aspects of the symbolic and artefactual context of devolution. *Chapter 4*, like the chapters discussed above, is based on analysis of actual discourse (in this case, interviews and the resulting narratives). We have included it in this section, however, on the basis of its subject matter and the remit of its analysis – i.e. the relationship between art and broader issues of culture, nationness and identity. *Chapter 6* deals with a particular discourse artefact, i.e. newspaper 'letters to the editor', and considers how citizens use this public realm to express and construct devolution-related identities and categories. *Chapters 5* and *7* (focusing respectively on flags and public commemorations/exhibitions) both discuss the question of contested symbolism and heritage within post-devolution Northern Ireland, while also considering more general issues around devolution, history and symbolism. We will now outline these chapters in more detail.

In *Chapter 4*, William Housley reports on a study carried out on art and devolution in Wales. It explores practitioners' understandings of 'visual art in Wales' and the notion of 'Welsh art' as national parameters that are both recognised and contested. The chapter analyses examples of artistic narrative as a means of describing the nature of these understandings and the various discourses used by artists in negotiating the relationship between the creative self and wider social, cultural and national boundaries. To this extent, Housley explores the narrative of the creative self in relation to wider discourses of nation. This case study, he argues, has resonance with the study of culture, marginalised collective experience, national renewal and cultural modernisation in Wales, the UK and beyond.

Dominic Bryan, in *Chapter 5*, also explores a particular context of post-devolution culture in his discussion of public symbolism and visual culture in Northern Ireland. Symbols such as flags and parades, play an important – if contentious – role in Northern Irish political and social life. However, the Peace Agreement and the newly devolved institutions offered the possibility for the development of symbolic representations of a new Northern Ireland. Whilst there were some obvious examples of this process, such as a new badge for the police service and a new emblem for the new Assembly, debates over the flying of flags appear as intense as ever. Bryan examines the strategies to resolve disputes over the use of flags and emblems and looks at the attempts by public agencies and institutions to symbolically create a new devolved dispensation. It concludes that contradictory policy approaches derive from conflicting conceptions of the Agreement and of the role and purpose of devolution in Northern Ireland.

In *Chapter 6*, Richard Fitzgerald and William Housley examine the increasing intersection between the discourse of public access media and political representation within post-devolution Wales. This chapter applies the principles of Membership Categorisation Analysis to analyse national identity, categorisation and interaction. Focusing on 'letters-to-the-editor', Fitzgerald and Housley explore the three interrelated issues of public access media interaction, political accountability and the discourse of national identity. They explore the discursive construction of motives mapped onto categories of political and national identity through public access media, within devolved Wales, and their relationship to other layers of social and political organisation. The authors then discuss perceptual shifts in the locus of political and national identity through a consideration of the perceived relationship of post-devolution Wales to both local and wider political and economic spheres (e.g. the UK and Europe).

Carol-Ann Barnes and Arthur Aughey (*Chapter 7*) consider the issue of modern British identity in terms of a 'fantasy echo'. This concept, drawn from Scott (2001) signifies the ambiguity of repetition of something imagined and an imagined repetition. 'Fantasy' discovers relations of identity between past and present; 'echo', on the other hand, tends to undermine the idea of enduring sameness. Political identities need a sense of historic continuity but the echoes of that continuity can be deceptive. Focusing in particular on the commemoration of the 200th anniversary of the Irish Act of Union, Barnes and Aughey discuss current debates about the values, character and shape of contemporary – in particular post-devolution – Britishness, within that interpretative framework, and critically assess the respective influences of fantasy and echo, continuity and change.

Specific Social Projects

The chapters in this group are concerned with the ways in which devolution shapes and/or facilitates the pursuit of particular social projects, ranging from gender representation and politics (*Chapter 8*) to regional marketing (*Chapter 9*) to the exclusivist national politics of the British National Party (*Chapter 10*). In all of these cases, devolution is shown to have impacted upon the form and trajectory of these projects, both through formal, constitutional mechanisms (particularly true for gender issues) and, more intangibly, through the changing social, political and discursive spaces of the post-devolution context.

In *Chapter 8*, Carmel Roulston discusses the impact of devolution on gender issues within the UK regions. Specifically, she examines the relationship between devolution and women's inclusion and representation in mainstream politics in Northern Ireland, Scotland and Wales. The chapter investigates how the programme of devolution in the UK has opened a space for dialogue and deliberation on the symbolic and substantive representation of women in the new political institutions. It explores how contextual factors within the three societies facilitated or delimited the formation of pro-feminist alliances around issues of effective representation of women's diverse needs and values. The chapter concludes by reflecting on the relationship between nationalism and gender identity, with particular reference to Northern Ireland, and on the continuing struggles for gender equality within the three societies.

Sharon Millar (*Chapter 9*) explores identity-making in the context of devolution in the UK and regionalisation in Europe from a marketing/business perspective. She argues that, since processes of localisation occur in a global context, the dimension of local/global may be equally or more apparent than that of regional/national, at least on a macro-level. This argument is explored using the websites of relevant government bodies in Wallonia, Belgium and in Scotland. Her analysis demonstrates the role of global corporate culture in identity-making by state institutions, whereby state institutions are constructed as business organisations; citizens and residents are customers/consumers (and, in Wallonia, stakeholders); and cities, regions, and countries are products in the global marketplace. Devolved and federal powers give local Parliaments a greater freedom to act within these trends, to 'go glocal' in the pursuit of economic and political success.

David Irwin (*Chapter 10*) tackles the seeming antithesis of the modern devolution process and the call for a centralised British state as espoused by the British National Party. While it would have been interesting in itself to reflect on oppositional positions to devolution, Irwin highlights a range of paradoxes and contradictions within the BNP position, most specifically from our perspective, the support of local and regional identities within a British nationalist context. The BNP recognises the multi-ethnic nature of the historical foundation of Britain, but not the multi-ethnic nature of its modern position; hence, their central policy of the repatriation of immigrants. Operating alongside this is, at the same time, a positive recognition of the Scots, Welsh, and Northern Irish positions within Britain. Regional traditions and histories, even regional languages, are to be given their role within a national British state. As Irwin notes, this is an unusual position and one which both pulls for and against devolution at one and the same time. The reality is, as he notes, that the BNP must continually construct and deconstruct world views to force some form of consistency into an inconsistent ideology.

Summary

Through examination of these thematics across the regions, the volume provides insights into a number of issues and questions. The central question is 'How does devolution impact upon individual/group identities; and what can this tell us about nature of the devolution process itself?' Hence, the chapters examine contemporary configurations of both 'national' identities, and 'Britishness' within devolved regions. This focus on identity also reflects the more general relationship between socio-political structures and individual/group identities; and in particular, the processes through which identities are transformed and/or maintained in the context of socio-political change. As indicated above, however, the collection aims to generate different perspectives, debates, and indeed, to raise new questions and avenues for research. Gerry Philipsen's final *Epilogue* reflections are also undertaken very much in this spirit. He conclude with the view that, rather than providing definitive 'answers' to the questions surrounding devolution and identity, this volume provides 'a remarkable resource for posing such questions and for sketching some possible lines along which answers can be anticipated'.

Chapter 1

Identity Categories in Use: Britishness, Devolution and the Ulster Scots Identity in Northern Ireland

John Wilson and Karyn Stapleton

Introduction

The distinction between national/regional and state structures in post-devolution UK has highlighted the existence of ethno-national identities alongside civic citizenship. That is, as well as being 'British', citizens are now arguably more likely to draw upon national or regional (or indeed 'ethnic' or 'cultural') identity categories (e.g. Jeffery, 2004). However, conceptualising what a devolved 'Northern Irish' identity category might mean, let alone its relationship to a sense of Britishness, is far from straightforward. In the first instance, as pointed out by McCrone (2002: 309, 317), the ascription of a British identity in Northern Ireland (NI) is inherently politicised. Moreover, Northern Ireland lacks an agreed national ideology or national identity (Graham, 1998), while those who do define themselves as British (broadly, unionists) have traditionally been seen as endorsing a civic, or state-centred ideology, which left little room for ethno-nationalist expression (Aughey, 1989, 1995, but cf. Finlayson, 1996).

All of this means that not only the British identity, but also the devolution process itself, is distinctive in NI. In this paper, we will discuss one form of 'British' identity expression; i.e. the Ulster Scots identity, which has recently gained prominence in Northern Irish public and political life. We will consider this as an emergent identity category, the expression of which is both facilitated and given impetus by devolution in NI. Then, in the main part of the Chapter, we will consider how, as an emergent identity, the Ulster Scots category is negotiated and constructed by 'grass-roots' citizens, thereby reflecting different aspects of the shifting socio-political context of contemporary NI. The analysis, then, will highlight two issues central to any consideration of devolution and identity: changing relationships between Britishness and regional/(ethno-)national identities and the emergence and articulation of 'new' and/or minority identities, in the post-devolution context.

Devolution and Britishness in Northern Ireland

Northern Irish Britishness

In NI, 'Britishness' itself carries political connotations. Here, as pointed out by McCrone (2002: 317), '"British" is a thoroughly politicised identity largely equated with political unionism'. This category also invokes salient ethno-religious, social and cultural dimensions (including 'the Protestant way of life'), all of which are predicated upon maintenance of the British Union (Racioppi and O'Sullivan See, 2001, Shirlow and McGovern, 1997). That the legitimacy of this union is rejected by a substantial minority of NI citizens (i.e. NI nationalists) further intensifies the unionist imperative to remain British. A British identity in Northern Ireland, then, cannot simply be equated with the state identity held in England, Scotland and Wales, insofar as it is, to a large extent, also constitutive of *ethno-national identity* in the NI context. Hence, the potential decoupling of state and (ethno-)national identities instigated by the devolution process (e.g. McCall, 2002a) raises particularly interesting questions for the British identity in Northern Ireland.

Additionally, NI Britishness/unionism has traditionally been based upon a state-centred ideology of civic citizenship within the UK, in contrast to the more 'ethnic' or 'cultural' conceptions of Irish nationalism (Aughey, 1989, 1995, Miller, 1978). As expressed by Aughey (1989: 18), 'the identity of unionism has little to do with the idea of the nation and everything to do with the idea of the state'. Other writers (e.g. Finlayson, 1996, McCall, 2002a) have argued that there is, in fact, a strong cultural force to Northern Irish unionism/Protestantism. However, it remains the case that, while displaying a strong attachment to NI and to 'the Protestant way of life', Northern Irish unionists have, in the past, shown little evidence of what may be understood as ethno-nationalist sentiment, expressed in cultural or ethnic terms (cf. Stapleton and Wilson, 2004a). Hence NI Britishness/unionism has often been perceived as a 'negative' identity, predicated primarily upon what it is not (Irish, Roman Catholic, nationalist) rather than what it is or could become (McCall, 2002a). However, recent socio-political developments, particularly those wrought by devolution and the peace process, have fundamentally altered the notion of what it means to be British in NI, and have forced a new scrutiny of this very concept (Finlayson, 1999, Mitchell, 2003).

Devolution in Northern Ireland: An Overview

The Belfast Agreement of 1998, which introduced Northern Irish devolution, could not be seen, like the other regional arrangements, as simply transferring constitutional powers to a coherent political entity. Rather, as part of a peace agreement, devolution in Northern Ireland aimed simultaneously to effect conflict resolution *and* constitutional reform (Carmichael, 1999, Hayes and McAllister, 2001, Horowitz, 2002). However, set in a context of socio-historical conflict and contested political structures, and constantly threatened by interparty animosity, the process of Northern Irish devolution has been faltering and unstable. The Northern Ireland Assembly, set up under the Belfast Agreement, has been suspended on four separate occasions since its establishment, and was formally dissolved on 28 April 2003, following its most recent suspension in October 2002.[1] After over three years of attempts to reinstate the political institutions, the British and Irish governments have recently issued an 'ultimatum'-type document setting November 2006 as the final deadline for Northern Ireland's political parties to agree to re-enter government together. Many are sceptical, however, that this deadline will be met.

Socially and culturally, these problems are also apparent. In relation to questions of identity, there was little likelihood that devolution at the global level would engender a unified 'Northern Irish' identity, in the same way that devolution in Scotland or Wales may be expected to intensify 'Scottish' or 'Welsh' identification. In fact, there is an implicit tension between the goals of *cultural diversity*, enshrined in the Belfast Agreement, and of a *common identity*, suggested by the devolution process (see MacGinty and Darby, 2002, Wilson and Stapleton, 2003). High levels of polarisation and division remain in Northern Irish society (see KuusistoArponen, 2001, Shirlow, 2001, 2005, Wilson and Stapleton, 2005, 2006, forthcoming). In fact, there is increasing evidence that sectarianism and community segregation have *intensified* since the beginning of the peace process (Shirlow, 2005), with much of NI society remaining polarised along ethno-national and religious lines. Such polarisation was also highlighted in the most recent elections to the (then suspended) NI Assembly in November 2003, and in the Westminster elections of May 2005, both of which demonstrated significant and increasing polarisation of the electorate, at the expense of the 'middle ground' NI political parties.

Devolution and Cultural Challenges to Britishness in NI

Within post-devolution NI, Britishness, as indicated above, faces a number of particular challenges. All of these, we would argue, have provided an impetus towards cultural reconfiguration and the need to find new modes of identity expression among the Protestant/unionist community.

Firstly, the peace process is seen by many within Northern Ireland (and in particular, by an overwhelming majority of Protestants) as having enhanced – and indeed continuing to enhance – the status of nationalists *vis-à-vis* unionists (*Northern Ireland Life and Times* survey, 2002). This is perceived not only in the political sphere, but perhaps even more strongly in the cultural sphere, where Irish nationalist culture is perceived as an increasingly powerful and ascendant force, both within NI and on the wider world stage (Graham, 1998, Mitchell, 2003, Murray, 2000, Rolston, 1998). The significance of culture as a status marker is intensified by the nature of the Belfast Agreement itself, which, through its

---

[1]   Northern Ireland Assembly website http://www.ni-assembly.gov.uk/.

consociational nature and 'parity of esteem' principles, facilitates the promotion of single-identity politics (Brown and MacGinty, 2003, MacGinty and Darby, 2002, Wilson and Stapleton 2003). Hence, post-devolution Northern Ireland has seen an increased emphasis on political and cultural symbolism and a polarisation of attitudes towards the public display of community symbols (Brown and MacGinty, 2003, MacGinty and Darby, 2002).

As well as challenges faced by nationalist culture and symbolism within NI, unionists must also deal with a rapidly changing relationship to mainstream Britishness. Even before devolution, unionists have suspected that Britain is no longer politically interested in or committed to Northern Ireland (see Dunn and Morgan, 1994, Finlayson, 1996). These views have intensified post-devolution in the face of substantial government concessions to nationalists and the perception by many unionists that devolution has weakened NI's place within the Union (see Wilson and Stapleton, 2006). However, devolution also raises another fundamental challenge for unionists; namely, the need to articulate a distinctive cultural identity *within* the Union. As outlined earlier, concepts of Britishness in Northern Ireland have been largely based on a civic ideology, in which, for the most part, ethno-national and state identity have been co-constitutive. In the face of increasing regionalisation, however, it may no longer be enough for Northern Irish unionists to proclaim themselves 'simply British'. In the absence of an existing agreed 'Northern Irish' identity, there is a need for Protestants/unionists to forge a distinctive cultural identity based, for example, on history, heritage, territory and culture. This, then, would provide NI Britishness with a viable ethno-nationalist identity among the devolved regions; thereby consolidating its place within the UK, while simultaneously maintaining a cultural and political distance from Irish nationalism.

In this Chapter, we argue that the rapid growth of Ulster Scots as an identity category and cultural discourse in NI can be seen, at least in part, as a response to this need (Stapleton and Wilson, 2003, 2004a). We are not claiming here, that Ulster Scots has emerged *because of* devolution, but rather that its 'uptake' at grassroots level reflects many of the issues and challenges facing contemporary unionism, which are highlighted and intensified by the socio-political transformations wrought through devolution and the peace process. Indeed, in many ways, devolution could be said to have hastened socio-political developments already underway within unionist/ Protestant culture; e.g. growing perceptions of alienation from 'mainland' Britain and, in particular, from the British government (Dunn and Morgan, 1994); and the growing confidence and relative ascendancy of Irish nationalist culture (Rolston, 1998), both of which have gathered pace since the early 1990s. Interestingly, during this time, there has been a marked rise in cultural movements among Northern Irish unionists, an increasing emphasis on heritage and culture, and notably, a shift 'from British to Ulsterish' (Finlayson, 1996: 97; see also McCall, 2002b, Nic Craith, 2001).

However, devolution gives added impetus to such movements generally, and in particular, to Ulster Scots. Crucially, the devolved structures also facilitate the movement through the provision of official recognition and institutional/financial support. Thus, Ulster Scots may be seen as one particular outworking of issues raised by devolution across the UK; i.e. the reconfiguration of Britishness in relation to other identity categories, reconfiguration within those categories themselves, and the articulation of 'new' and/or minority identities within this context. In our analysis below, we consider the ways in which Ulster Scots is being configured at the micro-level of identity construction among grass-roots citizens and communities. Before this however, it is necessary to briefly outline the background to the movement.

The Ulster Scots Movement

Although grass-roots interest has existed for some years, the Ulster Scots movement only came to public consciousness in the early 1990s. The movement, which draws its supporters overwhelmingly from the Protestant/unionist community, highlights the historical links between Scotland and Ulster and works to raise awareness of the Ulster Scots legacy in contemporary Northern Irish/Ulster society. There is also an emphasis on the links between Ulster and the USA, specifically, the contribution made by the Ulster Scots (or 'Scotch Irish') emigrants in shaping American culture, society, politics and economics.[2] As a cultural movement, Ulster Scots is concerned with a broad range of activities and artefacts, including language, music, history, dance, literature, historical pageantry, cooking and visual art. However, it is often perceived as being primarily, if not solely, about the Ulster Scots language (i.e. a form of Scots) (see Nic Craith, 2001, Radford 2001, Stapleton and Wilson, 2004a, Wilson and Stapleton, under review). While such perceptions mask the full breadth of Ulster Scots culture, it is undeniably the case that the Ulster Scots language has received most public attention (much of it negative; see below); and also that it has been the language which has been the target of much of the institutional support afforded Ulster Scots under devolution.

Institutional support for Ulster Scots was established within a 'parity of esteem' discourse, articulated within the principles of the Belfast Agreement. Under this principle, Ulster Scots gained formal recognition as a part of the British and Irish governments' commitment to linguistic and cultural diversity in the devolved institutions. As part of the new North/South Language Body, *The Ulster Scots Agency* was set up to '*promote the study, conservation, development and use of Ulster-Scots as a living language; to encourage and develop the full range of its attendant culture;*

---

[2]   For example, it is claimed that seventeen of the 43 US Presidents are of Ulster descent. Particularly in the eighteenth and nineteenth centuries, a number of Presidents can be shown to be of direct Ulster Scots (Scotch Irish) lineage. (*Ulster-Scots and United States Presidents.* Information leaflet [n.d.] produced by the *Ulster Scots Agency*).

and to promote an understanding of the history of the Ulster-Scots'.[3] In addition, the Ulster Scots language received international recognition when it was officially recognised as the Scots language in Ireland by the UK Committee of the European Bureau of Lesser-Used Languages (EBLUL) (see Nic Craith 2001).

In post-devolution NI, Ulster Scots is an important item on the social and political agenda (Nic Craith, 2001, Stapleton and Wilson, 2004a, Wilson and Stapleton, 2003, under review), with the language and culture being formally recognised and granted official support and endorsement. However, Ulster Scots is inevitably opposed by many in NI, who see it, variously, as a political football, a tool of separatist politics, a 'reactive' and 'inauthentic' language and culture, and even a threat to community relations. We do not intend to discuss these issues here (but see Stapleton and Wilson, 2004a). We note them because they form an important part of the socio-political backdrop against which Ulster Scots is being articulated; i.e. a post-devolution culture where, more than ever, culture operates as a 'battlefield' on which political goals are pursued (see Rolston, 1998).

The Present Study

In this Chapter, we adopt the increasingly influential *discursive* approach to place and cultural identities (e.g. Barker and Galasinski, 2001, Billig, 1995, Condor, 2000, De Cillia *et al.*, 1999, Dixon and Durrheim, 2000, Meinhof, 2002, Hester and Housley, 2001, Reicher and Hopkins, 2001, Stapleton and Wilson, 2003, 2004a, 2004b, Taylor and Wetherell, 1999, Wilson and Stapleton, 2005, 2006, forthcoming, Wodak *et al.*, 1999). This approach rejects the notion of pre-existing sociological or psychological constructs of identity and allegiance (see Reicher and Hopkins, 2001) and looks instead at how identities are negotiated within and through discourse. From this perspective, place/cultural identity is seen not as a pre-defined category, but rather as a discursive formation that is shaped by ideological structures and meanings, and (re)produced in everyday talk/interaction. This approach also emphasises the need to analyse *real-life discursive data*, in which people structure and interpret their own identities, through the negotiation and use of particular categories and labels. In constructing their cultural identities, then, speakers may be seen as forging a place within a set of culturally available discourses and structures, while simultaneously negotiating these structures to produce personalised versions of identity (see e.g. Stapleton and Wilson, 2004b, Taylor and Wetherell, 1999, Wodak *et al.*, 1999).

Hence, we argue that in order to examine the significance of Ulster Scots as a form of ethno-nationalist expression in post-devolution Northern Ireland, it is essential to look at the ways in which the category *is used* at the micro-level of identity construction. In their analysis of everyday identity categories, Antaki *et al.* (1996: 489) show that 'the reading of a category label is localized, and the only reliable evidence one can have is the way in which the participants themselves

---

3   http://www.ulsterscotsagency.com/aboutus-overview.asp.

manifest what is locally "live"'. Similarly, but with specific reference to national identity, Fevre and Thompson (1999: 45, cited in Hester and Housley, 2001) argue that '(Welsh) national identity is not pregiven, but is very largely constructed by people as they develop and express their understandings of situations, events and other people as they arise' (see also Kiely *et al.*, 2001).

The data below comprise the identity expressions of a series of self-defined Ulster Scots people, as collected from focus groups and interviews, conducted between February and July 2002 as part of a research project addressing the nature of Ulster Scots identity in contemporary society. The study participants were recruited from community and cultural groups throughout Northern Ireland and the border counties of the Irish Republic. These groups were contacted by post and invited to participate in a study of 'Ulster Scots identity', the recruitment criterion being simply that respondents *saw themselves* as being of Ulster Scots descent and/or felt themselves to 'be' Ulster Scots. Sampling was thus non-random and participation was completely voluntary (in most cases, involving only some members of the groups in question). Data collection took the form of focus group discussions (or one-to-one interviews) conducted by a researcher from the Institute of Ulster Scots Studies. Discussions/interviews were open-ended and loosely focused on what it 'means' to have an 'Ulster Scots identity'. Each session was audio-recorded and subsequently transcribed by the researcher.

Our particular analytic approach is broadly based on the Discourse Analysis (DA) framework developed by Jonathan Potter, Margaret Wetherell and others (Edwards 1997, Edwards and Potter 1992, Potter 2003, Potter and Edwards 1999, Potter and Wetherell 1987, Wetherell and Potter 1992). From this perspective, language is always used to 'do' things (e.g. blaming, excusing), in the process of which social phenomena, and indeed social reality, are constructed in particular ways. Drawing on (among others) postmoderninst and ethnomethodological insights, this approach highlights simultaneously the macro-level ideological structures that shape social meanings and accounts, and the micro-level processes of language and interaction, through which meanings are negotiated, events and actions are interpreted, and people 'make sense' of the world and their own location within it (see Wetherell 1998). Our analysis, then, focused both on the general discourses and narratives that structure the social category of Ulster Scots and on the contextualised realisations of this category as ascribed to self and others. Analytic foci included: self-narratives; cultural categories and references; self-positionings and ideological stances; patterns of alignment; modes of practical reasoning and interpretation; self-other constructions and delineations and points of reference and contrast (see Stapleton and Wilson, 2003, 2004a). For the purposes of this chapter, however, we focus specifically on the construction of Ulster Scots as an ethno-national identity category.

Analysis

For analysis, we have selected a number of extracts in which the speakers explicitly invoke ethno-national categories in order to locate the nature/origins of their Ulster Scots identity. As we will illustrate, these formations vary considerably from one extract to another, thereby producing a range of ethno-nationalist positions. For analytic purposes, we have grouped these under four thematic headings, based on our reading of the transcripts; i.e. 'not Irish', 'British', 'Scottish', and what we have termed 'partly Irish?'.[4]

1. Not Irish

Extract 1[5]

1.	R:	Um, would you all … did you personally (.) feel an Ulster Scots
2.		identity before being involved in these groups? (***)
3.	M1:	Yeah (.) Yeah, I was a former, I'm a former member of the Ulster
4.		Defence Regiment, and we had to fill in our passport (.) all the
5.		various literature and that. And say what (.) um, <u>citizenship</u> you had.
6.		And they wanted on your thing, not <u>just British</u>, but whether you
7.		were British-English, British-Welsh, British-Scottish or British-Irish.
8.		And (.) I know that a whole <u>lot</u> of us would've filled in British Ulster
9.		Scots. Cos, um, we didn't really <u>feel</u> British-Irish.[6]
10.	R:	Uh huh.
11.	M1:	But we're (.) uh, (.) it seemed … to put 'Irish' on your passport
12.		when you're going there to fight Irish Republican Army, like. (.) It
13.		didn't seem <u>right</u>. So, we always, <u>I</u> always did personally anyway.

In *Extract 1*, the speaker constructs Ulster Scots as a category of British citizenship, albeit one not conventionally recognised by the British themselves; hence, his difficulty in locating himself within the standard categories of British citizenship. There are a number of interesting features of this account. Firstly, it reflects the pre-eminence of the NI British state identity. M1's use of prosodic emphasis suggests that he was somewhat taken aback, or perhaps even indignant, that his passport form

---

[4]   It is important to note that, as in other identity constructions, these categories may (and often do) overlap; and further, that there is inevitably some meaning variation within the categories themselves.

[5]   For transcription conventions, please see appendix.

[6]   M1 designates 'Male 1' from a particular focus group discussion. However, it should be noted that the extracts are drawn from different focus groups. Therefore 'M1' (etc.) in subsequent extracts should not be taken as referring to the same speaker(s) on each occasion.

required more that 'just British' as a category label. Further, the citizenship options supplied here were not acceptable to M1 due to the inherent tension between the NI British and Irish identity categories. Without over-interpreting the data, this may also imply the failure of the (mainland) British to fully grasp the nature and dilemmas of a NI British identity. In fact, it would seem that a (nominal) Irish identity was being thrust upon M1 by Britain itself.

The over-riding theme of this account, however, is an opposition to Irishness. The speaker goes on to elaborate why an Irish identity was not only unacceptable to him personally, but also wholly irreconcilable with the goals and activities in which he was preparing to engage (i.e. fighting the Irish Republican Army). In this context, Ulster Scots functions as an alternative category label, which allows M1 to circumvent the citizenship dilemma of being (seen as) simultaneously Irish and British. Thus, its meaning is primarily oppositional; i.e. defined in opposition to an unacceptable identity attributed by others. A similar construction is illustrated in *Extract 2* below.

Extract 2

1.	M1:	Well, I personally think that, um (.) from the formation of
2.		Provisional Sinn <u>Fein</u>, and their pushing the Irish culture (.) has made
3.		me <u>very</u> much aware that (.) I was not (.) <u>I</u> was born an <u>Ulsterman</u> (…)
4.		I was an Ulster Scot <u>first</u>. And um (.) the fact that it was pushed (.)
5.		that uh, Sinn Fein tried to ram it down your throat that you were all
6.		<u>Irish</u> (.) I resented that very, very <u>much</u>. And I dug my heels in. And
7.		I, I would always <u>refer</u> to myself as an Ulster Scot. Y'know
8.		whereas previously, I (.) I was an Ulsterman. (.) Because the Ulster
9.		Scots identity is (.) <u>distinctive</u>. In that, you know? It's just
10.		*(laughs)* whenever they ram it down your throat (.) you just get tired
11.		of it day after day after <u>day</u>. And you have to identify yourself to,
12.		to stand <u>out</u> from that.

In this extract, Ulster Scots is again chiefly constructed as 'not Irish'. However, the account differs from *Extract 1* in a number of ways. Here, the Ulster Scots identity is a *cultural* alternative to the Irish identity, and is in effect, largely equated with 'Ulsterness'. Thus, M1 states that he 'was born an Ulsterman', this category providing the basis for his Ulster Scots identity, and also his rejection of any attributions of Irishness. Such attributions are presented very clearly as a threat from Irish nationalists/republicans, the largest republican party, specifically Sinn Fein (SF). That is, not only does M1 perceive SF as promoting the Irish culture, but more injuriously, as foisting this culture/identity upon all NI citizens (i.e. trying 'to ram it down your throat that you were all <u>Irish</u>').

In this context, the Ulster Scots category functions not merely in opposition, but also as an explicit *resistance*, to Irishness; and indeed to the threat of absorption into an Irish culture. This effectively articulates the separateness of Ulster, and moreover, as noted by M1 himself, provides a 'distinctive' identity, a means of 'standing out' from SF and their version of pan-Irishness. From this perspective, Ulster Scots might be seen as a pragmatic, or even a reactive, identity formation. However, the speaker's identity seems to entail more than a simple rejection of Irishness. His claim for contradistinction is not based on a straightforward citizenship entitlement (e.g. simply being British). Rather, it is formulated in terms of birthrights and heritage, which are based in a native Ulster, and which are being threatened by an increasingly dominant adversative culture.

In *Extracts 1* and *2*, then, Ulster Scots is defined primarily in contradistinction to Irishness. Of course, *any* statement of identity is implicitly also a statement of what that identity is not (see e.g. McCrone, 2002). However, what is notable in these extracts, is that a specific oppositional component (i.e. Irishness) is *explicitly foregrounded* as a defining feature of Ulster Scots. This is *not* to suggest that Ulster Scots is simply a reactive or negatively defined identity (see Stapleton and Wilson, 2004a). Rather, it illustrates the centrality of Irishness as a point of reference, and (perhaps understandably in the conflicted cultural terrain of Northern Ireland), the key function of Ulster Scots in demarcating an extant cultural and political distinctiveness. In *Extracts 3–5* below, we examine some of the ways in which the participants also draw on the category of Britishness in constructing an Ulster Scots identity.

2. British

While Ulster Scots is frequently seen as an expression of Britishness in Northern Ireland, the participants negotiate and qualify this relationship in a number of ways. For analysis, we have selected two particularly salient themes from our transcriptions. These are 'British, but Ulster Scots first' (*Extracts 3* and *4*) and 'British, but not English' (*Extract 5*).

British, but Ulster Scots first

Extract 3

1. M3: But young Protestants now, coming on (.) or young loyalists,
2.   or whatever they want to call themselves (.) they <u>are</u> keen to forget a,
3.   an identity (.) for themselves. And they <u>do</u> see Ulster Scots as a
4.   viable identity. A few years ago, you didn't know whether you
5.   were Northern Irish (.) or British, or whatever. But Ulster Scots
6.   <u>is</u> a viable, it <u>is</u> a place where they can (.) they can hang their, their
7.   coat on that there, and say '<u>I'm</u> an Ulster Scot (.) I'm <u>not</u> <u>Irish</u> (.) Um,
8.   I <u>am</u> British, but I'm an Ulster Scot <u>first</u>'. And, uh, it is, it's a place
9.   (.) there's a, you know it's a <u>home</u> for these people. Or a home for a
10.   <u>lot</u> of people.

In *Extract 3*, the speaker outlines the value of the Ulster Scots identity for the younger generation of what he broadly terms Protestants/loyalists. Here, Ulster Scots is presented as a developing, or emerging, identity; i.e. something that the younger generation are 'keen to forge'. Such an identity is seen as providing a distinctive voice, within the general category of Britishness. Thus, M3 suggests that while the NI British identity used to be ambiguous, Ulster Scots has established a 'viable' British identity (which incidentally, is explicitly 'not Irish'). The articulation of this identity ('I am British, but I'm an Ulster Scot first') consolidates the speaker's claim to Britishness, but also expresses a recognisable ethno-nationalist identity *within* Britain, comparable, for example, to many constructions of Welsh and Scottish identities. Moreover, M3 claims that having the means to articulate a distinctive Ulster Scots (but nonetheless British) identity also provides a sense of security; i.e. 'a home for these people'. In the following extract, similar themes are articulated by the interviewee, in this case with specific reference to the changing context of Britishness.

Extract 4

1.	M:	Mm. (2.0) I think (.) yeah, well I think I've always felt a
2.		closer connection to, to Ulster, as a sort of (.) whatever Ulster is, as
3.		an entity. (.) Um, and it's a more regional thing. I mean, I would feel
4.		more affinity with the idea of Ulster Scots (.) of (.) y'know our own
5.		Ulster Scots community here, and of the wider sense of Ulster Scots (.)
6.		um, probably more than anything else, really. (.....) that regional
7.		identity, for me, is the strongest (.) element of, of our culture.
8.		Because well, you say well (.) someone who feels British, for example,
9.		well what does that mean? (.) And it means, essentially, an amalgam
10.		(.) of different regionalisations. (.) So to me, 'British' (.) does, does not
11.		really have a meaning as such (...) A lot of the sense of Britishness is
12.		(.) well I suppose it's been (.) really dissipated, over the years. You
13.		know, and when we talk about the future, and regionalisation, and
14.		where we go with Europe, and all the rest (.) y'know nation states
15.		have less and less relevance. (.) But the bedrock of it all lies in your
16.		own culture, and your own identity.

Here, Ulster Scots is constructed as first and foremost a communal and personal affiliation, centred on the idea of 'Ulster'. However, while this account invokes a distinctive community, culture, and form of belonging, it also, through the concept of 'regions', locates this culture within a broader framework of Britishness. In fact, if Britishness is, by its very nature, regionalised (i.e. 'an amalgam of different regionalisations') then Ulster Scots is just one of a number of constituent, identities within that amalgam. However, the speaker clearly emphasises the value of (regional) distinctiveness. This is presented partly in reference to the 'dissipation' of Britishness as an overarching identity category, as well as the impacts of European regionalisation and the decreasing significance of the nation state. Hence, he constructs a 'new' version of Britain in which regional cultures are the 'bedrock' of identity. In this context, Ulster Scots is necessarily and intrinsically British, but simultaneously provides a regionally distinctive point of identification.

British, but not English

A second related feature of the construction of 'Ulster Scots as British' draws a distinction between Britishness and Englishness. As a number of writers have pointed out, these categories are frequently confused and/or conflated (McCrone, 2002). Despite, or perhaps because of, this, a number of our study participants constructed their own British identity in direct opposition to that of 'the English'. This is illustrated in *Extract 5*, but is also evident in the next section (i.e. constructions of 'Ulster Scots as Scottish').

Extract 5

1.	M2:	It <u>is</u>, uh, an <u>identity</u> thing. You know, it (.) when you hear,
2.		kind of (.) Ulster Protestants and such, saying '<u>I'm</u> <u>British</u>'. (.) Well,
3.		saying (.) I mean, we <u>are</u> British, but y'know (.) there's <u>more</u> than just
4.		saying you're British. Kind of, um (.) in this part of Ireland, this part
5.		of Northern Ireland (.) you're <u>not</u> <u>English</u> (.) Y'know, you're not <u>Welsh</u>,
6.		you're, you're not a <u>Londoner</u>. (.) You <u>are</u> from this part of the <u>world</u>,
7.		and um (.) I think there <u>is</u> an identity here, especially I think, if you go
8.		away, y'know, you realise, well it's <u>more</u>, I'm <u>not</u> just British. I'm
9.		British, but (.) I come from <u>this</u> part of (.) Northern Ireland. That
10.		there's Ulster Scots connections, and that you <u>identify</u> with Scottish
11.		people more. As <u>well</u>.
12.	M3:	Uh huh.
13.	M2:	If you're, if you're living in London, and you're meeting other
14.		people, you <u>tend</u> to meet people who are <u>either</u> (.) from Northern
15.		Ireland? Or, or from Scotland? And, uh, there, there <u>is</u> some sort of
16.		<u>connection</u> there, type of thing. Maybe it is an anti-<u>English</u> type
17.		thing.

In this account, M2 expresses an inability to articulate his own NI identity within a generic category of Britishness. In fact, he is somewhat scathing of those ('Ulster Protestants') who are content to accept this state citizenship without interrogating the 'meaning' of their identities. While he categorically claims a British identity for both himself and his fellow 'Ulster Protestants', he underlines the need to establish the nature of the British identity in this particular region. Thus, he delineates the NI British identity from a number of other categories (Welsh, English and London), in order to exemplify his stance that he must be 'more (than) just British'. His perception of a distinctive NI British identity centres on the 'Ulster Scots connections', as well as close identifications with Scottish people. M2 elaborates the issue of identification with reference to his own personal experience of working in London.

Here, he describes having formed connections with people from Northern Ireland and Scotland in the context of a possible 'anti-English type thing'. Hence, in M2's account, there is clearly a distinction between being British and being English, to the extent that a NI British identity can even be 'anti-English'. In the next section, this theme is explored further with reference to the category of Scottishness.

3. Scottish

In a number of our extracts, Ulster Scots is explicitly constructed within a category of Scottishness. These formulations draw on two potentially complementary narratives of origin; the most common being that of the seventeenth century Plantations, in which large numbers of Scottish families were settled in Ulster. However, an alternative perspective – i.e. that the Scots were in fact the first settlers of Ireland, and that the seventeenth century Planters were simply 'returning home', having been driven out of Ulster by the Celts (Adamson, 1991) – has also recently gained currency among some Ulster loyalists (see Nic Craith, 2001). Elsewhere, we have shown how these historical accounts work to structure personal and group identities (Stapleton and Wilson, 2003, 2004a). Here, however, we are interested in how the categories themselves are negotiated; i.e. how Ulster Scots is presented *as* Scottish. As illustrated below, there are two main contradistinctive formulations of this category; 'Scottish, not Irish' (*Extracts 6* and *7)* and 'Scottish, not English' (*Extracts 8* and *9*).

Scottish, not Irish

Extract 6

1.	M2:	(…) And um (.) <u>My</u> father always said he was born and reared
2.		in the Scottish province of Ulster. He never, ever accepted Ulster as
3.		ever being part of this island. (.) And uh, history <u>shows</u> that. I mean
4.		the only time Ireland was ever united was under the British Crown.
5.		And clear of that, when you go back this part, this place that you're
6.		sitting in now was Dalnariada (?), part of the Dalriada Kingdom of the
7.		Western Isles of Scotland and the North Eastern seaboard of the
8.		island (.) that we're still <u>in</u>.

Extract 6 clearly articulates the claim that Ulster is inherently Scottish, in both historical and cultural terms. The speaker also sets up a Scottish-Irish opposition through which Ulster is not only Scottish, but then, by definition, 'not Irish'. M2's account centres on his father's claim that he 'was born and reared in the Scottish province of Ulster'. As well as drawing on a powerful trope of belonging ('born and reared'), this construction presents Ulster as irrefutably a constituent part (i.e. a 'province') of Scotland. This construction in reinforced in his father's refusal to accept that Ulster was ever a part of the Island of Ireland. Moreover, M2 himself endorses and warrants

this position through a compelling rhetoric of historical evidence; i.e. in which 'history shows' that his claims are justified. This evidence effectively undermines the notion that the Island of Ireland is a natural political entity, highlighting instead the former amalgamation of (the Western Isles of) Scotland and (the north-eastern part of) Ulster within a *single kingdom*. The contemporary significance of this is stressed in M2's claim that he is still living within this historically defined entity. In this construction then, there is, in effect, little or no difference between, Ulster Scots and Scottishness, itself; they are simply two components of the same culture. In the next extract, we can see a similar construction of 'Ulster Scots as Scottish'.

Extract 7

1.	M1:	They wanted everybody to think that they were Irish. And that (.)
2.		Through the schools (.) they put through an Irish history (.) and you
3.		learned all about the history of Irish (…)
4.	M2:	I'm glad you brought that up (M1 NAME). I mean, I'd say if you
5.		DNA tested us (.) You'll not get no Catholic Irish blood in us. We've
6.		the Scottish right down through the line.

This extract follows a discussion in which the participants have claimed that Ulster Scots has been suppressed by both British and Irish governments in an effort to impose a pan-Irish identity on the people of Northern Ireland.[7] Thus, M1 points to the emphasis on Irish history in school curricula, which he perceives as an attempt to get 'everybody to think that they were Irish'. The speakers are adamant in their resistance to such an ascription, as illustrated (a few turns later) in M2's claim that there is 'no Catholic Irish blood in us'. This construction is notable in two respects. Firstly, rather than drawing on conventional claims of culture, heritage, and history, M2 appeals to the concept of DNA and/or genetic testing. In this context, his rejection of 'Catholic Irish blood' can be read within two discursive formations; i.e. both the metaphorical framework of 'blood and belonging' (see Ignatieff, 1994), and the more concrete, 'scientific' discourse of genetics and hereditary extraction. Together, these discourses construct an indisputable claim of ancestry and lineage, which is explicitly not that of the 'Irish Catholic' population.

The second interesting aspect of this account is the oppositional category set up to counter any notion of Irishness. Rather than claiming an *Ulster Scots* identity (which he has done and continues to do throughout the discussion), M2 here contends that, were he and his fellow participants to be DNA tested, they would show 'Scottish [blood] right down through the line'. Here again then, we see the Ulster Scots category being used as coterminous, or interchangeable, with the category of Scottishness. This construction is coherent within the framework, illustrated in *Extract 6*, that Ulster Scots is, in fact, simply a *geographical variant of* Scottishness. While not necessarily endorsing this

---

7   This is articulated as 'a conspiracy theory, if you like to put it like that, between Dublin and London (.) to, to suppress this Ulster Scots' (Transcript 1, p. 14).

position (i.e. that Ulster Scots *is* Scottish), the next two extracts also show the centrality of 'the Scottish connection' in defining the meaning of Ulster Scots.

Scottish, not English

Extract 8

1.	M2:	I think more people nowadays would be sort of questioning
2.		their (.) their <u>links</u> with Britain. You know. With the way Britain's
3.		sort of (.) the way the British nation's <u>gone</u>. They maybe don't see
4.		themselves as close as (.) say, maybe in the time of the <u>Wars</u>. (.)
5.		Because they see Britain as not just (.) as good a country as it <u>used</u>
6.		to be (.) and they'd maybe look more to Scotland rather than to
7.		England.

This extract is set within a broad context of Britishness. However (as in *Extract 4*, above), there is a sense that Britishness is somehow changing or dissipating, and that this has direct consequences for the British identity in Northern Ireland, such that people are now 'questioning their links' with Britain. M2 describes this development as arising from changes in the British nation itself, and specifically, from the impression that these changes in effect, signify a decline or deterioration (i.e. that present-day Britain is not 'as good a country as it <u>used</u> to be'). He further suggests that in the context of this waning British connection, people may 'look more to Scotland rather than to England'. Notably, M2's account appears to equate traditional NI Britishness with allegiance to England (cf. *Extract 5*, above), with Scotland providing an *emergent* alternative for political, and cultural allegiance. This contrasts somewhat with *Extract 9* in which Ulster Scots is seen as *historically affiliated* to Scotland, in opposition to England.

Extract 9

1.	M1:	The Clan that <u>I</u> would come from, the (NAME), for example, has
2.		been in Northern Ireland for hundreds and <u>hundreds</u> of years. (.) And
3.		the first time that Scots-Irish is written or mentioned, is by Queen
4.		Elizabeth the First. And she talked about the (NAME) on the North
5.		Antrim coast, there …
6.	M2:	It sounds like youse were a bit <u>loyal</u> there, were youse?
7.	M1:	Well, I don't know (***) (*laughs*)
8.	M2:	Youse <u>were</u>. Youse <u>were</u>. Youse were <u>traitors</u> to the Scottish
9.		<u>people</u>.
10.		(*General laughter*).

This sequence begins with M1's account of his Scots/Ulster Scots ancestry. Thus he claims that his family (Clan) have been in Northern Ireland for several centuries and, were in fact, the topic of first historical reference to the 'Scots-Irish'; made by Queen

Elizabeth I. However, this Scottish lineage is called into question (albeit facetiously) by M2 who suggests that because the (English) Queen Elizabeth referred to the family, they must have been 'a bit loyal'. The point is partially accepted by M1 who laughingly denies knowledge of the situation. Subsequently, M2 twice reiterates his contention, before declaring that M1's family were '<u>traitors</u> to the Scottish <u>people</u>'. While this exchange is demonstrably humorous in nature, it nonetheless shows a clear Scottish-English opposition in the speakers' negotiation of the Ulster Scots category. Indeed, in this construction, Englishness and Scottishness are antithetical, such that loyalty to England entailed betrayal of Scotland (and hence of the true Ulster Scots people). Again, this formulation illustrates the complexity of negotiating an Ulster Scots identity within a common category of Britishness.[8]

4. Partly Irish?

In the final section of our analysis, we examine instances in which speakers profess to share some features, or at least experiences, with the Irish and/or nationalist population. Thus through its geographical location, Ulster Scots is here seen as influenced by, or even incorporating, certain aspects of native Irish/Ulster culture. This mode of construction contrasts sharply with the 'Not Irish' category outlined in *Section 1*, and admittedly occurs less frequently in our data. Nonetheless, it illustrates a further interesting complexity in the negotiation of the Ulster Scots identity category. Below, we discuss two configurations of this idea; firstly that Ulster Scots people have commonalities with their Irish counterparts (*Extract 10*); and secondly, that Ulster Scots *is* both Scottish and Irish (*Extract 11*).

Commonality with the Irish

Extract 10

1.	M1:	Well, I think (.) it's got to the stage (.) I think amongst, I'll use
2.		the term Protestants (.) Ulster Scots (.) that whenever you refer to
3.		being British, you're really thinking about (.) y'know, the Royal
4.		<u>Family</u>, and the sense of value associated (.) um, around
5.		<u>democracy</u>. The principle of democracy, and the <u>Parliament</u>. (.) But
6.		I think, um (.) what has been said before (.) and we may not <u>like</u> it,
7.		but it's <u>true</u>, that um (.) as far as day-to-day <u>life</u> goes, we would
8.		probably have more in common with our <u>Irish</u> counterparts than
9.		we do with the average person in <u>Britain</u>. Like there are differences
10.		between us and the, the personalities and the way of life in Britain
11.		(.) So I think personally, yes, we <u>have</u> moved away a bit from
12.		Britain.

---

[8]   Incidentally, it also shows the salience of historical narratives and categories in everyday life, and indeed, the implications of these categories for contemporary Ulster Scots identities (see Stapleton and Wilson, 2003, 2004a).

M1's account here centres again on the theme of dislocation from Britishness. However, in contrast to *Extract 8*, he does not link this to changes in British society, but rather, invokes conventional symbols of Britishness (the Royal Family, democracy and Parliament), in his suggestion that NI Protestants have 'moved away' from Britain. While he does not explicate this process, however, he points to its manifestation in terms of personality and lifestyle divergences (between Northern Ireland and mainland Britain). Hence, M1 suggests that in everyday life, Ulster Scots people (and/or NI British Protestants) 'probably have more in common with our Irish counterparts than we do with the average person in Britain'. This account then, claims a commonality with the Irish community (whether in Northern Ireland and/or the RoI is not specified).

However, through this very construction, the Ulster/Ulster Scots and Irish categories (while not set up in contradistinction to each other) remain clearly delineated. The notion of 'commonality' necessarily presumes two or more distinct entities or groupings; as illustrated in M1's use of the pronominals 'us' and 'we' to designate the ingroup, and in his description of the Irish as 'counterparts'. Moreover, in his assertion that 'we may not like it, but it's true', the speaker acknowledges that the idea of shared features/experiences is likely to be unpalatable to many of the ingroup (himself included, via the pronominal reference 'we'). Increased commonality with the Irish, then, is presented as unpleasant, but inescapable, in light of the changing context of Northern Irish Britishness. In the final extract, however, we explore an alternative construction in which Irishness is partly incorporated *within* the Ulster Scots category.

Scottish and Irish

Extract 11

1.	M3:	Well, I suppose (.) (.) there's lots of things that we do here that
2.		you know wouldn't have come from (.) a, an Irish tradition, maybe.
3.		But that <u>would</u> have been brought directly from Scotland. Y'know
4.		we'd have the tartan, and maybe our festivals, and things like that.
5.		And I think that (.) these things are very <u>clearly</u> Scottish in origin.
6.		But then there's, I suppose there's a certain degree of (.) difference
7.		as well. Y'know that would make them <u>Ulster</u> Scots?
8.	F1:	Yeah, I mean the fiddling that's done here, for instance,
9.		would be different (.) slightly different from Scotland (***)
10.	M5:	That's right. (.) That's right (.) As somebody said earlier, we
11.		have our roots in both countries. That we're historically native to
12.		Scotland <u>and</u> Ireland.

Here, the speakers jointly negotiate a 'Scottish and Irish' construction of Ulster Scots. M3's account initially highlights the Scottish heritage in Ulster. Thus he lists cultural components which, rather than being Irish, came 'directly from Scotland' (and) 'are very <u>clearly</u> Scottish in origin'. However, he then acknowledges that some of these traditions actually differ to some extent from their Scottish equivalents; in fact, this difference is invoked as necessary to 'make them <u>Ulster</u> Scots'. F2's reference to different fiddling traditions in Scotland and Ulster provides further support for this claim. Notably, both speakers' formulations ('a degree of difference', 'slightly different') suggest uncertainty about articulating this distinction. However, it is clear that these speakers do not see Ulster Scots as coterminous with Scottishness (cf. *Section 3*, above). Their perception of a distinctive <u>Ulster</u> Scots culture/identity necessitates a recognition of Ulster/Irish influences. In fact, this idea is explicitly articulated by M5, who claims that 'we have our roots in both countries [and] we're historically native to Scotland <u>and</u> Ireland'. This construction not only incorporates the Irish category *within* that of Ulster Scots, but moreover, highlights the *indigenous* status of the Ulster Scots community on the Island of Ireland.

Conclusion

This chapter has considered the ways in which Ulster Scots is being constructed as an ethno-national identity category in post-devolution Northern Ireland. As such, it has sought to address the processes of identity negotiation and realignment in the context of this constitutional change. We are not suggesting here that devolution has single-handedly engendered these identity debates and reconfigurations. Conversely, nor are we claiming that ethno-national and other identities were pre-formed and stable prior to the constitutional reforms. Rather we take the view, now widely recognised across the human sciences, that identities, whether individual or group-based, are inherently negotiable and are continually being defined and redefined (see Benwell and Stokoe, 2006). Devolution, however, creates a context where identity issues and debates are highlighted and focused in specific ways (e.g. Condor *et al.*, 2006). The new political structures and changing public discourses (of nation, state, culture and citizenship) provide new categories of membership, belonging and allegiance, while simultaneously closing off or altering others. This leads to increased identity fluidity and a greater need to actively configure and (re)articulate the available categories (see McCrone, 2002).

These processes are even more sharply focused in Northern Ireland than in other regions of the UK, given the general lack of an agreed 'starting point' for negotiating a 'Northern Irish identity'. Against this backdrop, and given the ongoing controversy surrounding the 'authenticity' and/or 'politicisation' of Ulster Scots (see Stapleton and Wilson, 2004a), we believe that our analysis of this 'emergent' culture highlights a number of issues that are centrally relevant both locally, to devolution in Northern Ireland, and more generally, to the devolution project as a whole. Methodologically, our approach has been driven by the principles of Discourse Analysis, and is based specifically on the premise that a culture/identity can only be understood in terms of its relevance and use in everyday life; and via the discursive structures and processes through which it is constituted. This approach is similar to the concept of 'practitioner narratives', or the double hermeneutic of defining one's identity through an account what it is to have that identity (Benhabib, 2002: 6; Giddens, 1991). Hence we have attempted to explore, in a real sense, the 'category in use'; i.e. the ways in which people negotiate, identify with and *use* the Ulster Scots identity in their own accounts.

Our analysis has provided insights into this particular context of 'devolution and identity', while raising a number of further questions about the process. The first point to note is the strong emphasis on themes of culture and belonging in the discourse of Ulster Scots. The speakers repeatedly invoke notions of history, heritage, 'blood'/DNA, 'roots', 'difference', 'connection' and 'feeling Ulster Scots'. Indeed, even when the category is constructed in more pragmatic, contingent or oppositional terms (such as resistance to Irishness – *Extracts 1* and *2*; or 'moving away from Britain' – *Extracts 4, 5* and *10*), these actions/conditions are generally framed as *arising from* an underlying sense of cultural difference and identity. In this sense, Ulster Scots can be seen to function similarly to other ethno-national categories (Stapleton and Wilson, 2003, 2004a); an analysis which suggests that the Ulster Scots movement may well be motivated, at least in part, by the need to articulate a distinctive NI British identity within the devolved regions of the UK.

This raises the question of the relationship between Ulster Scots and Britishness itself; i.e. how should we view Ulster Scots in relation to contemporary (post-devolution) Britishness? In light of the above, it is tempting to view the movement, in a straightforward sense, as an emergent ethno-national grouping, which emphasises its own cultural distinctiveness against a backdrop of civic British citizenship (and this is, implicitly or explicitly, the thrust of many of the speakers' accounts; see, for example, *Extracts 4* and *5*). However, this view conceals a number of complexities that do not apply to the other ethno-national categories within the UK. Firstly, taking NI Britishness as a whole, it should noted that NI unionists have by no means universally embraced the Ulster Scots identity; many are still content to be seen as 'simply British'[9] and do not identify with the ethno-cultural associations of Ulster Scots (see McCall, 2002b). Hence, Ulster Scots cannot be seen as a regionally representative ('Northern Irish') British identity comparable to Scots or Welsh. From this perspective, it may be arguably more appropriate to view Ulster Scots as a minority identity within the UK, albeit an indigenous one, and one that places Britishness at its centre. The struggle to define and articulate this identity is reflected in the participants' own discourse, as exemplified in *Extracts 1–11*. These demonstrate a complex of identity labels, alignments and contradistinctions, each of which produces a particular configuration of Ulster Scots in relation both to Britishness and to other ethno-national categories (which are themselves configured in different ways within or in opposition to the category of Britishness). From a conceptual perspective, this analysis further highlights the discursive flexibility of

---

[9] 'Simply British' was the election slogan of the Ulster Unionist Party in the 2005 Westminster elections – admittedly part of a largely unsuccessful campaign which saw the party lose out heavily to its main unionist rival, the Democratic Unionist Party.

identity categories, and the complexities of identity negotiation in the midst of socio-political change.

McCrone (2002: 310) claims that in the post-devolution context, identities are becoming increasingly fluid, and can, in fact, be treated 'as a political statement about culture'. From this perspective, the 'emergence' of Ulster Scots as an identity label is interesting. Like other cultural identities, Ulster Scots potentially can be deployed for political ends, and indeed, in its narrow sense, this has often been a criticism levelled by critics of the movement, who claim that Ulster Scots represents a tool of separatist politics in Northern Ireland. We do not intend to discuss here the extent to which Ulster Scots is 'politicised' within the NI context (although, as we discuss elsewhere, in NI politics, *both* the Ulster Scots and Irish cultures can be used in this way – see Wilson and Stapleton, 2003). However, leaving aside the tit-for-tat politics of Northern Ireland for a moment, it is possible to see Ulster Scots as serving the broader socio-political function of cultural identity expression and legitimisation. UK devolution has, arguably, created the context for the emergence and public prominence of Ulster Scots, in terms of engendering debates about Britishness, heightening the distinction between cultural identity and state citizenship, and, particularly in the NI 'peace' context, through the provision of formal recognition and support for cultural diversity. Thus, for at least some sections of the unionist community, Ulster Scots is a means of asserting a viable and distinctive British identity within an increasingly regionalised UK.

The resistance, debate and controversy surrounding Ulster Scots also provides insights into the complexities of NI devolution; and, in particular, into the contested nature of NI identities – which is, if anything, sharpened in the post-devolution context. We believe that this latter point is especially relevant to the devolution process as a whole. While constitutional legitimisation of territorial/cultural groupings *may* result in increased recognition and acceptance of identity diversity, it can also provide the basis for heightened ethno-cultural distinctions and identity conflict. This issue is thrown into relief in a conflicted region such as Northern Ireland, but it has a more general resonance throughout the UK, as progressive devolution continually raises new questions about belonging, allegiance and identity.[10] With reference to our own analysis of Ulster Scots, we argue that in order to understand these and other questions of post-devolution identity, it is necessary to examine how the relevant issues and categories are being worked out, not only at the macro-level of political and public discourse, but also at the micro-level of talk, interaction, and self-identification; where people are negotiating, in 'real time', the form and expression of their own identities within the changing socio-political framework.

---

[10]   It is also relevant to EU regionalisation policy, whereby ethnically contested regions are increasingly gaining constitutional recognition against a backdrop of bureaucratic centralisation.

Appendix: Transcription Conventions

(.)	Brief pause (less than one second)
(n)	Timed pause (more than one second)
(***)	Unintelligible material
(…)	Some omitted material
	(underlining) Prosodic emphasis on word or phrase
___	
R:	Researcher
M1:	Male 1 (etc.) (focus group)
F1:	Female 1 (etc.) (focus group)
M:	Male interviewee (one-to-one interview)
F:	Female interviewee (one-to-one interview)

Chapter 2

Ideologies of Language and Community in Post-devolution Wales

Nikolas Coupland and Hywel Bishop

Introduction

Sociolinguistics has recently developed confidence in its ability to engage in ideological critique. Language ideology is a powerful new perspective in sociolinguistics, emerging mainly from linguistic anthropology but linked to the critical tradition in linguistics and discourse analysis. Ideologically focussed sociolinguistics has introduced uncertainty as well as insight, not least because ideological critique is intensely reflexive and sceptical about intellectual practice. It tends to be subversive of long-established perspectives, and this includes painting canonical sociolinguistics as potentially naïve or old-school. It locates 'traditional' sociolinguistics, appropriately enough, as a product of its structuralist and Modernist origins. Scepticism comes easy of course, and it is sometimes evident that critical sociolinguistics, for all its purgative potential, it overconfident in its own ideological awareness, and even superiority. All the same, the turn to ideology has exposed some important fault-lines in sociolinguistic theorising, not least around the traditional topic of language planning and its more recent connections to linguistic human rights.

In this Chapter we cast a critical-ideological eye over some key language planning initiatives and linguistic rights campaigns in contemporary, post-devolution Wales. We do this by trying to expose some of the unwritten assumptions and implications behind two core concepts – 'language' and 'community' – inescapably central ideas in sociolinguistics – as they are woven into two interconnected sets of influential discourses in Wales. These discourses are ideologically salient within the post-devolution context, since they are bound up with notions of national/cultural identity, and are played out, in different ways, through contemporary socio-political structures and groupings. The analysis is located within a critical sociolinguistic framework.

The first discourse that we will examine is that of the Welsh Assembly Government, which has established an ambitious and in many ways impressive political and cultural agenda around the Welsh language and its planned resurgence. We draw on one particular document for this purpose, *Iaith Pawb*, 'Everyone's Language'

(2003).[1] Colin Williams (2005: 6) reminds us that *Iaith Pawb* should be seen as a strategic statement of policy, a 'statement of doctrine', and not strictly as a language planning document *per se*. But we are precisely interested here in how the Assembly articulates and rationalises its language strategies, and in understanding how they sit in a wider sociolinguistic context. The second discourse is that of the language and housing pressure group, *Cymuned* ('Community'), which formed in Spring 2001. Its leading figures are Simon Brooks, editor of the Welsh-language magazine *Barn*, and Gwynedd councillor Seimon Glyn. Its slogan is *Dal Dy Dir* ('Hold Your Ground'). *Cymuned* claims to have support from across the political spectrum in Wales, and one spokesperson was quoted in February 2001 as saying that its policies are 'supported by virtually all Plaid Cymru members in the north and west of Wales' (*Western Mail*, 21 February). *Cymuned* articulates radical priorities in defence of the Welsh language and what are often referred to in English as the 'heartland' Welsh-speaking communities of rural north-west and south-west Wales, and in Welsh as *Y Fro Gymraeg*. In *Cymuned*'s case we draw from diverse web-published sources where the group sets out its well-rounded, coherent but controversial policy stances.[2]

What we hope will emerge from our review is, firstly, some general sense of the prevailing debate in Wales about sociolinguistic affairs. How is the case for an expanding Welsh language made, and against what assumptions? What notions of 'the good' do the respective discourses and texts draw on? As part of this, what conceptions of *community* do they foreground, and how and for what purposes is the idea of community mobilised? What kinds of moral discourses are generated? Wales is often held up as an interesting sociolinguistic laboratory, where we can see rather universal dramas of minority language shift and revival being played out, and indeed where the drama nowadays seems to be working towards a happy ending of sorts. Wales is regularly cited as a rare and refreshing instance of what Joshua Fishman called 'reversing language shift'. This is the seeming near-miracle, in a globalising world, of a minority language, in the back yard not only of the totalising English language but of England itself, holding its own and revitalising. It is not only a matter of Welsh hanging on 'against all odds' – *yma o hyd* ('still here'), in the resonant nationalist phrase – but of Welsh apparently growing and regaining lost ground in Welsh social life. But our critical focus on *language* in these discourses makes us ask what social phenomenon is actually revitalising here, and indeed what 'vitality' implies in the Welsh language context.

What we think will emerge most strongly is another division of voices – between a generalised voice of the Welsh Assembly and *Cymuned*, taken together (notwithstanding their sometimes significant points of disagreement), and the sceptical voice of critical sociolinguistics. That is, we will suggest that public discourse in Wales about language and community generally aligns with an outmoded framing of sociolinguistic issues, one that is becoming largely untenable within a more contemporary critical-ideological sociolinguistics. That perspective holds that the

---

[1]   http://www.wales.gov.uk/subiculture/content/iaith-pawb-e.pdf.
[2]   See http://www.cymuned.net/index.php.

key concepts of *language* and *community*, as they are deployed in language rights and language planning discourses in Wales, are in fact not well-founded. They are grounded in assumptions about sociolinguistic conditions that have already lapsed – in Wales as elsewhere in the Late-Modern west. They are reductive concepts that serve the purposes of political rhetoric more than the demands of critical scrutiny.

On the one hand then, the chapter's concerns might seem to be rather esoteric. While Wales and Welsh appear to be 'doing very well' according to traditional conceptualisations of language in society, we (authors) might seem to be hung up on which versions of sociolinguistic theory are most robust or critically adequate. But in fact we think that the difficulties we draw attention to in the chapter will soon enough become difficulties for language intervention initiatives on the ground in Wales. It is a matter of whether the key concepts of language and community (and no doubt others) either can or can not ultimately bear the weight of language policy and planning processes in Wales. We suggest they can not, and we try to identify a different, more circumspect starting point for a meaningful sociolinguistic debate.

Community

The planning and implementation of what is called language revitalisation in Wales is being done on behalf of 'the community', and in some regards on behalf of (specific Welsh) 'communities'. Phrases like 'community regeneration' and 'the protection of communities' abound in the textual sources we have chosen to examine. Semantic slippage around the notion of 'community' has been commented on by several critics, well beyond Wales:

'"Community" is one of those words ... bandied around in ordinary, everyday speech, apparently readily intelligible to speaker and listener, which ... however, causes immense difficulty' (Cohen, 1985: 11). Raymond Williams (2003) points out how 'community' as a concept has no detractors. It tends to feature in political discourses where an author wants to construct a sense of fellow-feeling and positive consensus. Communities are often represented as bodies of uniform action or judgement or preference or need. So, discursive appeals to community are difficult to resist, although what is precisely implicated in them can be hard to identify, and it is sometimes illusory or merely vapid. Communities referenced in political discourses may be unrecognisable in terms of what we experience as 'community' and 'communities' on the ground.

In Wales, 'heartland communities' can nevertheless provide a powerful focus for policy initiatives developed in their name. The phrase appeals to a hierarchy of presumed cultural authenticity, distinguishing a set of favoured enclaves where the 'heart' of Wales beats loudest. These communities are rooted most deeply in the 'land' of Wales, building on a productive association between supposed national distinctiveness or identity and images of *gwlad* – 'land', as in *Hen Wlad Fy Nhadau*, the 'Land of My Fathers' of the Welsh national anthem (see Dicks, 2000, Garrett *et al.*, 2005, Gruffudd, 1999). Phrases like 'Welsh-speaking communities' or even the innocent-sounding 'small communities' tap into a familiar ideological seam of meaning which predisposes us to find intense cultural value in communities, often with the idea of the Welsh language embedded in this idea. The idea of 'smallness' is itself conventionally if rather meaninglessly attributed to Wales.

Consider these extracts from *Iaith Pawb*, the first of which begins by retrospecting on information on Welsh language use from the 1991 census:

Extract 1

The state of the language in communities where it was spoken by over 70 percent of the local population aged 3 years and over in 1991 is worthy of particular attention. These are communities where the density of Welsh speakers means that the language is more likely to be spoken in social, leisure and business activities and not be confined to the home, chapel and school. In these areas Welsh is a living, everyday language, spoken, heard and seen in the community; it is part of the fabric of the community. Censuses and surveys over recent decades have shown a continuing decline in the number of communities where more than 70 percent of the population speak Welsh. Continuing decline could arguably threaten the existence of the Welsh language since it would no longer have a natural environment in which it was spoken as a matter of course in the range of social contexts.

Extract 2

The decline of Welsh-speaking communities is a cause of concern to the Assembly Government, but it is part of a wider problem of economic change, population movement and social dislocation which afflicts large parts of Wales, rural and urban, and not merely Welsh-speaking areas. But we have no doubt that the dynamic health and evolution of the Welsh language will be seriously threatened if it ceases to be a language with a strong presence in the community.

The Assembly Government is clear about the crucial importance of maintaining Welsh as a living community language if the language is to thrive and flourish. A social and economic future for Welsh-speaking communities equates to a viable future for the Welsh language, and this Action Plan outlines how we intend to achieve this policy aim.

Findings from the decennial census are reported in terms of demographic units at varying levels of inclusiveness, from electoral wards upwards, and to that extent it is perhaps unsurprising that *Iaith Pawb* frames its discussion of Welsh language distributions in terms of 'communities'. But it is still striking how firmly and assertively *Iaith Pawb* consolidates 'communities' as a focus for its policy-making. Extract 1 conjures an image of rather homogeneous communities that have the Welsh language in their 'fabric', in all salient dimensions of 'social, leisure and business' lives. We comment on the claimed 'livingness' and 'naturalness' of Welsh later, but it is clear – perhaps most obviously in Extract 2 – that protecting 'communities', and guaranteeing them 'a social and economic future', as well as a Welsh linguistic future, is an explicit objective for the Assembly.

Both extracts move from referencing 'communities' in the sense of distinct, small territories and populaces marked as count-nouns, to 'community' in a more abstract, non-count sense, through the phrase 'in the community'. That is, the extracts represent small communities as being filled out by local practices and values which constitute 'community', which is presumably a positive condition of sociality and mutual connectedness. The phrase 'living community language' in Extract 2 validates the Welsh language as a key dimension of this local social nexus.

We would not at all want to deny that there are identifiable zones, regions and in one sense or another 'communities' in Wales which face particularly extreme levels of social and economic deprivation. There clearly are, and they are, for example, currently being targeted by European Union 'Objective One' funding for deprived areas such as the south Wales Valleys and the rural west of Wales. Wales continues to report some of the very worst UK conditions on indicators of health and prosperity. But it is not feasible to map these patterns of structural socio-economic disadvantage onto a romanticised notion of 'communities'. It is clear, for example, that some of the most extreme circumstances of social deprivation in Wales exist in regions where a lived sense of communal mutuality and coherence has been ripped apart by rapid and chaotic deindustrialisation – particularly through the closure of heavy industrial plants involved in coal and steel production. Community is at risk as much in cities and towns in Wales as in rural areas, for example through largely unrecognised problems of racial divisiveness (see Williams *et al.*, 2003). Rural 'heartland communities' certainly confront their own distinctive difficulties, often linked to housing costs and Welsh language politics, as we shall see. But 'community', if it has any specific meaning at all, is not an apposite construct on which to hang general socioeconomic or sociolinguistic policies in contemporary Wales.

Sociolinguistics is very familiar with the idea that dense and multiplex social networks are breeding grounds for maintaining and building linguistic distinctiveness. The concept of 'speech community' has for a long time served as a unifying concept in sociolinguistics, where different sorts of cohesiveness have been assumed to exist – probably several at the same time – among people in identified communities (Patrick, 2004). 'Speech community' has implied people, as community members, drawing from a shared repertoire of language forms and speech varieties, or people expressing some shared socio-psychological allegiance to the local group through some pattern of linguistic marking. Yet the concept of speech community is under great critical pressure in sociolinguistics nowadays (see Rampton, 1998). The extent of linguistic and indeed cultural uniformity in any one so-called speech community is an empirical issue that is too-easily glossed over by the concept of community itself. Indeed it has always been structured *diversity* that has emerged as the hallmark of sociolinguistic speech communities, rather than any demonstrable form of uniformity. Taking social identity as a function of speech community is nowadays considered risky, when research typically foregrounds what is (perhaps equally riskily) called *identity hybridity*, or complexity in the contextualisation and expression of social identities. The assumption that 'community' in any specific sense – cultural, linguistic or affective – neatly coheres a group of people, whose social lives consist in blandly recycling normative social actions and subjectivities, is under strong attack in sociolinguistics. Rampton (2006) in fact identifies 'the linguistics of community' as being a lapsed phase in sociolinguistic theorising.

These are empirical questions, however, rather than matters of fashion in theory. We need to ask how 'community-like' is the prototypical Welsh 'heartland community', if we can identify it. An earlier Assembly document, *A Bilingual Future – Dyfodol Dwyieithog*, a 'policy statement' prepared in 2000 by the First Minister, Rhodri Morgan, and Minister for Culture, Sport and the Welsh Language, Jenny Randerson, makes fleeting mention of the village of Maentwrog in north-west Wales. It comes up in this sentence: 'Local flexibility will be a key element of the action plan because what is suitable for Maentwrog is unlikely to be appropriate for Monmouth.' It implies that Maentwrog is a reasonable exemplar of a 'small heartland community', to be contrasted with Monmouth, an affluent and very anglicised town in the south-east of Wales. So empirical questions might include whether and to what extent inhabitants of Maentwrog fulfil the ideal and ideologised criteria for authentic standing as 'a heartland community'. The research has not been done, but there are reasons to be sceptical. From its web presence, for example, Maentwrog seems to be a rather globally connected 'community'. The Yahoo search engine actually finds 8830 entries for Maentwrog. One of them is for The Grapes Hotel, where, the site says, 'Gruff, Danielle and all the Staff offer you a warm welcome'. The Hotel website is in English only and seems targeted partly at international hill walkers and mountain bikers. Another Maentwrog listing is for The Old Rectory, which is, it says, 'so beautiful in fact that it has featured in many films, the most recent being "First Knight" starring Richard Gere and Sean Connery. The old stone bridge that adjoins our gardens appears in that film'. We tolerate this digression only to make the point that it is entirely possible – and necessary – to have a global reach and outlook in Maentwrog, and that it is likely that heartland communities are generally *not* as sealed and homogenous as the Assembly's discourse of community might imply.

The Welsh Assembly is of course not unaware of the limitations of this rhetoric in connection with complex Late-Modern living, and it sometimes manages to ambiguate its assumptions about community. This is evident in Extract 2 where we get a fleeting representation of global processes impinging on Wales – Wales's problems being 'part of a wider problem of economic change, population movement and social dislocation'. In the extract, these wider problems are linked to 'urban' as well as 'rural' areas, and 'Welsh-speaking' is also fleetingly disconnected from the problem of communities. But *Iaith Pawb* has been generally responsive, as Colin Williams (2005) points out, to the pressure exerted by lobbying groups such as *Cymuned*. *Iaith Pawb* generally endorses the language-community link, particularly when it addresses the problem of population movement into 'heartland' Wales and the potential for attrition of Welsh. Extract 3 is from a section of *Iaith Pawb* dealing with so-called 'welcome packs'. These are an information and cultural learning resource for distribution to 'newcomers' (who are also elsewhere referred to as 'incomers'):

Extract 3

The Assembly Government is keen to increase the opportunities for newcomers and non Welsh-speaking adults in Welsh-speaking areas to learn the language, so they can fully participate in all aspects of life in their new community and contribute to supporting and sustaining one of the most distinctive features of that community ... People moving in to Welsh-speaking communities in Gwynedd and the Denbigh/Conwy area were provided with packs which introduced them to the linguistic profile and heritage of the area and provided details of how to learn and respect the language.

In Extract 3, learning of Welsh is said to afford full participative access to 'all aspects of life' of the 'new community'. There are remarkably strong assumptions here about the culturally determining potential of language, which we consider again below. But 'communities' once again emerge here as powerfully realist social structures, endowed with strong and 'distinctive' qualities in their 'profile', linked through to a 'heritage of the area' and deserving 'respect'. Community is clearly therefore a moral construct in this discourse, subsuming forms of practice that are not only legitimate in specific cultural spaces, but are entitled to assert their distinctiveness and impose it onto newcomers. The phrase 'the linguistic profile and heritage of the area' constructs a determinate sociolinguistic singularity which 'welcome packs' purport to be able to characterise and to 'introduce' to 'newcomers'. Although Extract 3 uses the noun 'opportunities' and the verb 'introduce' to characterise the Assembly's (or more likely local estate agents') processes of inculcating cultural doxa, these clearly *are* doxa, and the initiative is one of cultural pedagogy towards sociolinguistic and social assimilation.

Free of the discursive and institutional constraints that bind the Assembly, *Cymuned* itself is able to publicise a far more direct stance on intergroup relations, on 'within-community' versus 'incomer' conflicts, and on socioeconomic and sociolinguistic stakes. Extract 4 is from the front page of *Cymuned*'s website; Extract 5 is from a document titled '*What is Cymuned?*':

Extract 4

Cymuned is an anti-colonisation pressure group which works on behalf of Welsh-speaking communities. We are working to ensure that the current unacceptable colonisation of the Fro Gymraeg is brought to an end, that local people can get on the housing ladder, and that inward-migration to our communities is at sustainable, healthy levels ... We believe that a strong Fro Gymraeg is essential for a strong Cymru/Wales, and that keeping our language as a living community language in the Fro Gymraeg will help support and motivate Welsh speakers in other parts of the country.

Extract 5

Traditional Cymraeg-speaking communities face a real problem at the start of the twenty-first century. It is not that the language is dying of its own accord, and it is not that people do not wish to speak it, but rather that a very vibrant and rich minority culture is being threatened by a combination of socio-economic factors.

While the idea of 'welcome packs', endorsed by the Assembly, implies ingroup priorities and cultural ownership by 'small communities', *Cymuned* frames its politics in terms of 'colonisation'. Extract 4 explicitly contrasts in-migrants with 'local' people, and represents the communities in question as 'our communities'. *Cymuned* is clear that the communities of 'Y Fro Gymraeg' are its targeted concern, as opposed to the Assembly's hesitation between espousing this focus and an all-Wales focus, which its policies must at some level be seen to address. *Cymuned*'s claim that 'a strong Fro Gymraeg is essential for a strong Cymru/Wales' either claims a metonymic status for *Y Fro Gymraeg*, standing for all-Wales, or else implies that 'the real Wales' or 'the Wales worth defending' is located there, at least as a stimulus to political action by Welsh-speaking people living elsewhere. In Extract 5, *Cymuned* locates the core problem as defending 'traditional Cymraeg-speaking communities at the start of the twenty-first century', styling itself as an anti-globalisation movement and giving priority to cultural 'richness' and tradition over deleterious demographic and economic forces invading from outside.

Cymuned directly articulates principles of minority rights, often located in an ecological discourse of sustainability, for example referring to a loss of linguistic and cultural diversity. Extract 6 is taken from a Policy Document, written by Jerry Hunter as a *Presentation to the UN Working Group on Minorities, May 2002*. Extract 7 is from a document titled *Holiday Homes Policy*:

Extract 6

I would like to draw your attention to the problems faced by the Welsh-speaking minority of Wales and the fact that one of the most fundamental rights of Welsh-speaking communities is being threatened: the right to exist and the right to continue to exist.

A combination of social and economic factors, aided and abetted by governmental inaction and a lack of political will, is now threatening to destroy this linguistic minority completely.

Extract 7

The issue of holiday homes ownership is a controversial subject in Wales. Many people in rural Welsh-speaking communities cannot afford to own property. The situation is made worse by wealthy individuals, often from England, buying up property in scenic villages and thus further pricing the locals out of the housing market.

Cymuned believes that the right of Welsh citizens to be homed should take precedence over the rights of wealthy individuals to own property in Wales for entertainment purposes. There is room to allow a small proportion of the housing stock in Wales to be put aside to allow other European citizens property for entertainment and relaxation, but this should only be allowed within the context of a sustainable host community.

Extract 6 interprets a 'right to (continue to) exist' as a linguistic and cultural minority's right to exist uninfluenced by incomers, projecting a scenario of cultural death through Welsh language attrition. Extract 7 opposes 'the right of Welsh citizens to be homed' to 'the rights of wealthy individuals to own property in Wales for entertainment purposes'. Several more specific semantic oppositions are constructed, for example between (local) 'citizens' and (incoming) 'individuals', between 'being homed' (not 'housed') and 'owning property', and between the motives of 'existing' and 'for entertainment'. Moral authority attaches to the first element in each opposition, where citizenship is coded for social entitlement in a context of responsibility, 'home' is coded for social solidarity, and 'existing' is coded as a basic human right in contrast to the opportunistic hedonism of 'entertainment'.

In other parts of *Cymuned*'s discourse, ecological and moral assumptions come more to the surface. Extract 8 is from the same source as Extract 6:

Extract 8

Statistics clearly show that Welsh as a community language is being undermined. One of the indigenous languages of the United Kingdom is being threatened with extinction, and thus the multinational, multicultural and multilingual society of the United Kingdom is being threatened. Moreover, the minority of people who speak Welsh as their first language are being denied the right to continue as a distinct cultural and linguistic group.

The general principle of intervening in the free market for moral reasons is well established in the realm of ecology. It has long been recognized that economic and industrial forces must be regulated in order to protect threatened ecosystems and thus preserve the natural wealth of the world... The same holds true for preserving the cultural wealth of the world and protecting threatened linguistic minorities like the Welsh-speaking communities of Wales.

(......)

The disappearance of Welsh-speaking communities shows that a minority community in a developed, democratic country can be pushed to the brink of extinction by governmental refusal to recognize the dangers posed by a free-market economy to economically weak minority communities. If individual economic might is allowed to triumph over the rights of minority communities, then those communities will cease to exist.

These extracts show that *Cymuned* is adept at drawing from a tradition of sociolinguistic theorising that interprets language diversity as a direct equivalent of bio-diversity, using the ecological case to defend 'minority language rights' or 'linguistic human rights' (Skutnabb-Kangas, 1998, Skutnabb-Kangas and Phillipson, 1994, Tollefson, 1991; see Pennycook, 2004 and May, 2005 for general reviews, and May, 2001: 252ff. for a discussion of rights in the Welsh context). But Stephen May's introduction to the 2005 collection explains how the language ecology and linguistic human rights movements are under extreme pressure in sociolinguistics, partly through critiques of their intellectual underpinnings and partly because of problems linked to applying their stances in local circumstances. Some elements of this critique, which we cannot review in detail here, are the tendency to freeze out historical factors, a tendency to romanticise cultural uniqueness, essentialising of the link between a language and a social identity, and a blindness about how support for one set of rights might infringe another set of rights. These are in addition to a narrowness in conceptualising 'the language', which we come on to, below. The point is not that language ecology arguments are 'incorrect' or even that they are necessarily 'impractical'. Cymuned's moral case in opposition to 'the free market' in population movement, house pricing and language choice 'triumphing over' established sociolinguistic and perhaps cultural practices is coherent and poignant. But as an ideology, it presents great difficulties to a nationally-responsible administration which must look beyond the concerns of 'heartland communities' to other groups in Wales and to wider moral concerns.

Back in *Iaith Pawb*, the Assembly's hesitant policy towards 'communities' perhaps inevitably sometimes results in phatic and empty rhetoric. This is partly because the Labour administration needs to acquiesce to a distinctively *New* Labour stance on community. Some commentators (Driver and Martell, 1997, 1998, Fairclough, 2000, Gould, 1998) have argued that New Labour is strongly influenced by 'communitarian' philosophy. In contrast to liberalism, which, as Calder (2004) points out, tends towards individualism and the assertion of individual rights, communitarianism sees individuals as primarily defined within and through their relationships with others. Community is therefore a 'moral starting point' (MacIntyre, 1985: 220). But as Fairclough (2000) points out, 'responsibility to the community', from a New Labour perspective, refers not so much to the responsibility of business and market forces to the community and its members, and more to individuals' moral responsibilities to their own communities. We reach what Loughlin and Williams (in press) refer to as the 'communitarian social state' – an approach that attempts to add elements of social solidarity and community to the neoliberal reforms of the 1980s. In clear contrast to *Cymuned*'s socialist/nationalist stance on state responsibilities to protect heartland Welsh communities, we therefore find *Iaith Pawb* arguing tortuously that 'the community' needs to look to maintaining its own distinctiveness and (Welsh) language, as in Extracts 9 and 10:

Extract 9

The philosophy underpinning our regeneration strategy is that the solution to a community's problems essentially lies within the community itself. Our aim is to empower and enable the communities to decide for themselves what needs to be done to regenerate their areas and to involve them in developing and implementing agreed local delivery plans... Ultimately, however, it is for the community to recognise that if the language is to survive at the community level, the community itself must take responsibility.

Extract 10

The third strand in our strategy will focus on the right of the individual to use the language of their choice and the responsibility of organisations within Welsh society to acknowledge and facilitate the individual's right to do so. The Assembly Government is committed to Wales becoming a truly bilingual country and our policies will continue to encourage individuals to learn Welsh and empower them to use the language. But the language will not flourish on the back of institutional support alone – however strong that support and commitment may be. The Assembly Government and its partners can work to create the right conditions, but individuals themselves must recognise that they too have a responsibility to the language by passing it on to their children and by having the confidence to use it in the widest possible variety of social and business settings.

Language

Sociolinguistics would need to turn its back on fifty years of empirical and theoretical research to accept a notion of 'a language', or therefore 'the Welsh language', as referring to an unproblematic monolith. Over the whole of this period mainstream sociolinguistic research has set itself ideologically against hegemonic assumptions that 'a language' can be identified as a single variety or inventory of linguistic forms operating across a social matrix. The most straightforward contrary case can be put through recognising complex systems of diversity running through the field supposedly occupied by the concept of 'a language'. Sociolinguistic interests in accents and dialects, where any one speech variety is viewed as having its legitimate place in the system alongside others, provide the obvious case of diversity, but another is the vast range of linguistic styles and communicative genres that make up 'a language'.

It is clear in the extracts we have considered so far that 'the Welsh language' remains implausibly monolithic in public discourse in Wales. The Welsh Language Board has as its primary, Welsh name *Bwrdd Yr Iaith* ('The Board of/for The Language'), with a confident determinacy of reference. But we have to ask what forms and patterns of linguistic use are actually in question when we talk of 'a revitalising Welsh language'. We know that the upturn in reported numbers of people using Welsh at the 2001 census (notwithstanding the ambiguities of the census questions and criteria about 'use of Welsh' – see Aitchison and Carter, 2004) derives from increased Welsh-speaking among young people, mainly in the urban south-east of Wales, who have learnt Welsh as a compulsory curriculum subject to age 16. This is in itself an impressive and encouraging trend. But the issue of which *varieties* of Welsh are coming more into circulation, and what communicative *purposes* are being realised through Welsh, when, where and by whom, remain largely unknown.

The quantitative framing of 'revitalisation', for example in the Assembly's target of increasing 'the number of Welsh speakers' by 5 percent by the year 2011, skates over everything that matters in qualitative sociolinguistic dimensions. 'More use of Welsh' is uncritically taken to be the central criterion for 'a stronger Welsh bilingualism' and perhaps for 'a more distinctive Wales', but we need to ask what persists and what is changing, inside the shifting demographics of 'Welsh speakers', in terms of communicative functions, national subjectivities and cultural values.

We have already mentioned the risk of essentialising the language-to-identity link, and it is remarkable how glib are the assumptions made about this relationship, even by leading authorities on Welsh-English bilingualism. Aitchison and Carter, for example, make an impassioned plea for creating 'an association between being Welsh and speaking Welsh, for only with that firmly established is there real hope for the emergence of a truly bilingual Wales to replace the old polarised split between a Welsh-Wales and Anglo-Wales'. In fact they are in favour of 'convincing all of the people of the centrality of the association of Welsh identity with the language' (2004:144). This stance at least acknowledges that there is more sociolinguistic revitalisation than a numbers game, but it ignores the fact that ethic/national affiliation in Wales has a life beyond the minority language. In fact we have recent data (Coupland *et al.*, in press, Coupland *et al.*, submitted) showing that strong levels of affiliation to Wales exist geographically and socially *throughout* Wales. If there was an 'old polarised split between a Welsh-Wales and Anglo-Wales', it has now lapsed. Indeed, in our data, strong affiliation spreads well beyond the boundaries of the nation, including vibrantly pro-Welsh subjectivities expressed by expatriate, returning emigrant and long-term in-migrant groups. These findings lead us to be highly sceptical of there being any generalisable split, socio-psychologically speaking, between 'local community' and 'incomer' or 'outsider' groups, and this is a very welcome finding. We also find that competence in using Welsh is only one of several social factors that are connected to high levels of affiliation to Wales.

Yet *Iaith Pawb* consistently recycles the Welsh language-Welsh identity associative myth and the quantitative priority for 'the language', as we have seen above but see again in Extracts 11 and 12:

Extract 11

The Welsh Assembly Government believes that the Welsh language is an integral part of our national identity. The Welsh language is an essential and enduring component in the history, culture and social fabric of our nation. We must respect that inheritance and work to ensure that it is not lost for future generations.

Extract 12

We believe that the long-term well-being of the language is dependent on enabling as many pre-school children and young people as possible to acquire the language and as early as possible. Accordingly, we want to sustain the growth of the language which has been achieved over the past two decades among school-age children, improve the rate of language transfer from Welsh-speaking parent to their children and encourage those who have used or acquired the language at school to retain and use it once they have left.

But we want to look beyond mere numbers of people who can speak Welsh. We want Wales to be a truly bilingual nation, by which we mean a country where people can choose to live their lives through the medium of either or both Welsh or English and where the presence of the two languages is a source of pride and strength to us all.

These and earlier extracts are replete with metaphors that portray Welsh not only as a unitary phenomenon, historically unchanging and 'essential' to Welsh 'culture and social fabric', but as a living organism which grows and can have health problems. Metaphor is language's medium and the organic metaphor for languages themselves is thoroughly familiar. However, other than as a reified cultural icon, 'a language' exists only as an abstract lexico-grammatical resource, a particular way of operationalising language, a meaning potential waiting to be activated by speakers and listeners. What exactly is activated and 'how that language means on that occasion' are very much matters of the local moment and context. So, for example, there is nothing inherently and necessarily 'Welsh' about the meanings that 'the Welsh language' activates. It is a familiar experience in Wales that the English language can animate Welsh cultural distinctiveness in its different forms, but also that a Welsh linguistic code can animate cultural meanings and values imported from elsewhere. There is a broad tendency for the world's languages to animate speech genres and meanings that have a *global* rather than a local frame of reference. Television quiz shows and reality shows, or global music formats, carry rather uniform cultural values, whatever the language in which they are coded, and this is true in Wales too.

'More Welsh, earlier', as prioritised in Extract 12, elides any analysis of what really could be culturally distinctive in the use of the Welsh language, or indeed other languages, and what values might more convincingly underpin a language education programme. Our argument is not at all that Welsh does not matter as a vehicle for cultural transmission. We agree with Raymond Williams who has repeatedly emphasised the unique historical continuity and literary heritage of Welsh, and who saw in those qualities a powerful case for promoting 'the language'. 'The Welsh language', or more accurately 'specific ways of using Welsh-language resources', do have great potential to articulate Welsh sensibilities and to constitute Welshness. But so do other linguistic codes and other semiotic forms of cultural performance, and 'what matters about Welshness' does not follow as a simple consequence of marshalling Welsh lexis, syntax and phonology. We also agree with Raymond Williams's view that Wales's 'costume past' and a loose sense of our supposed Celtic authenticity are not sufficient as a basis for cultural engagement (Williams, 2003: 178). Williams pointed to the fact that there are multiple historical 'truths' about Wales, and that Wales may be best distinguished by how it has played off one cultural formation against another, and learned to manage repeated waves of 'penetration' by hegemonic Englishness. The most enduring theme in his analysis of

'Welsh identity' is his conviction that we must respect 'the complex of forced and acquired discontinuities' and the 'profoundly and consciously problematic' (2003: 20) nature of Welsh cultural life.

There is always the argument that language planners and language rights activists 'cannot afford' to indulge in 'complex messages' of this sort. But this is marketing discourse and a critical analysis has to question what is achievable and what is being achieved in the 'revitalisation of Welsh'. It seems from some of our own research that there is a growing attachment in Wales, as well as from Welsh-identifying people living outside Wales, to 'ceremonial' functions for Welsh. This is when people endorse the view that Welsh is an appropriate code to use in personal names, institutional titles, in singing the national anthem and in the mini-rituals of greetings and leave-takings. Welsh of course functions widely in 'full communicative' functions as well as ceremonial ones. But our data show that there is a regular perception that Welsh 'belongs' in ceremonial functions rather more than in communicative functions, for example in the workplace (see the sources cited earlier). In our view this is not necessarily the 'disappointing' finding that it might seem to be, particularly when we realise how richly Late-Modern discourse draws on ceremonial and performative functions. Welsh 'in performance' seems to be an entirely predictable format, and one that inevitably follows from the metalinguistically and reflexively intense circumstances that language planning promotes.

The documents we are examining here show no awareness of functional or cultural complexities behind 'the Welsh language'. The phrase a 'truly bilingual' Wales surfaces in Extracts 10 and 12, as well as in the Aitchison and Carter quote, above. Extract 12 offers a definition of 'truly bilingual', in terms of *choice* – 'a country where people can choose to live their lives through the medium of either or both Welsh or English and where the presence of the two languages is a source of pride and strength to us all'. The second part of this formulation seems to imply (importantly for a 'doctrine of plenary inclusion', as Colin Williams refers to *Iaith Pawb*) that the simple 'presence' of both languages, whether many individuals speak them or not, might be symbolically sufficient for the nation. But the first part of the definition conjures a sociolinguistic fantasyland where code choice is free and non-normative. This is the 'true bilingualism' of the parallel text, where individuals (in classic New Labour mode) exercise 'choice' over which language code to use, as lifestyle options, as the moment takes them.

Quite to the contrary, sociolinguistic research on multilingualism has generally emphasised how language codes tend to be allocated to particular discourse functions in 'speech communities', typically in complementary distribution to one another. It has also shown how language codes in bilingualism are routinely mixed and switched, often within single utterances. To posit a wholesale equivalence between languages, and languages held as discrete and fully-formed codes, is sociolinguistically naïve or else disingenuous. But we also know that claims of this sort tends to be hegemonic claims. They are usually made by elites who have some interest in (discursively) minimising the extent and value of sociolinguistic diversity and complexity, in favour of standard(ised) varieties which they themselves tend to command as cultural resources and capital. This is not how the Welsh Assembly Government comes to the debate, although there is a risk here, similar to the risks that follow from ideologies of linguistic purism. It is that linguistic varieties deemed to be 'incomplete' (e.g. partially learned, code-mixed) or 'non-standard' (e.g. regionally or class-marked) might be excluded from the 'truly bilingual' ideal. Just at a time when the Welsh establishment needs to be openly welcoming *any* and *all* forms of Welsh practice, any and all levels of competence and varieties involving Welsh, it is highly unfortunate for an untenable bilingual ideal to be being promulgated. The idea of 'choice' does not mitigate the problem, because we know that 'communities' (whatever they might be) develop norms of production and interpretation around language variation, according to which ways of speaking come to be seen as 'how language can be used'. The further risk, then, is that *structural* inequalities enter the sociolinguistic scene, in part because of an ideology that is blind to these socio-political operations.

On *Cymuned*'s part there are oddly similar risks. Their discourse foregrounds the minoritised status of Welsh so forcefully that, in its defence, it too homogenises 'the Welsh language' and its 'essential' link to Welsh cultural distinctiveness. *Cymuned* of course does not suggest that 'choice' is available. Its rhetoric is about curtailing the influence of English incomers (restricting their 'choice') and asserting the 'naturalness' of Welsh in 'heartland communities'. But this stance too is in danger of misfiring. The 'natural' sociolinguistic condition of 'heartland communities' is undoubtedly more bilingual and diverse than *Cymuned*'s discourse suggests. We know that purist ideologies generate counter-purisms, and that language activism constructs an ideological climate in which the positive subjectivities of non-Welsh speakers and even 'incomers' (see above) could easily be undermined. Alastair Pennycook (1998) points out that to divide languages into dominant and dominated, minority and majority, can only succeed to a certain degree, and inevitably leads to an oversimplification of power relations. The Assembly's denial of power issues, in its appeal to 'free choice', is clearly inadequate. But so is *Cymuned*'s unilateralist view of power, when it is evident that 'market forces' and globalisation effects are felt within 'the heartland' as well as outside it – in Maentwrog as well as in Monmouth or Manchester.

Discussion

Benedict Anderson (1983) is usually credited with developing the clearest critical perspective on how language is one part of the cultural apparatus for *imagining* distinctive nations. We have shown how, in some particular respects, public discourses of language and community in *post-devolution* Wales reflect rather particular imaginings of Wales and of Welshness, and how these might serve their particular political needs more than they shed light on sociolinguistic processes and opportunities. We take the view that discourse about language and community in the public sphere in Wales needs to be much more critically sophisticated and nuanced than, according to the materials we have examined here, it currently is. We hope there will be emancipation in greater awareness, and we would expect that recognising sociolinguistic complexities will let more air – and more people and more bilingual practice – into the rather claustrophobic ideological machines of 'Welsh language regeneration'.

The contrary case, which *Cymuned* would put, is that critical reflexivity is a distraction when 'there is a language to be saved'. It is impossible for sociolinguists not to be drawn to *Cymuned*'s politics, and there is the undeniable fact that language activism has brought about significant 'improvements in the Welsh language's health' (to use the commodifying and organic metaphors). Their ecological perspective, as we noted, still has considerable support within sociolinguistics, and, as we noted, it amounts to a far more coherent discourse than that of the Assembly, stretched and deformed as it is by different political considerations. *Cymuned*'s central linguistic argument is that, in the case of 'heartland communities' in Wales, preserving linguistic diversity primarily means ensuring that Welsh can continue to enjoy its local majoritarian status, even if this needs to be achieved by 'incomers' adopting Welsh. The urgency of *Cymuned*'s rhetoric is persuasive and there is the possibility that their strategies are correct, if the criterion is whether numerical trends will be enhanced in favour of Welsh in the near future.

But the ideologies of sociolinguistic retrenchment and language engineering do not sit fully comfortably with eco-principles, and they are not unalloyed 'goods'. We are seeing significant sociolinguistic shifts in Wales at present, whereby Welsh speaking is coming to be associated as much with young people as with the old, and with urban as much as with rural Wales. Welsh is taking on a less socially regimented character. There is a good deal to celebrate in these trends, as well as reasons to regret the continuing 'shrinking of the heartland'. Varieties of Welsh are no doubt evolving, just as new functions for its use are coming to the fore. There is an ecological 'naturalness' to these changes, which will be hard to resist through legislation, 'welcome packs' or patterns of economic investment. There is the risk that, in trying to shore up authentic sociolinguistic Welshness, we will in any case end up with forms, meanings and practices that have evolved internally. The core notion here is *meaning*, and language planning is far less capable of determining what is *meant* by language than what forms language use takes.

The national project that political devolution has handed to Wales in many ways comes at an odd moment – a time when national boundaries are being redrawn, when the securities that nationalisms once brought are being undermined by global realignments (Bauman, 2001a), and where nations, especially 'small' ones, have to find new niches and market values to remain viable. Central concepts here are flows (of people, ideas and symbols) and new interdependencies (economic and cultural). The contemporary context of post-devolution Wales, then, offers an arena in which sociolinguistic and cultural identity issues are highlighted and are being worked out in a context of political and cultural change. The concepts of 'Welsh communities' and 'the Welsh language' have been and will inevitably continue to be reshaped by these massive realignments, and social and sociolinguistic policy-making may be the more successful for working through how Wales and Welsh can ride these changes – productively, creatively and enthusiastically – rather than simply set out to resist them. Raymond Williams backed 'the true nation, the actual and diverse people [of Wales]', through whom 'the cultural struggle for actual social identities' and 'the political definition of effective self-governing societies' (2003: 197–8) can take place. We strongly approve of his commitment to authenticities, because arguments against glib authenticities are not arguments against the possibility of authenticity itself (Coupland, 2003). In this same spirit we would argue that it is the moment for Wales to build an openness of perspective around who we are in terms of 'community' and 'communities' (perhaps diverse, welcoming, loyal, quarrelsome and inconsistent) and around what makes us legitimately and distinctively Welsh in the domain of language – perhaps multi-valenced, combative, performative, and impossibly and irreverently multilingual.

Chapter 3

Vernacular Constructions of 'National Identity' in Post-devolution Scotland and England

Susan Condor and Jackie Abell

Introduction

The political process of UK constitutional change was accompanied by a set of moral panics concerning potential, possible or impending crises of national identity. Concerns were expressed that devolution would lead to a decline in 'British identity' which would in turn further undermine the legitimacy of the UK state. Similarly, concerns were expressed that the establishment of a Scottish parliament would precipitate a rise in 'Scottish identity', which would in turn lead to increased calls for Scottish political independence. However, the most colourful rhetorical formulations involved the spectre of a rise in English national consciousness threatening not only the constitutional status quo, but sometimes the very foundations of civilised society, as illustrated by John Barnes's comments to the House of Commons Select Committee on Scottish Affairs in 1998:[1]

> I think that we tend to feel that [English] people are more rational, more cool, more calculated than, in fact, they are, and I think with some skill, you could find a demagogue, shall we say, an Enoch Powell,[2] who could stir those passions in some rather strange quarters [...] I think these passions are there to be moved, and I think there are some very ugly forces who would love to move them.

Although these kinds of argument were typically presented as statements of mere common sense, existing academic analyses did not necessarily confirm the presuppositions on which they rested. For example, the idea that the legitimacy of the British state depended crucially on the construct of 'British identity' overlooked

---

[1]   Hansard: House of Commons Select Committee on Scottish Affairs Examination of Witnesses, 24 June 1998 (paragraph 276).

[2]   Reference to the MP who in 1968 made a controversial speech against immigration. The immediate response included displays of popular support from some Trades Unions, and his immediate sacking from the Conservative Party. Powell's 'rivers of blood' speech has subsequently come to be attributed with a dual legacy, as popularising 'racialist' understandings of Anglo British nationhood, but also as prompting a subsequent consensus on the part of mainstream British political parties against such formulations (Favell, 1998).

the enormous variety of ways in which Britishness is, and has been, understood (R. Cohen, 1994, Davies, 1999, Samuel, 1998) and the capacity for political institutions to be legitimated without direct recourse to the construct of 'identity' (cf. Kenny, 2004). The association in Scotland between Nationalism as a political force and national identity as a psychological condition appeared to owe more to the categories of formal political rhetoric than to those of common-sense (A. Cohen, 1996). Images of English people lacking reflexive awareness of the atavistic potential of their dormant national passion paradoxically represented a popular stereotype used at the time by English people themselves (Condor, 1996).

This chapter reports findings from a study conducted as part of an extensive programme of research, funded by the Leverhulme Trust, designed precisely to monitor the effects of constitutional change on orientations to national identity in England and in Scotland.[3]

National Identity in the Vernacular

It is so common now to encounter the term 'national identity' in political rhetoric or academic writing that it is easy to suppose that it constitutes an enduring feature of the lexicon of nationhood (cf. Billig, 1995). In fact, the term is of surprisingly recent provenance, rarely being used in the UK before the late 1980s. 'Identity' is a notoriously polyvalent term and a consideration of its use in the current literature on nationalism reveals a common tendency to elide the 'national identity' construct with pre-existing academic categories such as nation, nationality, nationalism, national character, citizenship, or imagined community. In addition, the ambiguities of the referent of the term 'identity' afford slippage between 'the nation' as an object of literary or political rhetoric and assumptions concerning the subjective self-consciousness of individual citizens.

This inconsistency in the use and understanding of the national identity construct may have contributed to a relative lack of direct empirical work on the ways in which ordinary social actors construct themselves as nationalised subjects. In practice, most scholarly accounts of national 'identities' in the UK have been based on the author's own interpretation of social structure or symbolism (e.g. R. Cohen, 1994, Edensor, 2002, Haseler, 1996, Kumar, 2003, Weight, 2003). Studies of talk and text have tended to focus on elite representations, in popular and high literature (Giles and Middleton, 1995, Pearce, 2000), the media (Creeber, 2004, Fitzgerald and Housley, 2002, Jacobson, 2002, Rosie et al., 2004) or political rhetoric (Billig, 1995, Chambers, 1989, Reicher and Hopkins, 2001).

Of course, some research has focussed on ordinary social actors' orientations to nationhood, using either survey or interview methodology. However, a good deal of this work has still tended to treat 'national identity' as an analysts' construct rather than a participants' resource. For example, social psychological work on national

---

[3]   The 'Nations and Regions' programme, coordinated by David McCrone http://www. institute-of-governance.org/forum/Leverhulme/levbrief.html.

identity has often been informed by general theoretical perspectives provided by social identity and self-categorization theory (e.g. Reicher and Hopkins, 2001, cf. Billig, 1996), and a dominant strand of sociological enquiry approaches the national identity problematic from a symbolic interactionist perspective (e.g. Bechhofer *et al.*, 1999, Kiely *et al.*, 2001, McCrone *et al.*, 1998).

Whilst we would not question the validity of these approaches in their own terms, in this chapter we adopt a rather different perspective. Following Billig's (1995) injunction that 'the psychological study of national identity should search for the common-sense assumptions and ways of talking about nationhood' (p. 61), and drawing on insights from discursive approaches to national representation (e.g. Hester and Housley, 2002, Windisch, 1990, Wodak *et al.*, 1999), we consider the ways in which ordinary social actors may construct nation-ness as a matter of subjective identity. To refer back to the quotation on page 1, we may note the prevalence of psychological assumptions and terminology: of rationality, calculation, skill, passion, and strategic intentionality. In this chapter we consider how ordinary social actors may – or may not – orient to nation-ness as a psychological state or trait, as a matter of knowledge, awareness, rationality, emotion, habit, character, agency, self-control and so forth (cf. Antaki and Widdicombe, 1998, Edwards and Potter, 1992, 2005).

Billig's suggestion that research should focus on 'common-sense assumptions and ways of talking about nationhood' begs the question of '*whose* common-sense?'. Billig's (1995) own account of the common-sense nature of 'British national identity' has subsequently been questioned for its implicitly Anglocentric focus (Abell *et al.*, 2006, Rosie *et al.*, 2004). A more general consideration of the question, 'whose common-sense?', reveals a lacuna in the extant academic literature on national identity. Although a good deal of work has considered how constructs such as nationhood and citizenship may be understood differently within and between different state bureaucracies or populations (Brubaker, 1992, Conover, Crewe and Searing, 1991, Favell, 1998), authors tend to treat the process of national *self-identification* as a pan-cultural universal. Comparative research has considered how people may vary in terms of the strength of their identification with a national category, or in terms of the object of this identification (for example, in a UK context, whether an individual identifies themselves as British, Irish, Scottish, Welsh, English, Pakistani etc.). However, it is generally supposed that the socio-psychological process, and subjective experience, of identification (whether understood as an outcome of self-categorisation processes, of the proffering and receipt of identity claims, etc.) is invariant (see A. Cohen, 1996 and Reicher and Hopkins, 2001: ix for explicit statements).

In contrast, our work adopts a comparative approach that follows from a general theoretical concern over the cultural specificity of societal and self-representation (Billig *et al.*, 1988) and over national representation in particular (Condor, 2001). Our particular concern has been to investigate the pervasive, and often subtle, differences that currently exist between discourses of nationhood used in Scotland and in England. Our analytic perspective involves a commitment to ethnomethodological indifference (Garfinkel and Sacks 1970) and to symmetrical accounting procedures (Bloor, 1976), which rather than evaluate vernacular accounts and displays of national identity against some prior definition or theoretical model, seeks instead to understand them in their own terms.

An initial study drew attention to a potential incommensurability between the ways in which nationhood was understood in relation to values of cultural integration and assimilation in pre-devolution Scotland and England (Faulkner *et al.*, 2002). Subsequently we have considered how people in post-devolution Scotland and England may employ different lay geographies and historiographies, and understand the construct of Britain in different ways (Abell, *et al.* 2006, Condor and Abell, 2006). In this chapter, we consider how ordinary social actors in Scotland and in England orient to nation-ness as a matter of identity.

The 'Nationals and Migrants' Study

Study Design

The data considered here have been taken from a five-year panel study conducted jointly with David McCrone, Richard Kiely and Frank Bechhofer at Edinburgh University.[4] The study involved repeat-interviews with people born and living in Scotland (N=60) and in England (N=100) conducted between 2000–2004. Panel respondents were recruited with a view to ensuring maximum sample diversity. Key sites in England and in Scotland were first selected on the grounds of their contrasting character: Glasgow and rural Perthshire in Scotland; Greater Manchester and rural East Sussex in England. Within each site, panel members were then recruited through a combination of open and theoretical sampling to ensure heterogeneity in terms of age, gender, political affiliation, and socio-economic status.

A narrative interview technique was employed whereby the interviewer started out by asking the respondent to 'tell me something about yourself', and once the respondent appeared at ease would start to shape the conversation to issues germane to the research interests, such as local, national and European identity, social inclusion and constitutional change. Interviews ranged between 45 minutes and 4 hours, with most lasting approximately 90 minutes.

Analysis and Reporting of Findings

Discursive psychologists sometimes elide the activity of 'analysis' with the account provided of the specific extracts presented in an academic article (Antaki *et al.*, 2003). For present purposes, however, we would wish to distinguish the summary report of our findings presented in this chapter from the analytic procedure by which an understanding of the data was originally arrived at.

Following the standard recommendations for inductive qualitative research (e.g. Silverman, 2000), analysis started at the point at which the first interview

---

[4]   Whilst the study was conducted jointly, the responsibility for the present analysis is, of course, the authors' own.

transcript became available. Throughout the analytic process, attention shifted from a consideration of the micro-features of particular recorded exchanges (informed by membership categorisation analysis, discursive psychology and frame analysis), coherence within accounts (informed by narrative analysis) and generalisability between rhetorical contexts and respondents (employing strategies based on the grounded theory techniques of constant comparison and deviant case analysis). Working hypotheses were regularly tested using truth tables and category counts (Seale, 1999). Emergent theories concerning patterning of response types were, in turn, used to direct subsequent sampling and interviewing procedures towards a search for disconfirming evidence. Where possible, conclusions based on this particular data corpus were subsequently tested against other data sets.

Since it is impossible in the space of a single chapter to do justice to the nuances of national representation and identity display in nearly 300 interviews, we shall limit our account in two respects. First, as noted above, we shall focus on the ways in which nationhood was (or was not) constructed as a psychological matter of identity. Second, in the interests of economy of exposition, we will focus only on those accounts provided by white people who either claimed not to support any particular political party or who claimed liberal-left political views but who did not affiliate themselves with Nationalist political parties.[5]

In order to balance a description of micro-features of particular exchanges with an appreciation both of intra-respondent variability and of narrative coherence, for purposes of exemplification, we shall focus on interview accounts provided by three particular respondents. All were middle class, in their mid forties, resident in urban areas (Glasgow and Manchester), all supported the Labour party, all claimed a 'strong' sense of national (Scottish and English) identity. In all cases, respondents are talking to a co-national (Richard Kiely in Scotland, and Jackie Abell in England). It should be emphasised that we are not suggesting that these particular interviews constitute 'typical' cases. Like all vernacular accounts of national identity, they are highly idiosyncratic (cf. A. Cohen, 1996). However, the particular features to which we shall draw attention do pertain to factors that analysis indicated to be common within, and often distinctive to, the national samples from which they were drawn.

---

[5]   Although this necessarily compromises the generalisability of the present analyses, the respondent group considered here in fact represents a majority of the total sample. Some measure of curtailment was necessary for reasons of economy of exposition, and the strategy adopted here has the benefit of maximising the comparability of the samples. In addition to the fact that there exists no obvious English equivalent to the SNP, Conservative party affiliation tends to be associated with political nationalism in England, and with unionism in Scotland. Whilst these are clearly interesting issues in their own right, space constraints prevent us from considering them here.

Vernacular Discourses of National Identity in Scotland

Respondents in Scotland typically spoke at some length about issues relating to nationality, citizenship and their own sense of national identity. In extract 1(a) Jenny is responding to a direct question concerning her *'sense of being Scottish'*:

Extract 1(a): 'It's a sense of identity'

1.	R:	We've touched on it a couple of times in the interview, you feel a
2.		sense of being Scottish, and this may be a difficult question to answer
3.		but why?
4.	J:	Why? Why do I have the pride or why do you have the feeling?
5.	R:	Or both?
6.	J:	It's a sense of identity, isn't it, really? I think that's what things come
7.		down to. It's whatever makes you feel comfortable and whatever puts
8.		you at ease. If you've got the choice between a scabby, rusty bike and
9.		a nice red, shiny bike, you'll choose the red, shiny bike over the other
10.		because you can feel proud of it. You can get on it and be the envy of
11.		all your friends. Not even the envy, you'll just be the same as all your
12.		friends. You have something in which, you have something that
13.		reflects, that you're part of, that you're proud to be part of. That's
14.		why, I think, that's why I feel so strongly about it. I'm so proud of my
15.		country. I'm so proud of my countrymen, not only those are living but
16.		those that have gone before and the contribution that's been made over
17.		the centuries. I'm just so proud to be part of that, albeit that I had no
18.		input in it whatsoever. I'm proud, by association.
19.	R:	Do you mean by that em?
20.	J:	Fleming, figures in history. Even right down to the unsung. The girls
21.		that worked in the munitions factories down in Clydebank and risked
22.		their lives night after night when the German bombers kept confusing
23.		the moonlight on the tarmacadammed road, but they still went. You
24.		just feel this incredible fierce pride.
25.	R:	You do feel pride?
26.	J:	Yes, I swell with pride. See when the old ones get together and they
27.		tell stories about the Blitz, I just think my God you were great wee
28.		ladies. Or even forget the Blitz, the fact they dragged themselves out
29.		the gutters and poverty in the east end of Glasgow or the Gorbals or
30.		wherever they were brought up particularly where there's deprivation.
31.		These wee ladies aw grafted their way through and brought up
32.		families, aye, they're terrific. The fishermen and the guys who went
33.		out in the boats from Peterhead, all the way through the First World
34.		War. Anything to do with it, I just feel an enormous source of pride
35.		because they're just stalwart. They just got on wi' things, no whining,
36.		just got right on with the job in hand.
37.	R:	So you don't just feel the sense of being Scottish simply on a basis that
38.		you happen to have been born in Scotland?
39.	J:	No, because I have met people who would love to be Scottish and they
40.		were born many thousands of miles away and have no Scottish blood
41.		whatsoever because it's an admirable quality.

There are clearly many potentially interesting aspects of this account. However, rather than attempt an exhaustive analysis, for present purposes we shall focus on the way in which Jenny presents being Scottish as '*a sense of identity*' (line 6), and in particular what, following Wittgenstein (1958), we might term 'mental state avowals', that is her use of psychological language, of '*pride*', '*feeling*', '*choice*' and '*envy*'.

Emotion and Rationality

The first, and possibly most obvious, consideration relates to the way in which Jenny's account of her sense of national identity is bound up with displays of positive sentimental attachment. Although Jenny initially orients to a potential distinction between the state of '*feeling*' Scottish and of having a sense of '*pride*' (line 4), in her subsequent account she treats the former as a direct function of the latter. Although Jenny's response is more strongly-worded than most of the interview accounts, it is nevertheless typical of the way in which respondents interviewed in Scotland treated claims to a strong '*sense of identity*' coupled with '*pride*' as the preferred response to a question concerning their '*feelings*' about '*being Scottish*'.

In so far as she casts national identity as a matter of emotional expression, Jenny appears to be employing a 'romantic' ideology of nationhood, in which her display of emotion attests to the authenticity of the identity in question (cf. Shields, 2005). However, we may note that Jenny is not treating her sense of emotional attachment to Scotland and to Scottishness as antithetical to rationality (cf. Edwards, 1999). On the contrary, by constructing her national identity as a matter of calculated 'choice', Jenny couples the experience of pride with matters of rationality and values of self-determination: '*If you've got the choice between a scabby, rusty bike and a nice red, shiny bike, you'll choose the red shiny bike over the other because you can feel proud of it*' (lines 8–10). In addition, we may note how Jenny casts her personal sense of national pride not as a reflection of her own chauvinistic prejudice, but rather as a rational appreciation of the objectively '*admirable quality*' (line 41) of Scottish nationality. This is accomplished through the narrative figure of the envious and respectful foreigner who, having no obvious stake, may be taken as arbiter of the objective value of Scottish culture and character. This was a common trope in accounts of Scottish national identity, and we see Jenny employing the same device again in extract 1(e).

Personal and Social Identity

Jenny's account of her subjective experience of national identity as '*whatever makes you feel comfortable and whatever puts you at ease*' (lines 7–8) corresponds with Anthony Cohen's (1996) depiction of 'personal nationalism', in which nationality serves as a vehicle through which to express immediate, authentic, personal experience. Elsewhere in her interview, Jenny constructs her sense of Scottish nationality as not simply compatible with, but as saturating, her sense of individual selfhood, using a metaphor of 'blood': '*That's who you are, that's your DNA chain, all the way through. You cannot deny blood* [...] *it's a fundamental*'. However, the sense of identity that Jenny projects is not merely a 'personal' identity understood as a sense of unique individuality (cf. Turner, 1987). Rather, an effective lamination of personal and collective identity is apparent in Jenny's casting of her own subjective experience as an exemplification of a normative case. On lines 23–24, Jenny ends with the gist statement, '*You just feel this incredible fierce pride*', and Richard uses an echoing technique as a prompt, '*You do feel pride*' (line 25). Jenny's response indicates that she interprets this question not as an indicator of the potentially accountable nature of her claim to 'pride', but rather as a request for clarification concerning the pronoun 'you'. Consequently, Jenny restates her position, but reformulates the generic 'you' into the personal 'I': '*I swell with pride*' (line 26).

At one stage, in the course of establishing her subjective sense of Scottish identity as a function of rational personal choice, Jenny employs an extreme case formulation (Pomerantz, 1986) noting how the possession of Scottish identity will make you '*the envy of all your friends*' (lines 10–11). In this original formulation, the category '*all your friends*' is presented as an interpersonal referent, with the implication that these people represent a benchmark against which to establish one's status as a unique individual (cf. Turner, 1987). However, Jenny immediately repairs this formulation, '*Not even the envy, you'll just be the same as all your friends*' (lines 11–12). Jenny's elision of the categories of Scottish compatriots and '*all your friends*' is significant for two reasons. First, it illustrates a tendency, relatively common among respondents in Scotland, to treat national identity (normally 'Scottish' but occasionally 'British') as functionally equivalent to local, concrete social relationships. That is, national identity is equated with what social scientists might gloss as 'civil society'. Although Jenny's interview was somewhat idiosyncratic in her use of literal and metaphoric references to family as a running theme, it was common for respondents in Scotland to make passing references to kith and kin, and to their local area of residence or birth, to warrant or illustrate generic claims concerning Scottish people, Scottish society or Scotland as place.

Second, we may note how Jenny constructs Scottish national identity as a matter of common category membership: a sense of 'being like' other people: '*you'll just be the same*'. This representation of social identification as involving a sense of substantive or functional equivalence with other ingroup members is, of course, central to the social psychological construct of self-categorisation (Turner, 1987), which has recently been applied specifically to matters relating to national identity by Reicher and Hopkins (2001). Again, it was common for respondents in Scotland to treat their own sense of Scottishness as a matter of shared character, culture and identity with other co-nationals. Elsewhere in her interview, Jenny oriented to a normative presumption that a condition of being-like constitutes a general psychological need (extract 1(c)). As we shall see in the next section, this sense of identity as sameness is also used rhetorically to link the immediacy and present-tense quality of friendship and kinship networks with the Scottish nation as a geographically and historically distanciated imagined community.

Synchronic and Diachronic National Community Membership

From line 13 onwards, Jenny starts to work up an account of her *'sense of identity'* in terms of a sense of communitarian belonging, or being *'part of'* (line 13). Initially, she constructs the object of this identity as a non-specific *'something'* (line 12). She then reformulates this as a matter of place attachment, *'my country'* (lines 14–15), and then upgrades this to a sense of attachment to a national people, *'my countrymen'* (line 15). The category *'my countrymen'* is then extended beyond a sense of synchronic community (Anderson, 1983), to constitute a quasi-ethnic group with a common and historically enduring heritage *'not only those are living but those that have gone before'* (lines 15–16). National-historical elisions are accomplished by tense slippages, as Jenny moves from an account of past heroism to current character (*'aye, they're terrific'*, line 32; *'they're just stalwart'*, line 35).

On lines 17–18 Jenny temporarily forges a distinction between personal and national identity: *'albeit that I had no input in it'*. However, this statement is in practice formulated as an inoculation device, allowing Jenny forcefully to reassert: *'I'm proud, by association'* (line 18). On line 19, Richard requests further clarification: *'Do you mean by that em?'*. In response, Jenny works up a vivid and substantive account starting with an allusion to a conventional stereotype of Scottish historical accomplishment in science and technology, but then switching to a focus on the heroism of the *'unsung'* (line 20), her rendition of diachronic Scottish national community involving what MacCormick (1982 p. 249) has described as, a 'communal past, including shared suffering and shared achievement'.

In addition, we may note how Jenny presents her sense of pride in Scottish national identity as identification with what, following Anderson (1983 p. 16), we might gloss as 'a deep, horizontal comradeship': that is, a sense of common identity, purpose, belonging and character that transcends class or generation. To this end, the categories of class and of war-heroism are customised to fit precisely within the imagined contours of the Scottish nation. At no stage does Jenny orient either to variations within the Scottish experience, nor to the possibility that shared histories of economic privation or Blitzkrieg might provide a basis for imagining extra- or trans-national forms of community.

This rhetorical work of national categorisation does not, however, undermine what Anthony Cohen (1996) described as the 'iconic intimacy of Scottish collective identity, its proximity to the circumstances of everyday life' (p. 810). At the same time as constructing Scottishness as a singular horizontal community, Jenny's shift from a 'Great Man' to a 'People's' history is accompanied by a rhetorical feminisation of imagined national community, and a casting of the local (Glasgow, the Gorbals) as exemplificatory of the entire Scottish nation.

Self and Other

It has, of course, been commonly observed that both personal and social identities are often defined in comparative terms, and that national identity may be commonly defined in relation to an imagined 'other'. Although it is generally agreed that any national ingroup may be defined against a variety of potential outgroups, commentators have particularly noted the tendency for Scottish identity to be defined primarily in contrast to the category English. This tendency was, unsurprisingly, clearly evident in the current corpus of interview data.

Jenny's account of her thoughts and feelings concerning '*the English*', reproduced in extract 1(b), illustrates a particular dilemma of identity display that was commonly apparent in the interview accounts. On the one hand, respondents in Scotland oriented to a perceived normative requirement to differentiate a Scottish self from an English other, and *vice versa*. Moreover, the perceived requirement to display a sense of positive ingroup distinctiveness (cf. Tajfel, 1978) was such that displays of positive or neutral sentiment towards 'the English' were routinely treated as a potential threat to the speaker's claim to Scottish identity (Stevenson *et al.*, 2004). On the other hand, speakers displayed concern to avoid the stigmatised identity of 'anti-English' prejudice on behalf both of themselves as individuals and of the Scottish nation as a whole. This dilemma was routinely managed using rhetorical strategies that will be familiar to any student of the strategic aspects of 'prejudiced discourse' as outlined, for example, by van Dijk (1984).

Extract 1 (b) 'the English' as other

1.	J:	This is awful, this is really, really quite awful, right, but I would feel a
2.		link with anybody before I would feel a link with the English.
3.	R:	Do you know why that is?
4.	J:	I've no idea. I think it's probably learned behaviour. I think it's
5.		probably grown up from hearing about the Highland Clearances. I
6.		think its probably grown up from over the years from sitting watching
7.		footage of Culloden and seeing the Butcher of Cumberland coming in
8.		and going like a mad thing round the place.

In lines 1–8 we see Jenny combine an explicit account of her psychological sense of social distance from English people with use of linguistic demonstratives of distance ('*the English*'). At the same time she displays a recognition of the potentially counter-normative status of these sentiments, thereby inoculating herself from possible charges of unreflexive prejudice. When prompted for an explanation, her first response involves reference to childhood socialisation ('*I think it's probably learned behaviour*', line 4), projecting responsibility onto her teachers or the media,[6] and disclaiming any current, conscious act of will on her own behalf. Soon after, however, Jenny switches tack, and treats her lack of felt '*link*' as a rational response to the English '*attitude*', initially treated as a matter of perception ('*they come*

---

[6]   This particular extract illustrates the propensity for variability within accounts: earlier Jenny had volunteered that she had not learned about Scottish history at school.

across') but then immediately upgraded to a statement of objective fact concerning English national character (*'they feel superior'*):

11.   I think the English have got a dreadful habit, and I say that, and it's
12.   very broad brush, of adopting the moral and the social high ground at
13.   everything, they come across, they feel superior to everyone and I find
14.   it offensive, that attitude.

Jenny is here implicitly orienting to a distinction between patriotic pride deriving from a rational recognition of national virtues (such as that which she proclaims on her own behalf) and an *'offensive'* *'attitude'* or irrational *'habit'* of *'adopting'* a stance, and *'feeling'* of superiority. Once again, Jenny combines her account with a display of recognition of the stereotyped nature of the assertion (*'it's a very broad brush'*, lines 11–12), and shortly afterwards mitigates her categorical account through the use of re-fencing, whereby 'the English' are re-specified in such a manner as to exclude people from Newcastle or Liverpool. Her hyperbolic formulation, *'I love people from Newcastle ...'* both displays her own non-prejudiced character and provides an implicit point of negative contrast with *'their fellow countrymen'*:

16.   As I say I love people from Newcastle and I love people from
17.   Liverpool, ((coughs)) excuse me, because they don't
18.   display certain qualities that are displayed among their fellow
19.   countrymen.

It is worth noting that Jenny's comment, *'As I say I love people from Newcastle ...'* referred back to an earlier exchange in which she had not, in fact, referred directly to matters of *'love'*, but had rather said that *'Glasgow, Newcastle and Liverpool'* are *'very similar'* in their *'outlook and their opinions and the way they communicate'*. The implicit bridging inference is that sentimental attachment is necessarily and legitimately entailed with a sense of being-like.

Finally, Jenny presents her lack of felt *'affinity'* as a rational reaction to the factually *'brash'* and *'opinionated'* behaviour of *'the English'*, this time warranted with reference to personal experience *'on holiday'*. This particular narrative device is significant in view of the fact that Jenny had worked in England for a considerable period of time, although she had never been permanently domiciled there. Consequently, her use of the 'holiday' frame here would appear to be serving two functions. First it reinforces the elision of civil society with Scottish people by presenting encounters with 'English people' as occurring outside of the mundane experience of everyday life. Second, it allows Jenny to invoke a sense of shared experience with other members of her national ingroup (note the generic *'you'*).

20   You go on holiday. They're loud, they're brash, they're opinionated.
21   I just don't feel any affinity with English people. I feel it for my Irish
22   brothers and Welsh sisters, but I don't feel it for England as a nation.
23   I feel it for individuals but not for the nation.

Between lines 20–23 Jenny again displays her non-prejudiced character and signals the particularity of 'their' objectionable character by contrasting her feelings for *'English people'* with those for her *'Irish brothers and Welsh sisters'*. Finally, she re-formulates the object of her negative feelings from people to 'the nation': *'I feel it [affinity] for individuals but not for the nation'* (line 23). It was common for respondents in Scotland to deflect potential changes of anti-English prejudice by shifting the object of their talk to a depopulated or spatially-defined category (note, for example, Jenny's earlier attribution of psychological and behavioural traits to *Glasgow, Liverpool* and *Newcastle*), often presented in the form of euphemistic references to 'south of the border' or to references to England as 'neighbour' (as Jenny put it later: *'a near neighbour across the Hadrian's Wall'*).

Jenny did not simply represent a subjective sense of national identity as a matter of her own personal experience. Rather, the psychological experience of national identity was itself cast as a form of shared possession that positively differentiated 'us' from the English out-group.

Extract 1(c) 'They don't have an English culture'

1.   J: That's what's wrong with the English. They don't have an English
2.   culture. They've gone out and they've stolen everyone else's in the
3.   past. They weren't too keen on what the Indian community had on
4.   offer, you don't see them giving it large with the dance of the seven
5.   veils. So they just trample over things because they don't have it
6.   themselves, they envy what other people have.
[…]
14.   they envy this purity and the fact that; there was a form a dress.
15.   What's their form of dress? They dinnae have kilts, we've got kilts,
16.   the Irish have kilts and the wee Welshmen have the daft hats. Do you
17.   know what I mean? There's a social identity there, a cultural identity.

Unlike the other component nationalities of the British Isles, *'the English'* have national character, but lack indigenous culture, and hence a *'social identity'*. This lack of identity is treated both as causing a negative psychological state – *'envy'* – but also as symptomatic of a more deeply rooted, enduring, pathology of national character.

National Identity and Polity

We noted at the start of this Chapter how academics often use the term 'national identity' in a rather loose way, and fail to distinguish it from other constructs such as 'imagined community', 'nationality' or 'citizenship'. Our present concern with commonsense constructions of national identity was informed partly by the analytic insight that ordinary social actors themselves may, on occasions, forge distinctions between the constructs. We noted above how Jenny effectively treats her own sense of Scottish identity as functionally equivalent to a sense of common category membership ('being like'), of imagined community ('being for', 'being of') and civil society ('being with'). However, Jenny did not treat all national issues, nor issues of political community, as matters of subjective identity.

We also noted at the start of this chapter how post-devolution moral panic discourses often treated the construct of 'British identity' as a proxy for the constructs of 'UK citizenship', or of 'attitude towards the British state' (e.g. Curtice and Seyd, 2001). Throughout her interview, Jenny consistently disclaimed any subjective sense of British identity, and provided two possible explanations for this state of affairs. First, she suggested that the salience of any aspect of identity might be contingent on experience of it having been '*challenged*':

Extract 1(d): 'I've never been challenged on my Britishness'

1.	R:	So, for example, we talked a little bit before about the idea of pride in
2.		being Scottish, pride in being British?
3.	J:	I've never thought about it because I don't consider it. As I say, I
4.		consider myself first and foremost Scottish. In saying that I've never
5.		been challenged on my Britishness. I've been challenged on my
6.		Scottishness.

Later, Jenny suggested that her failure to think of herself or call herself British represented a reaction to experiences of negative reception from others who confused the categories British and English (cf. Kiely *et al.*, 2005):

Extract 1 (e) 'I don't think they've got good PR overseas'

1.	R:	Would you ever think of yourself as being British?
2.	J:	No, I don't even put it on my passport. I put down that I'm Scottish.
3.	R:	Have you ever, in the past, I don't know 10 or 15 years ago, had a
4.		sense of being British?
5.	J:	No, never, never, and I don't know what that is. I don't know if
6.		it's because when I go to France, to try out my pathetic French
7.		on them and notice the complete change when they say
8.		'Anglais?' And you say 'non, Ecosse' and you're welcomed with
9.		open arms and we get free Kirs and we get the best of service
10.		wherever. Before that we would be cold-shouldered. I don't
11.		know if it's something to do with that. But I don't think they've
12.		got good PR overseas.

We may note that both of these explanations mirror the way in which national identity has been discussed in the academic literature as a function of an interactional process of claim and receipt (Bechhofer *et al.*, 1999, Kiely *et al.*, 2001, McCrone *et al.*, 1998). However, notwithstanding Jenny's strong claim to Scottish identity and her denial of any conscious sense of British identity, she did not oppose Scotland's continued membership of the British state. On the contrary, she equated political nationalism with irrationality:

Extract 1(f) 'the SNPs, these crazies'

1.	J:	[...] I would never like to see Scotland separate from the rest of
2.		the British Isles, that includes England, Wales and Ireland. I would
3.		never like to see them do that because I think it would be detrimental
4.		and I think that the factors that would impact on that is if you get the
5.		crazies involved, the SNPs, these crazies. You know, the ones that are,
6		the nationalists that are so fervent that they want to blow people up.

Note how Jenny's argument in favour of Scotland's continued connection to the UK is not based on appeals to 'identity', of 'pride' or, indeed, any form of positive emotional attachment. Rather her assessment of the '*detrimental*' nature of political independence is presented as an objective, reasoned position as opposed to the nationalists' inappropriate emotion (cf. Shields, 2005), their '*fervent*' (line 6), 'crazy', behaviour. Note also how, at this point, Jenny substitutes notions or values of identity or cultural community with references to territory (cf. Abell *et al.*, 2006). Her expressed concern is not for the separation of peoples, but for '*Scotland's*' separation from '*the rest of the British Isles*'.

The distinction between the rational language of polity and the emotional language of national self-identity is exemplified in our final extract, in which Jenny contrasts her sense of Scottish identity with her orientation to the UK and to '*Europe*' (meaning the EU), as a matter of contract as opposed to solidarity:

Extract 1(g): 'First and foremost, I am my mother's daughter'

1.	J:	[...] As I say, Scotland, as a country, had its own culture, had its
2.		own language, had its own hierarchy, had its own parliament
3.		before we were ever given it back and we were somewhat
4.		absorbed. Again, there was reasons behind that and reasons for
5.		that in the 1745 uprising and whatnot, you know, the backlash
6.		to that was a pulling down from the way of all that and I think
7.		its important that we do remember that, OK, we belong to the
8.		UK but we did have something before that and we are still
9.		independent people with an independent history, independent
10.		of England, Wales and Ireland. We do have a very separate
11.		(pause)
12.	R:	You mentioned that yes; we do belong to the UK

13	J:	Oh absolutely, and Europe.
14.	R:	Those are things that you still
15.	J:	I acknowledge that very much so, but, as I say, that's like, let's
16.		put it this way, as a single woman I was part of my mother's
17.		family. As a married woman I became part of my husband's
18.		family. First and foremost, I am my mother's daughter. That's
19.		what it comes down to. I acknowledge that I have other
20.		relatives and I'm very fond of them and I would like to think
21.		I'm kind to them and loyal and trusting and all the other good
22.		qualities that you should show but, at the end of the day, I am
23.		my mother's daughter.

Between lines 13–23, Jenny works up a 'blood is thicker than water' argument, through which her sense of attachment to, and identification with, Scotland is likened to primary familial bonds. In contrast, her sense of 'belonging to' the UK is treated as a rational appreciation of a political fact (*'I acknowledge'*, line 15), and any expression of positive emotion or loyalty a matter of dutiful display of *'good qualities that you should show'* (lines 21–2) such as those you would perform in relation to someone else's family. The distinction between the two types of attachment is also displayed through pronoun use: *'we'* and *'I'* used in relation to Scotland, and *'them'* in relation to the UK and Europe.

In lines 1–13, Jenny presents an account of her identification with Scotland as an historically-extended imagined cultural and political community, using historically-expanded 'we's' in conjunctions with purely-contemporary 'we's', in such a manner as to carry forward historically a sense of ultimate distinction between 'us' and the UK: *'we belong to the UK but we did have something before that and we are still independent people'* (lines 7–9). The kind of historical accounting that Jenny uses here, in which Scotland is attributed with primary, original and hence authentic national status, in contrast to the UK, which is treated as a relatively historically recent, and essentially contingent, political construction, was relatively common among respondents in Scotland (Condor and Abell, 2006). We may in addition note how, through the use of passive tense forms, Jenny presents both the UK status of Scotland and the advent of devolved governance as the result of external agency rather than autonomous national responsibility: *'we were somewhat absorbed'* (lines 3–4), *'we were ... given it back'* (line 3).

Vernacular Discourses of National Identity in England

Respondents in England were generally less inclined than those in Scotland to talk at length about national issues in general, and their own sense of national identity in particular. Constitutional change did not appear to have impacted on the extent to which people in England treated nationhood as a delicate topic (cf. Condor, 2000), as reflected by the indicators of production difficulty in the accounts reported in this section. In England, interview talk about national issues tended to be highly volatile, subject to rapid topic shading (Hurting, 1977) and drift (Hobbs, 1990). The category of nation itself tended to be very fragile. Rather than being construed as a 'deep horizontal comradeship', accounts of nation were liable to fragment as the speaker attended to class, ethnic or regional diversity.

In addition to these general differences in orientation to nation as a topic of conversation, there were very evident differences in the ways in which respondents went about claiming a personal sense of national self-identity. Whereas respondents in Scotland treated their claims to national identity as inferentially thick and referentially promiscuous, respondents in England tended to delimit the inferences to be drawn from their national identity claims by adopting a semi-detached footing, and by forging explicit distinctions between cognition and emotion; between identity and character; between personal and social identity; between public and private; between place and people; between national identity and civil society. Moreover, whereas in Scotland the meaning of national identity was normally established in contrast to an external (English) other, in England individuals sought to establish the meaning of their personal claims to national identity through a contrast with the 'typical' English case, or through a radical distinction between past and present. According to this system of accounting, English national identity effectively functions as its own 'other', being constructed *in relation to* the other UK nations, but defined and evaluated *against* itself.

In the following pages we shall be using extracts drawn from two interviews. In extract 2, Karen is making a relatively strong claim concerning her sense of English identity.

Extract 2: 'How objective can I be'

1.	K:	I do, I think have a very strong sense of my Englishness as opposed to
2.		Britishness, I would say, now, don't ask me why, cos I, I,
3.	R:	You do, or you don't?
4.	K:	I do.
5.	R:	You do.
6.	K:	I do think I do have, yeah, I mean, if you ask me 'How do you think of
7.		yourself?' I will say 'English'.
8.	R:	Really?
9.	K:	Yes, I would. I know that's terrible and it's not PC, but it's true.
10.	R:	Why is that terrible?
11.	K:	I've not been actually brought up to think like that, either, my parents
12.		are very, like, you know, we live in Great Britain, and, that sort of
13.		thing.
[...]		
30.	R:	Why do you say English rather than British?
31.	K:	I don't know. I don't know, don't know really.
32.	RJ:	Have they got different associations for you?
33.	K:	Erm.

34.	R:	Do they make you think of different things?
35.	K:	Well I think they do, really, I mean, I like to think it's the sort of
36.		feeling like erm, I carry, erm, most of my Scottish friends, I think, and
37.		you know, other Irish and Welsh friends would say that they were
38.		actually those things. Not British, and, I'm, you know, on your thing,
39.		you always have to put British, don't you, nationality, sort of thing,
40.		but, erm, if I'm asked a question in a form filling, like in what country
41.		were you born, I wouldn't put Great Britain, it wouldn't come to me
42.		automatically to put Great Britain, it would be England. I don't know.
43.		Don't know why, really.
44.	R:	Was it, are you kind of proud to be English, does that make you feel
45.	K:	No. No.
46.		((laughter))
47.	K:	I don't think I am, really, I'm not erm, I don't feel, like ashamed of
48.		being English, perhaps, from when I'm mixing with all these groups of
49.		people, with a terrible history
48.	R:	'I'm sorry, I'm sorry'
49.		((laughter))
50.	K:	I don't feel bad about it, but I don't, neither do I feel fantastic, you
51.		know, I, I am, I was born in the right place at the right time, sort of
52.		stuff. I don't, I don't, I mean, you know, how objective can I be, but, I
53.		don't think I feel like that, no, I'm, sort of, I would have been equally
54.		happy to be any of the other British people, you know, Scottish, Irish,
55.		whatever, you know, or perhaps even more happy to be one of them (.)
56.		don't know, I like their accents.
57.		((laughter)).

As we noted in the introduction, a good deal of contemporary research on national identity in the UK focuses on questions of self-labelling. In this respect, one fairly self-evident difference between Karen's and Jenny's accounts pertains to the different ways in which the speakers orient to the distinction between categories of national (English, Scottish) and British identity. Jenny, in common with many respondents in Scotland, treated 'British' as functionally synonymous with 'English' and, as such, the 'other' against which Scottish identity is defined. In contrast, Karen, like most other respondents in England, treats the category 'British' as a 'common ingroup'. Rather than treating Wales, Scotland and Ireland [sic] as 'others' against which to define the national ingroup, Karen adopts a stance of empathy, displaying recognition of the existence, and sensitivities, of the minority UK nations.

In addition, differences are apparent in the ways in which the two respondents orient to the act of claiming a national as opposed to a British identity. Whereas Jenny treated her own claim to Scottish as opposed to British identity as unproblematic, Karen treats a claim to British identity as the '*PC*' (line 9) or formally correct response to a request for information concerning one's 'nationality' ('*you always have to put British*', line 39). Although this kind of response was relatively distinctive to respondents from England (in so far as it was rarely displayed by respondents in Scotland), it was not 'typical' in the sense of representing a consensual position. On the contrary, even among our restricted sample (which excluded people with conservative or far right political affiliations) people varied in the meanings that they associated with the categories 'English' and 'British', and the extent to which they displayed a preference for one label or the other.

Rationality versus Emotion

Possibly the most obvious difference between Karen's and Jenny's accounts lies in the way in which the two respondents treat national identity in relation to emotionality, rationality and accountability. As we noted above, respondents in Scotland almost universally oriented to a perceived normative requirement to claim a strong sense of self in nationalised terms, the authenticity of which was established by displays of emotional attachment. In contrast, respondents in England were inclined to treat all strong avowals or public displays of national self-identity (whether 'British' or 'English') as indicative of irrationality and reprehensible chauvinism and particularism. In place of the envious or appreciative foreign voyeur whose reflected appraisals engender legitimate Scottish national pride, foreigners typically figured in English accounts of nationhood in the guise of critical appraisers, and possibly victims, of English national hubris.

As a consequence, respondents in England typically combined national identity avowals with attempts to manage their personal face as a rational and moral individual by forging a distinction between national self-identification as a matter of 'being' as opposed to 'feeling', of rational self-knowledge as opposed to sentiment. Hence Karen, when questioned concerning whether she experiences a sense of pride, reflects, '*how objective can I be*' (line 52), and in our third set of extracts, Peter displays concern over his '*awareness*' (extract 3c line 6) and of the '*accuracy*' of his self-labelling (extract 3c lines 8–9). In addition to managing the imagined negative appraisal of national 'others', this stance often involved a strategic attempt to differentiate a rationally-national English self from the passionately-driven English other who, in a manner similar to John Barnes (quoted on page 1), respondents commonly imagined to be susceptible to the influence of 'ugly forces'.

Elsewhere we have discussed how this bifurcated sense of rational-self reflecting on national-self may be employed when respondents in England attempt to position themselves as individuals in relation to the national stigma of imperial guilt (Condor and Abell, 2006). In this respect, it is worth noting how Jenny's image of a communal national past characterised by shared suffering and shared achievement (reported in extract 1) was accomplished by strategically bracketing Scottish imperial involvement for the purposes of moral calculation (see Condor and Abell, 2006, for an analysis of this aspect of her interview). Karen, in contrast, like most respondents from England, treats national reputation as permanently sullied by the stigma of Empire, placing an inevitable social distance between herself and those people who possess '*a terrible history*' (line 49).

In place of claims to legitimate national pride respondents in England typically employed avowals of 'acceptance' of nationality as a fact of nature or biography: '*I don't feel bad about it, but I don't, neither do I feel fantastic, you know, I, I am, I was born in the right place at the right time, sort of stuff'* (lines 50–52). Discourses of self-acceptance enable the respondent to manage accountability by divorcing their national identity claim from matters of volition, choice or personal responsibility.

Self versus National Identity

Whereas Jenny, like many respondents in Scotland, presented an image of her sense of self as effectively saturated by, and entirely consonant with, her Scottish national identity, respondents in England almost always represented national identity as something worn lightly, and only partially inhabited. Like most respondents in England, Karen demonstrates a semi-detached orientation towards nationhood, projecting an image of self as reflexive individual out beyond the national identity to which she is laying claim.

This distinction between authentic personal self and nationalised self could be projected through a particular form of footing which, to borrow Goffman's (1981) terminology, forged a distinction between the self as animator (the person of the interview 'respondent') and the self as protagonist (the nationalised self of whom they spoke). In the interviews conducted in England, accounts of national identity were typically punctuated by 'floodings out' (Goffman, 1974), as respondents signalled the existence of a reflexive individual behind their accounts through the injection of ironising laughter, self-mockery and meta-discursive orientations to the act of giving the account (cf. Clark and Gerrig, 1990).

In addition, we may note two further ways in which Karen signals a distinction between the self-as-speaker and the nationalised self who constitutes the subject of her reflexive account. First, Karen attributes her claim to English identity to deep-rooted psychological processes to which her conscious self has no privileged insight: *'don't ask me why'* (line 2), *'I don't know. I don't know, don't know really'* (line 31), *'I don't know. Don't know why, really'* (lines 42–3), *'don't know'* (line 55). Second, Karen embeds within her account the narrative figure of the self-under-other-circumstances: *'I would have been equally happy to be any of the other British people, you know, Scottish, Irish, whatever, you know, or perhaps even more happy to be one of them (.)'* (lines 53–55). This formulation not only marries her claim to English identity with a display of a rational impartiality, but also enables Karen to project a sense of selfhood as essentially independent of the nationality into which, by a quirk of nature and historical fate, she just happens to have been born.

Being versus Being-Like

In extract 1, Jenny presented Scottish identity as an inference-rich category (cf. Sacks, 1992), and construed her sense of national identity as a form of self-categorisation, involving a functional equivalence with other ingroup members, and the possession of a common national character (cf. Reicher and Hopkins, 2001). In contrast, it is notable that, in extract 2, Karen does not spontaneously mention any *substance* to English national identity. This was a common feature of the interviews in England,

and attention to the detail of the accounts suggested that respondents were typically orienting to normative assumptions that homogenised images of national culture or character were both irrational and morally reprehensible.

In extract 3(a), Peter attempts explicitly to promote an image of Englishness in such a manner as to render the category inference-poor, and consequently to forge an absolute distinction between matters of national self-labelling (*'saying English'*, line 8; *'claim ... to be English'*, line 12) and those of personal character:

Extract 3(a) 'there's a whole range of differences in the English person'

```
 1.   P:    Well, there is a place called Britain, if we say there is, then there is, if
 2.         we accept it socially, then there is
 3.   R:    [Although one-]
 4.   P:    [There's some]thing inside me that makes me stick at saying British,
 5.         and makes me prefer to say English.
 6.   R:    What do you associate Englishness with?
 7.   P:    I don't know, I don't know if there is a thing called Englishness, I
 8.         mean, I don't mind saying English is where I'm from, but whether I
 9.         am an English person, I dunno. And like, you know, it's, it's not
10.         something I've thought about, but I, is should say, but then I
11.         ((laughter))
12.         maybe I, no, I should be able to claim England, to be English, and to
13.         be an English person, as a, as a type as far as you can generalise. But
14.         I've not thought what the typical English person is, or what they
15.         embody, maybe there's, maybe there's a kind of (.) a whole range of
16.         differences in the English person, you know
17.   R:    Mm.
18.   P:    I don't know.
```

We may note how, like Karen, Peter presents a bifurcated sense of self, projecting a distinction between the physically present (and immediately accountable) self as speaking subject, and the self of whom he speaks. Like Karen, Peter attributes his sense of national identity to automatic psychological processes for which he, as sentient agent, can bear no personal responsibility: *'There's something inside me that makes me stick at saying British'* (line 4). Like Karen, Peter imposes a distance between the figure of self as speaker and the nationalised self which constitutes the object of his introspective account by strategic displays of reflexive ignorance: *'I don't know, I don't know'* (line 7), *'I dunno'* (line 9), *'I don't know'* (line 17), *'it's not something I've thought about'* (lines 9–10), *'I've not thought'* (line 13). Whereas Jenny, like many other Scottish respondents, presents 'the English' as a people with national character but not identity, Peter, like many English respondents, presents himself as possessing national identity, but not national character. In fact, respondents in England often justified a preference for self-labelling as either English or British precisely on the grounds that they understood their category of choice to have the fewest substantive connotations. In place of a notion of national identity as a shared sense of 'being like', Peter projects national identity as a mere awareness of 'being', and as such essentially compatible with liberal values of individual rights to self-definition and self-determination.

We may also note how both Peter and Karen construct their subjective sense of Englishness as a matter of place identity: of 'being from', rather than as a form of imagined community (*'English is where I'm from'*, extract 3(a) line 8; see also extract 2, lines 39–42). In general, respondents in England tended to forge an iconic distance between ideal-typical Englishness and the particularities of their own subjective experiences and the circumstances of their everyday lives (cf. A. Cohen, 1996). Respondents typically distinguished not only themselves as individuals, but also their friends, families and localities of residence from 'Englishness' as an abstract construct. Sometimes 'real' England and Englishness was projected into an imagined elsewhere: the past, the South, the rural, other generations or social classes. Often, however, respondents treated the construct of Englishness as ultimately and essentially phantasmagorical.

At the start of the exchange reported in extract 3(a), Peter is treating the category 'British' as existing (only) in so far as *'we accept it socially'* (line 2). [7] However, his account should be distinguished from Jenny's account of the constructed nature of the UK (extract 1(g)). Whereas Jenny, in common with most respondents in Scotland, treats the factual existence and moral value of Scotland as a 'topos beyond argumentation' (to borrow Billig's 1995 phrase), Peter also displays a *'rational'* appreciation of the constructed status of *'English identity'*. In extract 3(a) he says, *'I don't know if there is a thing called Englishness'* (line 7). Later in his interview he makes this point more explicitly:

Extract 3(b) 'they're both kind of constructions'

```
1    P:    I know British is manufactured but then English is as well. Rationally
2          there is no difference between an English identity and a British
3          identity. They're both kind of constructions.
```

Personal Identity versus Social Identity

In the contemporary social psychological literature it is common for authors to treat nation-ness as an exemplary case of 'social' as opposed to 'personal' identity, of a sense of self as group member rather than a sense of self as unique individual. However, interview respondents in England typically cast their own sense of national identity as a matter of personal as opposed to social identity. In his account of 'banal nationalism', Billig (1995) enjoins the student of nationalism to 'attend to the little

---

[7]   In this respect Peter's account is rather unusual. Most respondents in England (other than those with far right political beliefs) accepted the category 'Britain', although not necessarily the British state, as part of the eternal natural order.

words' (p. 173). Accordingly, we may note the way in which Karen's and Peter's accounts are formulated almost entirely through the personal 'I' or 'me' in a manner that contrasts starkly with Jenny's use of the generic 'you' and 'we'.

In extract 2 we can see how Karen presents her personal sense of being English as an idiosyncratic quirk of character. Rather than representing her sense of English identity as a possession held in common with her compatriots, or even as a normative response to the question *'How do you think of yourself?'* (lines 6–7), she treats her identity claim as contrary both to societal norms *'I know that's terrible'* (line 9) and contrary to the socialisation and familial pressures she has experienced *'I've not been actually brought up to think like that'* (line 11). Whereas Jenny presents her sense of national identity as a response to the cultural context in which she grew up, Karen presents her subjective sense of national identity as independent of formative social influences. In addition, we may note how, for Karen, national identity impacts on real or imagined interpersonal relationships not by defining the boundaries of a common-ingroup, but as an axis of diversity. Karen's account of civil society is not circumscribed by English national identity. Whereas Jenny elided Scottish compatriots with the category of *'all your friends'*, Karen presented her *'friends'* as a poly-national assortment of individuals (lines 35–38). Concrete personal network aside, Karen imagines herself in relations of communication with others whose national identities differ from her own (*'mixing with all these groups of people'* lines 46–47).

Being-For and Being-Alongside versus Being-in-Common

We noted above how reports of national self-identity in England tended to be formulated in such a manner as to render them more consistent with liberal values of the unique, asocial and sovereign individual than with communitarian values of a 'people like us'. Respondents in England did display commitment to membership of an imagined community occupying a nationalised space. However, they differed from respondents in Scotland in so far as neither the population of nation-as-place ('England' or 'Britain'), nor membership of a concrete or imagined 'society', were generally construed as isomorphic with 'national identity'.

This form of representation is nicely illustrated by our final extract in which Peter casts the act of claiming a national identity as a matter of etiquette and of liberal civility, as much about respect for the authentic identities of others as it is for asserting one's own authentic sense of self:

Extract 3(c) 'I don't want to presume a commonality with these people'

1.	R:	What would you describe yourself then as nationally?
2.	P:	English
3.	R:	English.
4.	P:	Yeah.
5.	R:	Why are you English? What makes you say that? (.)

6.   P: Erm. Well, I suppose cos I'm kind of aware that, you know, there's
7.   people who describe themselves as Scottish and Welsh, and to try and
8.   describe yourself as British, is trying to identify, you know, I, I just
9.   think it's more accurate, really, and I mean, all this stuff about
10.   language, and stuff. It's all, you know, it's, it's, yeah, I think it's more
11.   accurate, and so I tend to say it.
12. R: Is that because
13. P: So I was almost to say, I'm from England, Pakistan, Scotland or
14.   Wales.
15. R: Mm. (.) So is that because you don't feel any kind of erm commonality
16.   I suppose for people in Scotland and Wales? Is it because you want to
17.   be seen as distinct?
18. P: No. Well, I don't know if I, I wouldn't presu- well I suppose, I dunno,
19.   I dunno
20.   ((laughter))
21.   maybe I'm not pres- no, no, no, no, but maybe I'm not presuming it, I
22.   don't want to presume a commonality with these people really.
23. R: Mm. (.) Mm.
24. P: That's very generous of me, isn't it?

Here, we can see how a subjective sense of obligation and relation to others is not being conveyed through a discourse of 'people like us', of common national identity, shared subjectivity, culture or history. On the contrary, Peter presents himself as an individual occupying a multi-national and poly-ethnic (Kymlicka, 1995) social space alongside others whose '*commonality*' he would not wish to '*presume*'.

Concluding Comments

Miller (1995: 17) has suggested that, 'to understand what we mean when we talk of someone having a national identity, we must first get clear about what nations are'. However, as McCrone (1998) has argued, such formulations may distract attention from the equally important question of what we mean by the term 'identity'. In this Chapter we have attempted to take this argument a step further, by suggesting that answers should not only be sought in formal social scientific theories of identity (national or otherwise) but might also be sought in social actors' own mundane sense making practices. At the start of this Chapter we noted how academic work has generally neglected the question of vernacular understandings of national identity, preferring instead to treat the national identity construct as an analysts' category, or to consider its use in formal political rhetoric. By way of conclusion, however, we may reflect on the potential implications of our analysis for academic theorising and political rhetoric.

Bauman (1990) noted that one role of social science is to 'prod sluggish imagination' by showing apparently familiar things from unexpected angles. Nothing is more familiar to us than national identity. By focussing on the status of national identity as an emic rather than an etic construct, we may draw attention not only to the variety of different versions available to contemporary social actors, but also to the potential cultural specificity of extant academic accounts themselves. In the present case, it is especially notable that accounts developed in Scotland, in which national self-identity is viewed as a product of claims and receipts, of self-categorisation processes, or as characterised by an iconic intimacy of the national with the personal, closely mirror vernacular theories and concerns of ordinary social actors in Scotland. In contrast, the ironising stance adopted by respondents in England, in which the ultimate moral and empirical status of nationhood is treated as problematic, and national self-identity treated in part as the product of deep-rooted psychological factors beyond the individual's personal control or conscious awareness, quite neatly mirrors Billig's (1995) account of the 'mindless' character of 'banal' national consciousness.[8]

Over the past few years, it has become commonplace for UK politicians to attempt to enlist the British population through appeals to their sense of 'national identity'.[9] However, the observation that the fact and value of national identity could be oriented to in quite different ways even amongst a restricted sample of white people with apparently similar political affiliations, suggests that these appeals may be received rather differently in Scotland and in England (cf. Billig, 1995). Our research suggests that nation-ness may be cast as a progressive moral value in Scotland, but as a retrogressive, atavistic and essentially irrational construct in England (Condor and Abell, 2006). Similarly the construct of 'identity', and of the relation between the individual and the collective may also resonate in different ways in the two countries. Our own research suggests that 'national identity' may be construed in communitarian terms in Scotland, but in liberal individualist terms in England.

---

[8]   It may be noted that this has implications not only for our statements of theory but also for the way in which we formulate our research questions. With hindsight it is worth considering how the problematic as spelled out in our own original research proposal – in which 'national identity' was treated as functionally synonymous with 'civil society' – in practice corresponds to the Scottish liberal vernacular: 'In some contexts the range of those defined as 'fellow nationals', as 'people-like-us', may increase, with the corollary that, say, English people in Scotland – or Scots living in England – are included and welcomed as members of the nation. However, in some contexts, more exclusionary definitions of national belonging may be articulated and acted upon'.

[9]   For example: *Who do we think we are*? By David Willets [then Shadow Secretary of State for Education and Employment], 8 October 1988; *Citizenship, identity and ethnicity in Britain and Europe* by Keith Vaz [then FCO Minister of State] Diplomatic Academy, Vienna, 28 February 2001; *British Identity* by Robin Cook [then Foreign Secretary], Centre for the Open Society, Social Market Foundation, London, 19 April 2001; *British Council Annual Lecture*, by Gordon Brown [Chancellor of the Exchequer] 7 July 2004; *A new England: An English identity within Britain*, by David Blunkett, Institute for Public Policy Research, 14 March 2005.

As we noted at the start of this Chapter, the construct of 'national identity' has recently come to colonise the field of nationalism studies to the extent that it is often used as a functional synonym for constructs such as nationality, citizenship and society. This may be seen to represent part of a larger move identified by Bauman (2001b: 140) by virtue of which,

> 'identity' has now become a prism through which other topical aspects of contemporary life are spotted, grasped and examined. Established issues of social analysis are being rehashed and refurbished to fit the discourse now rotating around the 'identity' axis.

However, it is worth noting that although Anderson (1983) is often credited with an account of 'national identity', he never in fact used the term in his seminal text *Imagined Communities*. A consideration of vernacular understandings of nationhood might warn us against automatically reducing a range of concerns about community, belonging, civility and citizenship to the common denominator of 'national identity'. We noted how Jenny, like many respondents in Scotland, dissociated her claims to Scottish identity from political concerns relating to the pragmatic or moral value of 'the Union'. Karen and Peter, like many respondents in England, treated national self-identity as an essentially private matter, which did not define either the boundaries of citizenship-community (cf. J. Stapleton, 2005) or the constitution of the concrete social networks within which they routinely interacted with others. Future research might do well to consider the various ways in which nation-ness may be construed as a psychological matter of identity in more detail. However, it is also important not to assume that a study of vernacular constructions of national identity necessarily serves as an empirical proxy for the analysis of 'imagined community'.

Chapter 4

Artists, Wales, Narrative and Devolution

William Housley

Introduction

Wales is a small country that is recognised as a distinct constituent nation of the United Kingdom. It is characterised by a number of differences that include the existence of the Welsh language, unique national institutions (e.g. the Welsh Language Television Channel[s] S4C, the University of Wales, National Museum and Gallery and specific national cultural events). In 1997, the electorate of Wales voted in favour of the establishment of a devolved National Assembly. This Assembly has specific 'devolved' powers that include the areas of health, education and culture. As stated previously, Wales is recognised as possessing a distinct culture within the fabric of the British Isles and Europe. It is popularly associated with the 'Celtic nations' of Europe and has certain cultural characteristics that stand in contrast to its larger and more powerful neighbour. Whilst this is clearly the case with respect to Cymraeg (the Welsh language) the case for other cultural practices has not always been so clear-cut. The case of the visual arts is a good example.

During the course of this chapter, I intend to explore some issues relating to the visual arts and wider changes within the national context of Wales. The chapter draws from a study on art and devolution in Wales that explored the perceptions and expectations of a number of established artists working within Wales. The study explored the relationship between art and Wales through a detailed analysis of accounts generated through in-depth interviews. Whilst this Chapter, in line with the study,[1] represents an exploratory analysis, it aims to identify important themes, issues and perspectives that constitute this relatively unexplored domain of sociological interest.

Whilst the focus of this research was directed towards the context of Wales it has resonance with other parts of the United Kingdom and Europe. At a general level the project was concerned with documenting artists' expectations and perceptions of devolution in Wales in relation to the organisation of the visual arts, funding,

[1]   The study referred to here, *Art and Devolution in Wales: Expectations and Perceptions*, was funded by the British Academy small grants scheme. Thanks is extended to the British Academy for their support.

cultural identity and representation. More specifically, the research aimed to explore artists' (and people engaged in the production, management and exhibition of artistic products) expectations and perceptions of devolution and change within the United Kingdom. The contributions, concerns and insights of the artistic community are often ignored during times of social and political change whilst the products of art are, paradoxically, used as a means of interpreting historical events. This research sought to identify the changes that members of the artistic community expect to take place within the artistic community itself, the changing relationship and profile of the arts within Welsh institutions and the general public and policy formation within the new devolved Assembly. The study also sought to identify and profile the artistic community's perception of devolution as an opportunity for art to take a greater role in Welsh life and raise its profile as an important area of social, cultural and economic activity.

Wales and National Identity

Theoretical and empirical work in the area of national identity and Wales has developed in recent years. Nationalism in Wales has been explored as a social construction (Denney *et al.*, 1991). Work by Fevre *et al.* (1997, 1999) has developed the exploration of nationalist groups and organisations and has understood some of their activities in terms of the protection of monopolies in social and economic resources. Further work on national identity in Wales has explored the relationship between configurations of identity and the challenge of 'inclusive politics' within new devolved political frameworks (Chaney and Fevre, 2001). More recent work has explored the construction and negotiation of Welsh national identity within primary schooling and childhood (Scourfield *et al.*, 2003). This work seeks to relate notions of national identity in relation to an emerging devolved civic sphere in Wales. Additional sociological work has explored the more mundane aspects of nationalism (Billig, 1995) and its interactional and situated characteristics in relation to Wales and identity (Housley and Fitzgerald, 2002).

Despite the plethora of sociological work on national identity in post-devolution Wales little focus has been directed towards the cultural sphere and its relationship with different forms of identity construction and representation. A notable exception to this point is Dicks's work on heritage, territoriality and imagined communities (Dicks 1996, 1997, 1999). Through a 'museographical case study' of the Rhondda Heritage Park, Dicks's work demonstrates how specific forms of representation of community and the Rhondda, in which marginality and peripheral [Welsh working class] experiences are paramount, are colonised through specific territorial discourses of 'Britishness' and 'Rhondda Valleyness'. In many respects this Chapter builds on the work above by exploring notions of Welsh cultural identity through a consideration of the visual arts; and more specifically through a reconsideration of the representations and understandings of the visual arts in Wales as understood by prominent art practitioners. In other words this work is concerned with the actual producers and creators of artefacts; the cultural *producers* whose creative activity, whilst appropriated, is not translated into the recognition of a legitimate artistic voice and source of knowledge and insight concerning a changing cultural identity within the space and place in which they live, work and create.

Wales, Devolution and Art

In recent years art in Wales has sustained its position as a contested domain and form of life characterised by controversy. The recent collapse of the Cardiff Centre for the visual arts, the ripping of the plans for the building of an Opera House in Cardiff Bay and various debates on 'cultural policy' in the newly established National Assembly have added to an air of debate, interest, frustration and, in some cases, anger. In terms of the visual arts, however, events surrounding venues and funding have not prevented something of a resurgence in the profile of the visual arts in Wales. In some cases this has taken on a direct and explicit connection with attempts to kick-start a wider cultural renaissance within post-devolution Wales. This move has, more often than not, provided a further space through which the contested and slippery concept of the Welsh nation can be imagined, realised, explored and represented. The relationship between devolution and the visual arts is perhaps one that is abstract. However, as an important dimension of the cultural apparatus and array of practices routinely appropriated by the discourse of culture, it has increasingly been subject to the gaze of the new devolved institutions of Wales and active intellectual commentary. In terms of devolved institutions in Wales, the Culture Committee of the Welsh Assembly has recognised the importance of the visual arts in relation to culture policy in Wales. In a discussion Chapter (Post – 16 Education and Training Committee – ETR 15.00, 28/6/2000) the former Cultural Committee arts and cultural advisor locates the visual arts within a wider discourse of Welsh culture. The discussion chapter states:

The culture of Wales is rich and deep in its diversity of expression. It is a performative culture where people are passionate to take part and enjoy others taking part – from sports to choirs to acting to brass bands to Eisteddfodau, mountaineering, films, water sports and rock concerts. It admires the skills of creativity, hard work, industry and innovation. It is hewn from the natural environment of Wales, its dramatic landscape, its education system and unique social and industrial history. Wales excels in the literary arts, in its visual culture, in its music making, its built heritage, its national institutions, its actors and its sporting achievements…Wales is defined by its ancient language, its modern diversity of peoples and its social compassion, but above all, by its passion for creativity. The Culture of Wales is in the process of re-shaping itself, of re-defining itself, perhaps even, of re-inventing itself for the challenging of the new century and in reaction of the new political situation in which it finds itself.

In terms of active intellectual scholarship and commentary, Peter Lord's *Imaging the Nation* (2000) represents a profound move towards both the *establishment* and *recovery* of a visual narrative for Wales. With reference to the history of the visual arts in Wales and the process of the collective recovery of a national visual narrative, Lord (2000:9) states:

> It has often been alleged that a national consciousness heavily conditioned by the needs of differentiation from a dominant neighbour is a characteristic Welsh weakness. As a result of the political and economic decline of that neighbour, a complementary growth in our own self-confidence, and a wider change in perceptions of nationality, it is the hope of many at the beginning of the twenty-first century that this essentially colonized state of mind may at last been transcended.

For Lord, the sensible recovery of a 'Welsh' visual heritage is part of such a process. This process is also occurring during a time of significant cultural, political, social and economic change in Wales epitomised by the devolution process and attempts at the re-generation of both physical and mental landscapes. Consequently, the visual arts, as part of a wider array of cultural practices in Wales, can also be seen to be a concern of the devolution process and the potential re-invigoration of region and 'nation'. This process has also been bolstered by Cardiff's bid for the European Capital of Culture in 2008 through which the interface between cultural concerns and economics has increasingly come into focus. Furthermore, in 2003 Wales was represented at the Venice Biennale. This represents a profound shift in cultural representation and identity at the level of the visual arts within a high profile international context. This event courted some controversy concerning the Welsh credentials of the artists chosen to represent Wales at the arts festival (Western Mail, 12/6/03). A central dimension of this debate was the connection of being born in Wales, living in Wales and the production of visual artefacts. This chapter deals with some of the issues that lie behind this particular debate and the wider discursive field in and through which it is articulated and understood. However, before exploring these issues some consideration of the methodological and analytical approach adopted in this chapter will be provided.

Analytical and Methodological Approach

Whilst the policy context and general profile of the visual arts and culture is of importance, this chapter seeks to explore the field of the visual arts in Wales in terms of a detailed analysis of prominent artists working and living in Wales. The method for selecting the artists interviewed involved the use of publicly available information provided by established institutions in Wales (e.g. the Royal Cambrian Society for the Visual Arts) and contacting well known and established artists living and working in Wales. Over twenty-two in-depth interviews with elite artist practitioners were undertaken. To this extent, the chapter draws from data gathered from figures established within the art world. This clearly confines the validity of any observations in terms of the generalisability of artistic perceptions and understandings to a type of 'core group' (Collins and Evans, 2002). However, they do represent a systematic analysis of narratives provided by members of a recognisable 'group'. Consequently, this chapter works with a series of exemplars grounded in a number of case-centred studies of prominent artistic practitioners.

The chapter utilises categorisation analysis and the notion of the creative self in relation to wider cultural discourse (Housley, in press). While it is not a core concern, the chapter also makes use of theoretical concepts and relevant policy documents. The chapter does not utilise narrative and interview accounts as a means of appealing to a quantitative sense of validity. However, the data are incorporated and reported within the context of a sociologically informed argument and debate about the visual arts and cultural change within a post-devolution setting. As such these materials and discussion report on new phenomena. The accounts presented and analysed here were selected from the wider data set which had been coded and analysed thematically. The examples that follow are representative of perspectives or art-world views that were identified from this data set.

The accounts identified in the data and the examples presented in this chapter were generated through interview. Whilst sensitive to the local character and generation of interview talk (Hester and Francis, 1994) and the role of question and answer pairings in constituting responses, the interview strategy was careful to recognise the elite artists interviewed as 'knowledgeable agents' rather than 'cultural dopes'. In other words, the artists were viewed as individuals whose wish to engage with the topics identified in the study was very much geared towards a mutually constitutive dialogical exchange in which the discursive characteristics of discussion, argumentation and the exchange of views were paramount to the method of enquiry and engagement. The examples of artistic world-view in post-devolution Wales presented in this chapter represent the three principal art world view types which emerged from the data. This work provides detailed enquiry into this under researched form of life, practice and social perception and perspective within a 'peripheral' European setting. The relationship between cultural activity and peripheral economic location is one that demands examination. However, whilst this is a latent theme of this chapter it is one that is not taken up, this deserves far more detailed attention and serves as a basis for ongoing and future research. This chapter focuses on artists' accounts and narrative in relation to identity and the social, cultural and political parameters of a 'peripheral', submerged and problematic national experience that manifests itself through identifiable discursive positioning and rhetoric.

The notion of accounts used here is one that is couched within the analytical framework of interactionist oriented analysis (Atkinson and Housley, 2003) as displayed by Plummer (1995) and the notion of accounts and membership categorisation articulated within the work of Harvey Sacks (1992). A central concern is how narratives and accounts are constituted in terms of a *vocabulary of art and social identification* where the 'definition of the situation' is of primary analytical importance. The analysis of these accounts will initially explore their topical organisation, content and the display of art world perspectives in relation to the situational contexts and understandings of national parameters, identity and political processes. This chapter seeks to explore the perceptions and expectations of visual artistic practitioners in relation to these matters through the analysis of these narratives. To this extent I follow the observation by Maines (2001:220) that:

> Narrative structures can be thought of as kinds of information technologies insofar as they are a mechanism for processing information ... Unlike those formed of wire, computer chips, or paper, however, narrative structures are formed by history. They begin with humans trying to make sense out of problematic situations and emerge years later as forms of meaning that contain the criteria for evaluating the credibility of information. They possess reified truth claims and taken-for-granted properties of what-everybody-knows. Like public opinion ... narrative structures are tied to a society's social structure, and thus their agency derives in part from the legitimising processes that inhere in societal institutional arrangements.

The analysis of artistic narrative in Wales has been explored from a more literary, as opposed to sociological, perspective in the form of Tony Curtis's *Welsh Artists Talking* (2000). In many respects the narratives produced in this book have much affinity with some of the analysis and discussion presented in this chapter. However, I intend to explore these narratives → accounts from a more sociological angle. In terms of the genesis of this project it was my intention to explore art in terms of *artists'* expectations and perceptions. This approach is one that is shared and consistent with Curtis's straightforward and unambiguous approach. Furthermore, the concern with narrative and voices of artists connects with important sociological work on the collective character of telling as a site through which wider representations, concerns and understandings of particular social groups can be grasped.

Narrative, Accounts and the Contested Reality of Welsh Art

In terms of self, creativity and identity and national forms of categorisation, it would be tempting to establish a matrix of types; upon which various quantified descriptive instances could be mapped, in order to establish a quantified portrait of national self-categorisation and its relation to creativity and artistic practice. However, in terms of the corpus of interviews of an artistic 'elite group' such a manoeuvre achieves little. Rather the narrative forms of understanding and description will be attended to in order to flesh out and render visible the perceptions that such artists possess. These accounts are rich sources of data for exploring arts worlds and practice in relation to wider configurations of social and national identity. The following data provide a means of beginning to explore such issues. The data represent responses to questions and discussion concerning the creative self and other matters in terms of a changing national context. Furthermore, the examples presented here represent forms of narrative in relation to art-in-Wales that reflect and display three principal ways in which art is represented within the wider corpus of interview data, gathered and analysed during the course of the study. The narrative examples do not reflect these types ideally but they do display how these types can be heard and observed within the general data and the specific examples presented in this chapter.

Extract 1: Artists in Wales or Welsh Art?

1.	I:	Talking about art in Wales in a kind of general sense
2.		is it possible from your point of view from your experience to talk
3.		about 'Welsh art' or is it only possible to talk about artists in Wales?
4.	A:	I think the second (.) I think you can only really talk about artists in
5.		Wales. Because I am one of the few artists in Wales who paint in
6.		Welsh.
7.	I:	Right. Can you tell us what you mean by that?
8.	A:	My knowledge of Welsh is not very great but there are people who are
9.		fluent in Welsh who paint in English or American. But I happen to
10.		paint in Welsh. When I say that I've been told I paint in Welsh.
11.		Because my pictures do reflect Wales. And they tie up with Welsh
12.		poetry and that sort of thing (.) that's what I'm told. It's rather nice to
13.		be told I paint in Welsh. All these other sort of fashionable avant-
14.		garde artists now (.) God knows what they paint in! It has certainly
15.		got nothing to do with Wales. There is no school of Welsh Art there
16.		never really has been. We have a small school in North Wales but the
17.		Welsh Arts Council soon put the kiss of death on that.

In terms of this narrative and account, the interviewed artist responds to the opening question concerning whether it is possible to talk of 'Welsh art' or 'artists in Wales'. In terms of creative others the second applies; however in terms of the interviewee's self-definition he refers to himself as being one of the 'few artists who paint in Welsh', although his understanding of the Welsh language is not as it might be. Thus, the artist understands Wales and art in terms of artists living in Wales, rather than 'Welsh artists', which is viewed as a rare phenomenon. This provides a form of self-definition that he not only subscribes to but also embodies. Clearly, this is an idiosyncratic and potentially contradictory state; Welsh being a language and painting being a practice that produces a profound visual effect. However, for *the interviewee*, this apparent oxymoron is transcended. His art, as described by 'others', is linked with the language of poetry and the Cymry; the two as a seamless and unproblematic reality. This self-categorisation is made firmly within the rare rubric of the Welsh artist. This form of self-categorisation and understanding is not only located in terms of others but also contrasted with other contemporary artists in Wales. The interviewee asserts that '... there is no school of Welsh Art there never really has been'. He also asserts that localised attempts to establish a college of Welsh Art in his vicinity of Wales were contested and stifled by other agencies active within the cultural field.

Thus, this form of self categorisation of creative act and artefact in terms of national structures is one that, on the one hand, preserves a notion of artists living in Wales but, on the other, displays a unique (or at least not commonplace) claim to being a Welsh artist. This is a rare quality embodied by the artist. Thus, the particularism of the concept of 'Welsh art' as opposed to the universalism of artists and art in general is negotiated by the fact that such an embodiment is rare, unique and not common. This condition is explained by the fact that a school of Welsh Art has, in terms of their perceptions, never existed and that attempts to establish one have been stifled. This explanation is qualified in later accounts during the course of the same discussion. For the artist, this is due to both historical reasons and contemporary practices. Historically he refers to the lack of patronage in Wales and the condition and relationship of the Welsh aristocracy with the Welsh people. Contemporarily, whilst there are Welsh artists and artefacts an attempt to unify or present a consistent visual presentation or narrative of such social facts had, until the contribution of Lord (2000), been noticeable by its absence. The following account (produced by the same artist) is initiated through a response to a question concerning the establishment of a recognised national collection of Welsh art.

Extract 2: Welsh art as problematic/possible

1.   A: Oh, well, no not really but they're damned if they're going to have a
2.   room for Welsh art. There is no room for Welsh art in the whole of
3.   Wales. There is no room for Welsh art in the National Museum. And
4.   they're buggered if there is going to be one as far as I can find out.
5.   I: Do you think that that also extends to other aspects of art? For
6.   example there isn't any kind of definitive Welsh school of art in Wales
7.   as far as I understand.
8.   A: There's no Welsh school of art (.) no. But there are Welsh artists. And
9.   how on earth can a country get interested in art if they cannot see the
10.   contribution over the last three hundred years of artists in Wales?
11.   And it is hopeless (.) they can't do it if they can't see what's going on.
12.   If there was a gallery of Welsh art in the National Museum of Wales of
13.   the last three hundred years mini buses of school children would
14.   come down from around the valleys and say: Damn we didn't know
15.   about this! And they would be interested as they see it. That is what
16.   is so pathetic.

In this account, which follows the previous discussion, the poor visibility of Welsh art is located and perceived in terms of contemporary practices; in this case, there being no gallery or any visible organisation for Welsh art. This point is one that connects with wider current debates in which prominent artists in Wales and members of the Welsh assembly have sought to explore ways in which the artistic legacy of Wales can be mirrored in the form of a designated space in the National Gallery. Clearly, there are others who see such a manoeuvre as 'nationalistic' and limited in scope;

one that does not fit well with more 'international'[2] theories of curation, organisation and display.

In terms of the account produced here this is almost a call for recognising the (contested) category of 'Welsh art'; the recognisability of such a demand literally being respected not only through a process of historical recuperation but also a syntagmatic visual display and tangible location within a National Institution. Furthermore, it may be observed here that the discourse of Welsh art and artist is one that is not exclusionary in principle but merely one that reflects or asserts a reality of nationhood and national experience; that is, an imagined reality in which the next generation would be able to recognise their own visual heritage. This forms a powerful account and narrative of national renewal and the recognition of submerged traditions, narratives and understandings that have been previously denied and currently thwarted. In this narrative, Welsh art, both its potential recovery and potential realisation, are couched in terms of a counter-hegemony; one potentially connected to post-colonial aspirations and the return of the repressed. In the following account, by another accomplished practitioner, a different understanding of Welsh art and art in Wales is presented. Here the possibility of Welsh art and art in terms of a universal set of signifiers is displayed.

Extract 3: Art, space and place

1. I: As a practitioner (.) as an artist (.) do you think it's possible to talk
2.   about Welsh Art or is it only possible to talk about art in Wales? Or is
3.   that too much of a hard and fast distinction?
4. A: Well (.) they probably both exist as concepts. I think that in many
5.   areas of the world (.) like in Mexico for instance (.) there would be
6.   such a thing as Mexican Art. In Santa Fé they have what they call
7.   'Western Art'. And in Wales there is bound to be Welsh Art just like in
8.   Yorkshire there *is* local art (.) based locally. And then there is art that
9.   transcends borders and is about human beings and our life our being
10.   and that inevitably transcends nationality. Now personally I think
11.   that that is greater because of its transcendence that that is a greater
12.   form of art. So every locality has its, what you might call parochial
13.   art. And then every so often someone working that parochial art does
14.   it so incredibly well that it transcends the barrier of parochial art and
15.   becomes something else. But I suppose they just coexist. But
16.   specifically in Wales I think that if a nation can only boast the art of
17.   its nationality (.) that is if it can only boast parochial art (.) that isn't
18.   much of a recommendation really.
19. I: So do you think there is a kind of tension between art as a universal
20.   enterprise and framing it within a category or a national identity or
21.   whatever?
22. A: Can I just add to that? Just to say that although I would tend to say

---

[2]   Ironically, postmodern theories of curation and display are increasingly international and almost universally acknowledged.

23.   that universal art (.) or you might say art that is unrestricted (.) is
24.   greater than parochial art (.) just to stress that point (.) that
25.   sometimes parochial art can arise to become profound. But ultimately
26.   it's a silly restriction to put a stamp of any particular nation on art
27.   that happens to come from there is a silly thing.
28.   I: In terms of art that that is done Wales (.) for example (.) thinking
29.   about it in a wider sense (.) though your work addresses
30.   transcendental issues which are perhaps of interest and of
31.   significance to human beings rather than specific sections of the
32.   population or groups and so forth (.) Is there any way in which your
33.   experience of being located in Wales does that have any effect on the
34.   type of work that you do? Perhaps in the past or the way you've
35.   developed or where you're going (.) is there any way in which your
36.   location does affect your work?
37.   A: I think there probably is an effect. But it's no more specific than a
38.   kind of psychic gloominess. There is a gloom. I think in this weird
39.   magical country of mists and heavy layers of cloud and hills. I think
40.   the gloom finds its way into my work. The ephemeral uncertainty.
41.   I: The environmental in one sense?
42.   A: Yes it's just that. Because that moulds a population as well. The
43.   weather changes the psychology of a nation doesn't it?

In terms of the account provided here the concepts of 'Welsh Art' and 'artists living in Wales' are understood to be ones that can 'co-exist'. In terms of the notion of national frames of artistic practice this is a form of life that is readily recognised and compared to 'Mexican Art' and, in Sante Fe, a form of artistic practice denominated as 'Western Art'. The account provides for an understanding in which Welsh Art is a perfectly realisable and recognisable concept and practice. However, the notion of Welsh Art being '… just like in Yorkshire' interpolates the notion of the visual nation as one that can be equated with the local or regional; art based in terms of the locale, as opposed to art that might resonate with notions of people, nation and submerged, sidelined, unrecognised experiences. Thus the potential for Welsh Art *is* recognised but within the terms of a particular discursive construction; that of the local as opposed to the national.

The second part of the account (L.8–18) responds to the question by displaying an understanding of art-in-Wales as a concept that reflects a universal conceptualisation of art. Here art, wherever it may be produced, transcends borders, 'about human beings and our life our being', a concept of spirituality and the aesthetic that transcends nationality. In terms of this account, it is the universal power of art to transcend boundaries that is of significance. The account continues by building on a mode of discursive representation in which Wales as a locale is then connected to a third part of a discursive chain, in this case the parochial (Wales → Local → Parochial). This form of discursive constitution of Nation is specified in terms of Wales 'specifically' (L.16) and not at the level of nations in general. It is qualified in terms of the assertion that 'if a nation can only boast the art of its nationality' (.) that is if it can only boast parochial art (.) that isn't much of a recommendation really' (L.

16–18). Clearly, the notion of Welsh Art, though not necessarily other forms of art couched in national criteria, is viewed as one that is local and parochial; particular as opposed to universal. The following account provided by a different artist represents a further transformation and discursive positioning of art subjectivity and relations. This involves a particular framing of creative-self in relation to artistic practice and identity.

Extract 4: Constructing identity and locating the creative self

1.	I:	I'll just shift topic, but I would like to come back to that. Do you see
2.		yourself as an artist in Wales or as a Welsh artist?
3.	A:	Well at the moment both. Going to London was interesting because
4.		there are more artists there than anywhere else and it's a very sort of
5.		cut and thrust place, you're very much aware of how people promote
6.		themselves as artists and as people as well, that's so much a part of
7.		it, especially nowadays. And everyone really is in the business of
8.		exploiting whatever, and rightly so as well, of exploiting whatever they
9.		have in their life that makes them different from every other artist
10.		that's around. Because that enriches their work if it is genuinely a
11.		part of them and part of their work it's a case of promoting it. If you
12.		go to London it's such a multinational and multiracial place, and the
13.		artistic community is even more so or at least as much so that people
14.		are in the business of saying 'I'm from here, this is me, this is what I
15.		bring to the picture, to this cultural pot that you are dipping into' so
16.		people are really quite upfront about it, where they're and what
17.		they're about. So in a way that did make me think about my own
18.		relationship to where I'm from.
19.	I:	By going away?
20.	A:	Well, by going to London specifically, but by going away
21.		generally, yes. It made me realise that the work I want to make is
22.		about the sort of places where I've lived. That hasn't always been
23.		Wales. It's been to do with the kind of places that have been
24.		important to me, which have often been coastal, isolated or remote
25.		countryside, the wilder parts of the world. And I have become aware
26.		hat that is what I want to talk about even if it's not where I'm making
27.		the images that I want to deal with, just because they are important
28.		to me.
29.	I:	Do you think there is such a thing as Welsh art, as an artist?
30.	A:	Well, on a basic level yes, of course. Are you saying that there are
31.		themes in Welsh art that make them different from themes that are in
32.		other art? That there is something inherent in the style and the
33.		approach of a style?
34.	I:	If you like.
35.	A:	In the visual arts I don't really know whether that's true. It's not as
36.		strong a tradition in Wales as say music or writing. Or at least it
37.		doesn't have as high a profile, but I think that's changing. But I don't
38.		define myself in relation to other Welsh artists any differently than I

39.   do to other artists that I'm interested in. Obviously there are Welsh
40.   artists who are very definitely addressing Welsh issues, but that is a
41.   different thing. When you say is there such a thing as Welsh art, I
42.   kind of think that that's meaningless. Is there a kind of school, a
43.   style, a way of thinking about work which is inherently Welsh, I'm not
44.   sure that that's true.

In terms of the narrative presented here, the creative self is located within a wider art world that allows the condition of being a Welsh artist and an artist in Wales. The relationship between the creative self, location and identity figures prominently within this account. Recent experience of working in London is referred to, here the art world is characterised in terms of 'cut and thrust' and the profile of a multicultural demographic is alluded to. Furthermore issues of identity are seen to be important within this art world (L.14–15, 16–17). This includes where one is from, self-definition and what one brings to the cultural pot of this multicultural scene. Thus various biographical and reflective resources are central to this *presentation* of creative self in this dense and busy art world. In this scene, the business of presenting one's creative self is central to promoting oneself as an artist (L.5–7) and involves using various cultural resources in order to accomplish not only visibility but *difference*. Difference can be understood in terms of achieving recognition of unique creative quality. This is the hard currency of creative cultural capital. Thus, in terms of this narrative, it is not merely a question of promotion leading to visibility or a high profile but also of exploiting resources (these may be biographical, where you are from and your work) as a means of accomplishing difference. Difference is therefore not merely accomplished in terms of works of art but also in terms of the biographical details, geographical details or 'whatever'. Indeed, the accomplishment of identity, and the production of works of art, in this scene or 'field' (Bourdieu, 1977), are presented as equally important; 'people promote themselves as artists and as people as well, that's so much part of it nowadays'. In terms of the artist's experience of the London art scene he suggests that this stimulated reflection on his own biography and identity.

This identity is one that does not exclusively link with the national parameters of Wales. It is one that includes Wales but also links with remote parts of the countryside, and isolated coastal areas. Within this narrative the possibility of 'Welsh artists' is acknowledged although it is one that is not of primary importance in terms of the creative self being presented. The notion of 'Welsh art' is viewed as meaningless (although this is prefaced by a view that this may change). However, what is of interest here is the way in which other forms of creative endeavour (e.g. poetry, music) are seen as being able to be subject to national parameters and boundaries. Art and visual art in particular is seen to have a problematic relation with the parameters of nation proffered in this account.

Welsh Art, Accounts and Type

In terms of the exemplar narratives analysed and discussed in this chapter, a number of points can be advanced. Firstly, whilst artists' experience and perceptions of the creative self in relation to wider social categories and processes are unique, they also exhibit certain typical characteristics. These typical characteristics do not constitute a single homogenous type. Rather they can be subdivided into particular positional/ perspectival types. The importance of these types is twofold. Firstly they represent a way of beginning to understand the discursive characteristics of the visual arts in Wales and secondly, they display the type of discursive moves and cultural understandings that can be inferred and associated with this particular art world. In some respects these can be understood not merely as types but as forms of social representation or frames that find resonance within elite artists' accounts.

Welsh Art

Within this discursive representation, grounded as it is in lived experience, the notion of being submerged, peripheral and contested is evident. In the case where this form of representation is exhibited in its most pure form (Extract 1) the phenomenon of 'Welsh art' is understood and portrayed as a rare entity. It is also constituted in terms that are deeply embedded and connected to Welsh life, landscape and, in an attempt to overcome the dichotomy and compartmentalisation of the verbal and the visual, language. Its contested nature and submerged, even oppressed, character is made recognisable through accounts that relay stories of organisational interference (by organisations viewed as sometimes colonial in attitude and action or at least unsympathetic). This sense is also relayed through accounts of a lack of organic organisation in terms of grounded and culturally aware sites of artistic pedagogy e.g. designated, established and developed Art Colleges in Wales. These narratives both seek to recuperate a submerged history of Welsh art production and identify agencies of cultural hegemony that exclude national facts and cultural 'realities'.

Art in the Locale

Within this discursive frame, artistic and creative practices occur within a whole range of locales; the city, the region and the nation. Whilst some nations can legitimately claim a national narrative for art others cannot. In the example here 'Wales' provides such a category. This is in stark contrast to the previous narrative form. Furthermore, art in the locale is a legitimate cultural and spatial formation that is not at odds with the principles of universalism and transcendence. Certain national parameters are viewed as restrictive, parochial and limiting. This discursive framework negates the 'potential' and 'actual' levels of experience being authentically accorded to the creative self within a meaningful national/cultural milieu as a primary or central concern of artistic endeavour. Furthermore, the principle of locale can also invoke notions of landscape and other geographical features in a way that does not necessarily equate with notions of national identity. However in the case of Wales and other national communities, landscape represents a powerful resource for national forms of identity appropriation, construction and representation.

Art as a Universal/Transcendental

Art as a universal is commensurate with certain modern ideas concerning the conceptualisation of artistic practice. In terms of the creative self and the negotiation of national parameters, the universal language of artistic endeavours and products overwhelm the particular considerations of national circumstances, experiences or influences. This represents one form of narrative of the creative self in which autonomy of the created and creator is assumed. However, not only does it eschew the many consequences of purely national concerns but it is also associated with social processes, for example, the allocation of scarce resources, patronage and so forth. In many respects the frame and social representation of art in terms of universalism provides an 'othering device' in talk and accounts of 'Art, Identity and Wales'. It is the antithesis to all those accounts that seek to situate artistic practice and organisation in terms of national contexts or experiences. The notion of universalism does not fit well with the post-modern ethic of diversity, plurality and the rejection of grand-narratives. However, the notion of cosmopolitanism may provide a means through which such accounts of national-cultural experience can re-engage with values and principles that stand outside particular concerns; a discursive means of straddling the universal and the particular during a period of cultural modernisation in Wales. Within this chapter, and the data set as a whole, cosmopolitanism was not an idea that had explicit purchase although it may provide a means through which the universal vs. particular may be negated. However, this discussion remains outside the parameters of this specific chapter.

Conclusion

None of the exemplar narratives here represents a 'pure form' of the narrative 'repertoires' or reflects the discursive positions described above. This is, of course, to be expected; such accounts are principled positions that are renditions, stand on behalf of and report and reflect on experience, practice and expert understandings. The readings of doubt and methodological scepticism do not form a focus for this specific chapter. The negotiation of the creative self in relation to frames of national identity conforms, in part, to specific biographical profiles. Time, history and experience are central components to the stories told here. However, the positioning of narratives, an expression of certain biographical details, is merely one part of the story. These narratives form meaningful accounts, and attempts to account, for both a contested history of creative production in Wales and the contemporary cultural field during a time of cultural and political reflection and change. As such they are worthy of the most careful consideration and scrutiny as such narratives can also be understood to represent collective 'positionings' (Maine, 2002). The frames of the reflective-creative self in relation to a changing apparatus of national definition is of import. In terms of the exemplar narratives explored here the tension between universalism and particularism features heavily. Furthermore, a notion of nation as parochial and nation as an important but submerged discourse of self-understanding and cultural articulation is also observable. The contested character of the field reflects contemporary social facts. The notion of Wales in the cultural sphere is not only contested but is also 'up for grabs'.

Thus, these exemplar narratives are not only passive reflections but represent accounts of 'structuralised' cultural practice (Thomas, 1937) that report on the way in which cultural institutions and artistic traditions are constantly being negotiated and are the product of a variety of sustained social processes and interactions. They form understandings and experiences that mobilise and make use of contested historical accounts and sociological profiles in order to situate the creative self in both contemporary circumstances and current debates. These current debates (a room for Welsh Art in the National Gallery, the distribution of resources, the promotion of specific representation[s] and the character of creative careers) are therefore both reflected and constituted by such accounts. They are constituted both in terms of the situated enunciation of narrative in the interview and their articulation and rearticulation by prominent artists within other domains of social commentary. Thus, this chapter analyses and reports on the character of such narratives and recognises their wider circulation and uses. These narratives display not only collectivised positions but also the circulation of discursive types that enable an understanding and contestation of the discursive and practical field of Art in Wales. These narratives also report on the presentation of the creative self in relation to wider social structures, parameters and scenes.

To this extent these narratives of the creative self, by prominent artists in Wales, represent crucial data for explaining, exploring and understanding artistic endeavour within post-devolution Wales. The practice of 'telling' as reflected in other works (e.g. *Welsh Artists Talking*) provides a resource through which the often relegated voices of artists can be both heard and mobilised as a means of contributing to this ongoing cultural debate. These *strong* narratives, like visual representations, become powerful resources for informing, shifting and shaping the discourse and contours of debate and cultural decision-making (e.g. debates and consultation organised by the Institute for Welsh Affairs, the National Assembly and BBC Wales). To this extent the narratives explored here represent typical discursive positions that are in circulation both in print, by word of mouth and other forms of social network. Indeed many of the narrative accounts reflexively display their positioning in terms of other cultural networks, artists and art scenes. Thus, whilst they are situated accounts, for members, they are positioned and connected to wider sets of collective experience and understanding.

A crucial feature of the accounts reported within the limitations of this chapter is the contested character of 'Welsh art'. It is characterised by contested boundaries ranging from explicit scepticism to individual embodiment. It may well be worthwhile to theorise that the narrative reality of contested boundaries reflects certain cultural and social realities of post-devolution Wales as well as the contested character of artistic practice in general. Clearly, a creative space in which a national conceptualisation of visual narrative can be advanced is one that is questioned as well as promoted. However, it also displays the way in which the discursive construction of such a tradition in Wales and other nations is founded upon a diversity of views and understandings. The development of a coherent narrative for the visual arts in Wales has now been established in the form of Peter Lord's book *Imaging the Nation* (2000) and calls to establish a place for Welsh Art in the National Gallery. Thus the emergence of a visual narrative for Wales is well underway. This represents an explicit and conscious attempt at imagining a 'visual nation' in a space where it had not previously been acknowledged. A crucial feature in building up and operationalising such strong narratives is recognition. There was simply no narrative through which various creative artefacts and individuals in Wales, both past and present, could be discursively realised, enunciated and represented. It may well be that such intellectual work can be compared to the ideal typical legislative function of the modern intellectual (Bauman, 1987). Indeed, the construction of a story, a presentation of a story for the visual arts in Wales, is realised within a context of difference, debate and rancour. However, by analysing the perceptions and expectations of artists in Wales we not only learn a great deal about art, identity and the nation but also the manner in which discursive representations of cultural sites, spaces and places are never 'true' or 'accurate'. They are always partial 'will to truths' that impose a version of events and discursive frames upon, in this case, a national story. They are themselves social, cultural and political acts that promote certain world-views and discourses concerning national identity and understanding. The picture from Wales is, I would suggest, little different from other historical and contemporary (e.g. Brit-Art) attempts at imaging, 'branding' or 'legislating' various creative practices in terms of necessary national 'fictions', boundaries of experience and collective historical experience. In the case of Wales this process is, however, tainted by other historical experiences, that testify to a submerged, sidelined and ignored visual story that has as much right to expression (and surely contestation) as other national fictions in other parts of the world. In many respects the discourse of art in Wales is one shaped by the experiences of the periphery and economic decline. In terms of this location, visual culture provides a resource through which new forms of national expression/prestige and identity can be realised.

In terms of social-cultural precedent, some comparison to other nations pursuing forms of national renewal and re-invigoration can be located. The intellectual debate in Ireland during the early part of the twentieth century testifies to this. The Celtic Revival of the 1880's explicitly sought to recover and construct a distinct Irish culture. An important aspect of this process was the pursuit of a construction of a national artistic tradition. The initial means through which this was to be realised was through the establishment of a national art collection. According to Herrero (2002:61) this was seen to encapsulate two functions; firstly, as a means of constructing an authentic and distinct Irish-Celtic visual narrative and secondly, as means of helping Ireland ascend 'modernity's hierarchy of nations'. Furthermore, it was the opinion of Irish intellectuals of the time (in particular the ideas of Hugh Lane encapsulated in a letter to the *Irish Times*, 15 of January, 1903) that the establishment of a national collection and the physical establishment of a national gallery would help alleviate the paucity of art education in Ireland. For Lane the establishment of a contemporary school of modern Irish Art was central to the modernisation process and the securing of Ireland's place alongside other established 'modern' nations. Herrero (2002) asserts that this was a form of practice, alluded to earlier, associated with what Bauman (1987, 1992) has described as the 'legislators of modernity'. For Herrero (2002) the active practice of pursuing such a course of action was an important process in establishing a form of cultural modernity for Ireland. This process was characterised by public debate concerning what the collection should include. The debate polarised around two principal positions; namely an 'introspective position' and an 'internationalist' position. This account of Irish intellectuals, the establishment of national collections and artistic practice, has strong parallels with the experience of Wales. In terms of the national context of Wales, attempts at legislation are observable and institutions developed and their consequences experienced. These processes have also been polarised around Herroro's internationalist *vs.* introspective lines and what I have identified as the universal *vs.* particular dimensions of the visual arts in Wales. The future of this debate and the potential of transcending such dichotomies by appreciating the existence of other forms of cultural understanding remains, at least at this stage of cultural re-invigoration in Wales, a possibility.

In terms of contemporary conditions in Wales, as in other parts of the world, visual culture and sites for the display of visual culture have been used and are being used to promote certain notions of identity, from post-devolution national identities to multiculturalism. The visual arts alongside other creative endeavours are also being marshalled as a resource for the regeneration of areas of economic decline. The new demand for the consumption of 'art' and its wider aesthetic and spiritual function in societies experiencing religious decline represents a powerful resource for social integration. Consequently, the fact that the narratives of visual culture are highly contested by the artists themselves demands examination. It suggests that such narratives for visual culture (and consumption) do not always equate with the understanding and experiences of the artists. In this respect the attempts to construct or legislate meta-narratives for various national visual cultures submerges (some) of the voices of those who produce the visual products, especially those whose biography and identity claims do not fit neatly with the contours of the new narrative. Furthermore, a concern with the creative production of artefacts by highly creative individuals, as opposed to mere consumption or re-production, represents a form of resistance to the colonisation of the life-world by the market, rudderless consumption and its resultant waste (Bauman, 2003). In short, certain strong visual narratives can be used by legislators in constructing certain versions of events and spaces through which collective experiences and understandings can be displayed and inform other (e.g. educational) practices. Thus it is important that such voices are heard in order to inform a narrative of a visual nation, that reports on the contested character of artistic practice and national cultural appropriation as one that is diverse rather than monolithic, contested rather than passively accepted, productive as opposed to all-consuming, vibrant rather than dull. The cultural modernisation of Wales and the agents and institutions associated with this process can learn from other precedents. However, in terms of late modernity, the legislation of visual narratives should be open to participatory scrutiny. A crucial dimension of such participatory scrutiny is to be found in the voices of those who produce visual artefacts in the first place. The discourse of '(post)modern cultural legislation' denies the author such rights; it does so by excluding valuable insights and understandings that if allowed visible and audible expression will surely result in a form of visual narrative of cultural renaissance and regeneration that represents both the unique collective experience of Wales and the diversity of late modern Welshness (Fevre and Thompson, 1999). This manoeuvre would avoid the polarising effects of introspection vs. internationalism and represent a more pluralistic path for the management and promotion of the current cultural renaissance in Wales.

Chapter 5

New Colours for the Orange State: Finding Symbolic Space in a Newly Devolved Northern Ireland[1]

Dominic Bryan

You might ask mockingly: 'A flag? What's that? A stick with a rag on it?' No sire, a flag is much more. With a flag you lead men, for a flag, men live and die. In fact, it is the only thing for which they are ready to die in their masses, if you train them for it. Believe me, the politics of an entire people ... can be manipulated only through the imponderables that float in the air.

Theodore Herzl Quoted in R.J. Goldstein *Saving Old Glory* (1995)

All Participants acknowledge the sensitivity of the use of symbols and emblems for public purposes and the need in particular in creating the new institutions to ensure that such symbols and emblems are used in a manner which promotes mutual respect rather than division. Arrangements will be made to monitor the issue and consider what action should be taken.

The Good Friday/Belfast Agreement, p. 20

There is no lack of awareness over the role of symbols in politics in Northern Ireland either amongst the public and politicians who are regularly engaged and enraged by issues relating to the use of symbols or amongst academics working in the area (Bryan, 2000, Bryan and Gillespie, 2005, Brown and MacGinty, 2003, Bryson and McCartney, 1994, Buckley, 1985, Feldman, 1991, Harrison, 1995, Jarman, 1993, 1997, Loftus 1990, 1994, MacGinty and Darby, 2002, McCormick and Jarman, 2005, Nic Craith, 2002, Rolston, 1991, 1992, 1995, 2003, Santino, 2001). Flags and emblems, as well as memorials and parades, are the language through which identity politics is expressed. The 1998 Multi-Party Agreement, aside from the fact that its name also seems symbolically disputed (Good Friday or Belfast Agreement), contains references to the use of symbols (quoted above) within the framework of the section on 'Rights, Safeguards and Equality of Opportunity: Economic, Social and Cultural Issues' (pp. 19–20).

[1] This research was undertaken as part of a project funded under the ESRC Devolution programme. Funding was also forthcoming from the Office of the First Minister and Deputy First Minister. Particular thanks should go to Gordon Gillespie and Neil Fleming for help in undertaking the research.

The Agreement appeared to offer political space for a 'new' Northern Ireland to develop, expressing a broadly agreed political way forward. Politicians had opened to them the possibility of re-presenting Northern Ireland to its people and to the outside world. MacGinty and Darby (2002: 152–164) have argued that a 'peace process provides the participants in a conflict with opportunities for new beginnings, many of them symbolic' (p. 159). Possibly the most obvious often quoted example, from another arena, came in 1995 when Nelson Mandela attended the Rugby World Cup Final wearing a Springbok Rugby shirt. By wearing a symbol so associated with the previous apartheid regime Mandela created a moment that became symbolic of a new South Africa. Mandela understood that in creating a new peaceful democratic environment in South Africa symbols were important and he was particularly adept at capturing broad political acceptance through his actions. The same was understood in Northern Ireland by many politicians and particularly engaged those working throughout the peace process.

One post-Agreement image that is often reproduced is the moment a few days before the referendum that John Hume and David Trimble joined U2's singer Bono on stage at the Waterfront Hall (20 May 1998). It has been viewed as a defining moment in the campaign to try to win a yes vote for Agreement. Such an image played well with the media and suggested a different possible political future. Similarly, a few days after the Agreement, Elton John performed at a concert in the grounds of Stormont, an event designed to symbolise the opening up of an area seen as a bastion of Unionist power. Pictures of Elton John holding his arm up to the crowd, in a pose similar to Carson's statue standing a short distance away with Stormont Parliament buildings in the background, were beamed around the world.

These events seemed to symbolise a new Northern Ireland. However, such images have been the exception rather than the rule. The then two largest political parties in the Assembly, the Social Democratic Labour Party (SDLP) and the Ulster Unionist Party (UUP) did not choose to map a way forward that was different from the past. Unionism in particular, as we can judge from policies on flags, has remained determined to re-present Northern Ireland simply as another region of the United Kingdom.

MacGinty and Darby have argued there were no moments that rivalled the Mandela Rugby shirt (2002: 165–166).

> There was no attempt to create a 'third way' or new entity on either nationalism nor was a national integration programme agreed. Instead, both nationalisms were deemed legitimate. The intention was to create a single political entity that could accommodate both identities, giving both access to power and managing their interaction through consociational institutions (MacGinty and Darby, 2002: 166).

Although the Agreement suggested that pluralism and diversity were at the heart of the new institutions, as MacGinty and Darby (2002) rightly point out, the political structures were really there to enable two identities, reflecting the power base of the four main political parties, two Unionist: the Ulster Unionist Party (UUP) and the Democratic Unionist Party (DUP) and two Nationalist: the Social and Democratic

Labour Party (SDLP) and Sinn Féin. The key wording can be found at the start of
the Agreement:

> The participants endorse the commitment made by the British and Irish Governments that,
> in a new British-Irish Agreement replacing the Anglo-Irish Agreement, they will:
>
> ... (v) affirm that whatever choice is freely exercised by a majority of the people of
> Northern Ireland, the power of the sovereign government with jurisdiction there shall be
> exercised with rigorous impartiality on behalf of *all the people in the diversity of their
> identities and traditions* and shall be founded on the principles of full respect for, and
> equality of, civil, political, social and cultural rights, of freedom from discrimination for
> all citizens, and of parity of esteem and of just and equal treatment for the identity, ethos,
> and aspirations of *both communities*; ...
>
> (Multi-Party Agreement 1998 p. 2, my italics).

At the heart of a possible new Northern Ireland, whether it is to exist in a devolved
United Kingdom, independently, in joint sovereignty with the Republic of Ireland,
or as part of the Republic of Ireland, is the need to create an agreed polity that
both allows diversity and pluralism but does so in a context that gives the state
legitimacy and minimises the environment for violence. As with the development of
all organisations, institutions, companies and states, symbols play an important role
in the processes of legitimisation and representation.

Under devolution, identities in Scotland and Wales are not uncontested but
political divisions nevertheless exist within a broadly shared set of ritual and
symbolic identifiers providing for an imagined or symbolically constructed
community. Northern Ireland has a wide range of ritual and symbolic identifiers,
many present in both communities, but they are more often contested than shared.
The Agreement offered the tentative possibility that the large Catholic minority,
which in the main has never accepted the legitimacy of the state, might move into
new political relationships within Northern Ireland. Would the Agreement provide
the basis for a change in a sense of community in Northern Ireland that develops
alongside being Irish and British? What strategy provides for improved community
relations and peace building? This Chapter examines the strategies to resolve disputes
over the use of flags and emblems and looks at the attempts by public agencies and
institutions to symbolically create a new devolved dispensation. It looks at policies
related to the flying of official flags on Government buildings and on other official
buildings controlled by local Councils. In addition, it explores the difficulties the
Northern Ireland Human Rights Commission has had interpreting the Agreement. It
concludes that contradictory policy approaches derive from conflicting conceptions
of the Agreement and the role of devolution.

Flags in Northern Ireland

The display of flags and emblems has been a site of contest since the foundation of
the quasi-state of Northern Ireland. Many existing public events and most occasions

of public presentation became sites of symbolic competition. They have often represented political fissure rather than any sense of cross-community cohesion. The Union flag and the Ulster Flag (cross of St. George on a white background with a red hand within a white six pointed star, with a crown above it) were used routinely on many official buildings. Flags on Government buildings were not only often flown on the officially designated flag days, there were also additional days to those in the rest of the United Kingdom, most notably the Twelfth of July remembering the Battle of the Boyne (Bryson and McCartney 1994:76–78). The Union flag was also flown from police stations, fire stations and other services as well as from many Protestant churches. Both Union and Ulster flags were displayed frequently on parades and particularly around the Twelfth of July celebrations. This relationship between the popular and official flying of these flags has an important bearing on the perception of flags in contemporary Northern Ireland.

In contrast the Irish Tricolour was never displayed in Northern Ireland at any official occasions of which I am aware. Neither, until maybe the 1970s, was the Tricolour greatly tolerated by the police when it was used on popular occasions. The Civil Authorities (Special Powers) Act of 1922 was used to restrict parades and other displays of a broadly Irish Nationalist character (Jarman and Bryan 1998: 41–53). In 1958 Home Affairs Minister Edmond Warnock announced the banning of a St Patrick's Day parade saying 'so long as this Government lasts and so long as I am Home Affairs Minister, I shall not permit the Republican flag to be carried in Derry City' (quoted in Farrell 1980:199). In the mid-fifties the Northern Ireland Parliament passed the Flags and Emblems (Display) Act (Northern Ireland) 1954. Section 2(1) gave the police the power to order a person who erected an 'emblem' to remove it, or for the officer to remove it, if the officer felt it would lead to a breach of the peace. If the person failed to obey the constable's order they would be guilty of an offence. This proposition was not in itself totally unreasonable, what made the Act controversial and partisan was section 2(4). This states that 'emblem' includes a flag of any other kind except the Union flag (Bew *et al.*, 2002:97, Patterson, 1999). Infamously this Act was utilised by the police in September 1964 when Rev. Ian Paisley threatened to walk up the Falls Road and remove the Tricolour from the front window of the offices of the Republican Party. The attempt by the police to deal with the flag led to serious riots. The controversial and infamous implementation of this Act led to its repeal in 1987.

Heightened conflict from the late 1960s onwards was routinely sparked by public displays of flags and other emblems. Public space was controlled and demarcated though parades, by the designating of 'No-Go' areas by paramilitaries, by the painting of murals as well as by state and non-state violence. Government and local council buildings remained the site for symbolic conflict. Once direct rule was introduced by the UK, government buildings within their designation more often flew flags on official days, which was, in effect, a reduction from the practice under the pre-1972 Unionist regimes but the Union flag still flew over police stations and law courts. Significantly, popular flying of flags over the Twelfth increased as territorial space in Northern Ireland became marked. Flags had long been flown on people's houses around occasions like the Twelfth of July but increasingly flags were put up on lampposts and left up all year round. At local Councils, most authorities in Unionist control not only flew the Union flag, and often the Ulster flag, everyday of the year, but did so on all buildings within the control of the council such as swimming pools and sports centres. Those same Unionist controlled Councils used their buildings to display banners opposing the 1986 Anglo-Irish Agreement.

In contrast a number of Nationalist councils stopped flying the Union flag and either flew a council flag or no flag at all. Bryson and McCartney (1994: 78–79) describe the unsuccessful attempts by the, Nationalist controlled, Derry City council to resolve the flag flying problem by flying the Crimson flag associated with the Protestant defence of the city in 1688–89. However, this did not satisfy unionists who saw the removal of the Union flag as the central issue.

This then was the broad 'symbolic environment' that existed at the signing of the Multi-Party Agreement in 1998. As noted above, the Agreement recognised the conflictual nature of symbols and 'the need in particular in creating the new institutions to ensure that such symbols and emblems are used in a manner which promotes mutual respect rather than division'. So a political opportunity was available not only to the political parties that were to form the Government but also to policy makers. Indeed, it could be argued that there was some obligation for those supporting the Agreement to improve the symbolic environment. Examples of public authorities changing their policies can be found. As early as July 1998 the Chief Constable of the RUC announced that the Union flag would only be flown at police stations on occasions such as Royal birthdays and not on public holidays, such as the Twelfth. Relatively uncontested emblems were produced for the new Northern Ireland Assembly (Linen Flax) and for the Northern Ireland Executive (the Giants Causeway). The Patten report on policing in Northern Ireland recommended that a new badge be produced as the Royal Ulster Constabulary became the Police Service of Northern Ireland (PSNI). This new emblem for the PSNI was an achievement as there had been significant disputes over it and a number of attempts to come up with new emblems. This new symbol represents a rare case where the UUP and SDLP, sitting on the Policing Board, worked closely to get agreement.

The above examples were fairly immediate outworkings of the Agreement. But the obligations within the Agreement also led to new legislation and strengthening of existing legislation. It is worth looking at the legislation because it allows us to ask whether changes that did take place were, in part, a result of legislation or as part of the new political environment. Of most significance was Section 75 of the 1998 Northern Ireland Act arising from the signing of the Agreement. It demands that public authorities have to have due regard to promote equality of opportunity and regard the desirability of promoting good relations.

Section 75.

1. A public authority shall in carrying out its functions relating to Northern Ireland have due regard to the need to promote equality of opportunity –

(a)   between persons of different religious belief, political opinion, racial group, age, marital status or sexual orientation;
(b)   between men and women generally;
(c)   between persons with a disability and persons without; and
(d)   between persons with dependents and persons without.

2. Without prejudice to its obligations under subsection (1), a public authority shall in carrying out its functions relating to Northern Ireland have regard to the desirability of promoting good relations between persons of different religious belief, political opinion or racial groups.

Also of relevance to the issue of flags is fair employment legislation. The Fair Employment and Treatment (Northern Ireland) Order 1998 makes discrimination on the grounds of religious belief and political opinion unlawful both in the work place and in the provision of goods, facilities and services. The Fair Employment Code of Practice states that employers are required to identify any practices that do not provide equality of opportunity (1.1.2). They should:

> Promote a good and harmonious working environment and atmosphere in which no worker feels under threat or intimidated because of his or her religious belief or political opinion, e.g. prohibit the display of flags, emblems, posters, graffiti, or the circulation of materials, or the deliberate articulation of slogans or songs which are likely to give offence or case apprehension among particular groups of employees (5.2.2).

The Code of Practice suggests that Employers might take affirmative action by considering:

> ending displays at the workplace of flags, emblems, posters, graffiti, or the circulation of materials, or the deliberate articulation of slogans or songs which are likely to give offence to, or cause apprehension among, any one section of the population.

As soon as the new Government was set up the flying of flags over buildings caused controversy. The arrangement for Government Departments under the Agreement left the UUP in control of three Departments, the DUP in control of two the SDLP in control of three and Sinn Féin in control of two. Unionist Minister ordered the flag to be flown outside their Departments whilst Sinn Fein Ministers ordered no flag to be flown. SDLP Ministers ordered the Union flag not to be flown on the Twelfth. This produced heated controversy in the Assembly and eventually a committee was set up to explore the issue. Amongst other incidents loyalists put Union flags on the lampposts around the Department of Education building in Bangor after Education Minister, Martin McGuinness, refused to have the flag raised. In general, there was such contention that the Secretary of State, Peter Mandelson decided to introduce specific legislation in Westminster. The Flags (Northern Ireland) Order 2000 designates particular days on which the Union Flag should fly on Northern Ireland government buildings.

Flags and Regulations (*Northern Ireland*) *2000*
Flying of flags at government buildings on specified days

1. The Union flag shall be flown at the government buildings specified in Part I of the Schedule to these Regulations on the days specified in Part II of the Schedule.
2. The Union flag shall be flown on the days specified in Part II of the Schedule at any other government building at which it was the practice to fly the Union flag on notified days in the period of 12 months ending with 30th November 1999.
3. In paragraph (2), 'notified days' means days notified by the Department of Finance and Personnel to other Northern Ireland Departments as days for the flying of the Union flag at government buildings during the period of 12 months ending with 30th November 1999.
4. Where a government building specified in Part I of the Schedule has more than one flag pole, the European flag shall be flown in addition to the Union flag on Europe Day.

Nine government buildings are named under the Order.

The following days were designated under the original order:

> *20th January: Birthday of the Countess of Wessex*
> *6th February: Her Majesty's Accession*
> *19th February: Birthday of the Duke of York*
> *A day in March to be notified by publication in the Belfast Gazette on or before 31st January annually Commonwealth Day*
> *10th March: Birthday of the Earl of Wessex*
> *17th March: St Patrick's Day*
> *21st April: Birthday of Her Majesty the Queen*
> *9th May: Europe Day*
> *A day in June to be notified by publication in the Belfast Gazette on or before 31st January annually Official Celebration of Her Majesty's Birthday*
> *2nd June: Coronation Day*
> *10th June: Birthday of the Duke of Edinburgh*
> *4th August: Birthday of Her Majesty Queen Elizabeth The Queen Mother*
> *15th August: Birthday of The Princess Royal*
> *21st August: Birthday of The Princess Margaret*
> *A Sunday in November to be notified by publication in the Belfast Gazette on or before 31st January annually Remembrance Day*
> *14th November: Birthday of The Prince of Wales*
> *20th November: Her Majesty's Wedding Day.*

In October 2001, this power was challenged in the High Court by the Sinn Fein MLA, Conor Murphy, partly on the basis that the Order was used for political purposes but also that it was 'not in keeping with the Good Friday Agreement', and that the Secretary of State had acted beyond his jurisdiction. Mr. Justice Kerr found for the Government. As for political motivations he declared that such decisions are 'the stuff of politics. It is not subject to judicial review.' Kerr J. also dismissed Mr Murphy's argument that the flying of the flag breached section 75 of the Northern Ireland Act 1998 (see above). The Secretary of State, according to Kerr J., is not a public authority within the meaning of the Order, and the flying of the Union Flag is not designed to favour one flag over another, but rather 'it merely reflects Northern Ireland's constitutional position as part of the UK'. Further, the new regulations for flying the Union Flag on public buildings will mean that Northern Ireland will fall into line with the rest of the United Kingdom and that means a reduction in the number of days on which it is flown. It was in Kerr J's opinion that the regulations which require that the Union Flag be flown on government buildings do not treat those who oppose it less favourably: 'The purpose of the regulation is ... to reflect Northern Ireland's constitutional position, not to discriminate against any section of its population'. As to the assertion that is was against the principles of the Agreement, partnership, equality and mutual respect', Kerr J. felt that by restricting the flying days to those practised in the rest of the United Kingdom the Secretary of State was striking a balance between acknowledging the constitutional position of Northern Ireland and those who opposed it. Accordingly, the regulations were not contrary to the Agreement.[2]

This solution then was not born out of an agreement between local political parties but imposed from Westminster. It was found to be legal but only in a rather limited way can it be said to represent the new political environment. Of course the chance that a more consensual solution could have come from the political process was made unlikely with the frequent suspension of the Assembly. As such, we cannot know if the committee within the Assembly would have come up with any new solutions. However, if we now look at the example of local Councils in Northern Ireland the possibility of alternative options arising do not look good.

Whilst the flags legislation provided a solution for Government buildings, albeit one some of the political parties found unsatisfactory, Council buildings were left out of the legislation. Policies in Northern Ireland's 26 Councils vary depending on which political party controls it. Unionists argue that the removal of the Union flag has just as much impact as it being left in place. Nationalists tend to favour flying both the Union flag and the Tricolour, flying a Council flag or no flag at all. This means there is a range of policies from the flying of the Union flag on nearly all Council buildings every day of the year, to flying no flags on any building or flying simply the Council flag. There are Councils that have chosen to follow the legislation for Government buildings and fly flags on designated days, even though the legislation does not apply to local Council buildings. A further question is whether there is a difference between flying a flag at the Councils' headquarters and flying a flag at a place of work. Whilst the headquarters is also a place of work it could be argued

---

[2]   Re. *Murphy's Application for Judicial Review* [2001] N.I. 425 (4 Oct. 2001).

that its ceremonial status places it in a different category to that of a work place for council workers.

Northern Ireland Local Council's Policies on flying official flags, 2004

Council	Location	Flags and Dates
Antrim Borough Council	On Council HQ and Antrim Forum	Union Flag flown every day
Ards Borough Council	On Council HQ and war memorials	Union Flag every day
Armagh City & District Council	On Council HQ	Union Flag flown on designated days
Ballymena Borough Council	On Council HQ & Town Hall	Union Flag flown every day
Ballymoney Borough Council	Borough Offices, Riada House, Joey Dunlop Leisure Centre, Town Hall	Union Flag flown on all premises listed on designated days plus 12 July & Christmas Day
Banbridge District Council	On Council HQ, Tourist Information Centre and Town Hall, Banbridge	Union Flag flown every day
Belfast City Council	City Hall, Duncrue Complex, Ulster Hall	Union flag flown on City Hall every day and on Duncrue Complex and Ulster Hall on designated days plus New Years Day, Easter Day, Christmas Day and Twelfth of July
Carrickfergus Borough Council	On Town Hall, Leisure Centre, Bentra Golf Club, Sullatober Depot	Union Flag and Northern Ireland Flag flown at Town Hall and Leisure Centre Union Flag only at other venues
Castlereagh Borough Council	On Council HQ	Union Flag, Ulster Flag and Council Coat of Arms flown every day
Coleraine Borough Council	On Council HQ (Cloonavin) and 3 Town Halls	Union Flag : Cloonavin every day the building is in use and ceremonial days if not in use, Coleraine Town Hall every day, Portrush and Portstewart Town Halls in July and August and ceremonial days
Cookstown District Council		No flags flown
Craigavon Borough Council	On Civic Centre	Union Flag flown on designated days
Derry City Council		No flags flown

Council	Location	Flags and dates
Down District Council	On Council HQ	Council Flag flown every day – Union Flag not flown on any occasion
Dungannon District Council	On Council HQ	Union Flag flown on designated days
Fermanagh District Council		No flags flown
Larne Borough Council	On Council HQ and Leisure Centre	Union Flag flown every day
Limavady Borough Council		No flags flown
Lisburn City Council	On Council HQ	Union Flag flown on designated days plus 1 July and 12 July
Magherafelt District Council		No flags flown
Moyle District Council		No flags flown
Newry and Mourne District Council		No flags flown Council flag being considered
Newtownabbey Borough Council	On all Council administrative buildings and leisure centres	Union Flag flown on all premises listed every day
North Down Borough Council	On Town Hall and Leisure Complex	Union Flag flown every day
Omagh District Council	On Council HQ	Council Coat of Arms flown at all times – Union Flag not flown
Strabane District Council		No flags flown

However, Section 75 of the 1998 Northern Ireland Act has forced local Councils to carry out assessments of policies. As such, Equality Impact Assessments on the policy of flying flags in Council buildings has being undertaken in Ards, Armagh, Belfast, Fermanagh, North Down and Newtownabbey. An Equality Impact Assessment in Newtownabbey did not lead to a change of policy and Union Flags remain on all Council buildings at all times. In Ards there was a long drawn out process that at one point led to a change in policy, which was then changed back. For at least some Unionist controlled areas there is a movement towards flying the Union Flag in accordance with the regulations for Government building designating flag days. However any small movement seems to have been pushed by the legislation and pressure from the Equality Commission.

A Council official speaking about the difficulty of dealing with the flags issue within the perspective of good relations, under part 2 of section 75, said: 'It still hasn't been specifically defined as to what good relations are. We have defined it ourselves in many respects – through training and through our own internal thoughts. .... It's tackling difficult issues in terms of flags and emblems and whatever else. But that's extremely difficult to go in cold to people who are, maybe, from a strong unionist persuasion and tell them that they can't fly the flag. It's difficult but you have to tackle difficult issues as far as we are concerned.' On guidance over flags and legislation one commented: 'There needs to be some guidance from central government on this as well for us as the Mandelson edict doesn't apply to councils, it just applies to central government bodies. What councils are quite good at is complying with law. If we say "You have to do this" they say, "Why, why do we have to do that?" But if it's actually in statute they say OK. Similarly with section 75, as soon as they realised it was a legal obligation in terms of the equality duty they went for it right away'. During our research a number of council officials mentioned to us the desirability of extending the Flags (Northern Ireland) Order 2000 to cover local Council buildings.

The Equality Commission has consistently stressed that displays of the Union Flag must be viewed in the context within which the flag is flown. Factors affecting the context include the manner, location and frequency with which the flags are displayed. Council buildings are of course work places. In the work place there has for some time been pressure on employers to provide an atmosphere militating against intimidation. This has meant that flags and emblems, and items like pictures of the Queens, have been taken down. There have still been disputes over employees wearing poppies, black ribbons or football and GAA shirts

In relation to article 19 of the Fair Employment and Treatment (Northern Ireland) Order 1998, which obliges employers to take steps not to discriminate against any person, legal council, Mr Hanna, giving advice to Belfast City Council, felt that the Council would be on safer ground if it restricted the flying of the Union Flag to designated flag days as is the practice in the rest of the United Kingdom. There is a risk that if challenged the Council might be in breach of article 19 if the flag was flown every day. It is worth pointing out that, despite Hanna's legal opinion, the practice of flying flags on Council buildings in the rest of the UK, and for that matter the Republic of Ireland, varies quite widely. Many local Councils fly the national flag on designated days but some do fly it every day (see Bryan and Gillespie, 2005: 82–89).

Overall, it is reasonable to conclude therefore that in terms of the use of official flags there has been very little evidence of any attempts to symbolise a new dispensation. Rather, the legal outworkings of the Agreement have made a difference. Legal provisions, particularly the 1998 Northern Ireland Act, previous and new fair employment legislations and an empowered Equality Commission have effectively brought some pressure to bear upon Unionist controlled Councils flying the Union flag throughout the year. Disputes over Government buildings were effectively clarified, if not solved to anyone's satisfaction, by legislation introduced in Westminster. Of course, the lack of an Assembly and Executive for much of the period since the Agreement has also meant that new symbolic practices emanating out of the Agreement were made more difficult, although, as mentioned above, new symbols were produced for the Assembly, the Executive and the PSNI.

There is another possible reason that the flying of flags has remained problematic. The consociational nature of the Agreement is about recognition of the aspirations of 'both communities'. This is reflected in the political structures and voting requirements within the Assembly. But it is also recognised in the outworking of the Agreement. If the Agreement is about the recognition of 'two communities' then this will influence legal and policy implications. This is most clearly viewed if we look at the issues that have divided the Northern Ireland Human Rights Commission (NIHRC). The NIHRC was asked to draw up a Bill of Rights for Northern Ireland that would reflect the Agreement. The Agreement recognised the rights of 'all the people in the diversity of their identities and traditions' but reflected the aspirations of 'both communities'. For the NIHRC one of the major difficulties was to balance individual rights against the apparent acceptance in the Agreement that two particular communities in Northern Ireland have rights.

The NIHRC produced a comprehensive consultation document *Making a Bill of Rights for Northern Ireland: A Consultation by the Northern Ireland Human Rights Commission* (2001) on a new Bill of Rights that, as the Agreement demanded, reflects the particular circumstances of Northern Ireland. The introduction to the consultation document encapsulates the issue:

> So it must recognise and guarantee parity of treatment and esteem for members of the two main communities. But it must also avoid the risk of institutionalising the division between these communities. And it must protect the rights of smaller communities and of those who do not want to be treated as belonging to any particular community (p. 7).

In a later document from the NIHRC, *Progressing a Bill of Rights for Northern Ireland – An Update* 2004, the issue received even more attention. The Commission had received many opinions on its preference to use the word 'communities' over 'minorities' particularly from other ethnic groups. In addition there were complaints that the previous draft of a Human Rights Bill had given rights to individuals as members of a community and not to communities themselves. The new drafting elaborates on these issues. It is worth quoting almost in full as it indicates the centrality of the use of the, undefined, concept of community. The Bill of Rights might include:

Section 3 Identity and community Rights …

… (2) The law of Northern Ireland shall include just and equal treatment for the identity ethos and aspirations of both main communities.

(3) Everyone belonging to a national, ethnic, linguistic, or cultural minority or community in Northern Ireland shall have the right, individually and in common with other members of that community, to his or her own culture, to profess and practice his or her own religion and to use his or her own language.

(4) The law of Northern Ireland shall guarantee the rights conferred upon minorities, and on individual members of minorities, by the framework Convention for the Protection of National Minorities.

(5) Everyone in Northern Ireland has the right to express their culture except when such expression:

a)   promotes hatred, fear or intolerance,

b)   constitutes a threat or act of violence, intimidation, harassments or discrimination,

c)   is contrary to internationally accepted human rights standards.

...

(7) The Government and public bodies shall, ..., adopt effective and appropriate measures to:

a)   promote equality in all areas of social, economic, cultural and political life among and between persons belonging to national, ethnic and religious, linguistic or cultural communities;

b)   preserve the essential elements of the identity of such persons, namely their nationality, traditions, religion, language and cultural heritage;

c)   promote mutual tolerance, respect, understanding and co-operation among all persons living Northern Ireland, irrespective of their national, ethnic, linguistic or cultural identity, in particular in the fields of education and the media; and

d)   protect persons who are or may be subject to threats or acts of discrimination, hostility or violence as a result of their national, ethnic, religious, linguistic or cultural identity (pp. 30–31).

The tension between group rights and individual rights has created huge difficulties for the NIHRC and it is a reflection of the Agreement. Quite simply, some believe that naming group rights will help manage the conflict whilst others believe the claims made for group rights are simply part of the struggle: particular communities are being indulged and the conflict being sustained. Harvey, a supporter of the consociational approach, has argued that '[t]he aim of this conflict management approach ... is to get the two main communities (that really exist) to work together over time within all the new institutions' (Harvey, 2003). He goes on to point out that an approach favouring 'multi-ethnic integration' carries little support in Northern Ireland and that the Bill of Rights must reflect the core idea within the Agreement that was voted on in a referendum. Wilson, a trenchant critic of both consociationalism and group rights in the form being suggested, has argued that the type of group rights being demanded are beyond those for which there is any international standard and reflects a communalism that blights politics in Northern Ireland (Wilson, 2003).

Harvey's view has been reflected in the attitudes of the main political parties in Northern Ireland since the Agreement and reflected in their approach to symbols and therefore in policies on the flying of flags. Even local Councils, that are after all reflecting more regional interests, show little evidence of attempting to express identities other than through national symbols.

Some Conclusions

Analysis of the use of symbols must involve an exploration of the way symbols work. The same symbol can be viewed and used in many different ways. There is no innate meaning to a symbol. Humans give symbols meanings. Thus a flag can simultaneously be the marker of official and legal sovereignty and also the marker of local territory. It can be emblematic of democracy but also the harbinger of fear. The display of a symbol can be defended as freedom of speech whilst also be criticised as intimidation. This is particularly evident in Northern Ireland where political divisions over the nature of the polity have often been expressed though violent conflict.

In theory at least, there was potential for the flying of official flags to represent the aspirations drawn up in the Agreement. However, in spite of the broad language of recognition of diverse communities and an attempt at the politics of a new Northern Ireland, the Agreement is consociational in nature and the disputes over the flying of official flags has characterised this. Neither unionist nor nationalist politicians have argued in a coherent fashion that the symbols used might represent a wider community or diverse communities, simply that they should represent the Unionist community and/or the Nationalist community. Changes that have taken place in official flag flying practice have been driven by legislation. In many ways this mirrors what has taken place more generally in public space. In disputes over parades, new legislation, the Parades Commission, and changes in policing have altered the management of public space in a way that reduces the number of times boundaries and interfaces are crossed, and gives access to both identities into the centre of towns, such as Belfast and Derry. This new legal dispensation has changed the use of symbols in public space but in the main, not through agreement, but through enforcement.

In strand one of the Agreement on the devolved institutions in Northern Ireland there are written in 'safeguards to ensure that *all section of the community* can participate and work successfully together' (p. 5) but the 'cross-community arrangements' then detailed rely on nationalist and unionist members of the Assembly designating themselves as such. What is distinctly missing from the discussion is the creation of new political identities through the Agreement. An alternative strategy could have discussed: the need for neutral or agreed symbols. This strategy, used in police reform, would conceive the new political arrangements as needing their own distinctive civic identity to which the diverse communities could show allegiance. This some authors have characterised as civic nationalism.

> This nationalism is called civic because it envisages the nation as a community of equal, rights-bearing citizens, united in patriotic attachment to a shared set of political practices and values (Ignatieff 1994:3–4).

There have been other projects which appeal to the development of a civic political identity in Northern Ireland as a *raison d'être*. But if one looks at the main spheres that we would normally expect to find such events we are short on examples. There is no new flag, there have been precious few high profile events where the First and Deputy First Minister have attended jointly, there has been no way yet found to develop common commemorations of the past (Brown and MacGinty, 2003: 100–101) and sporting events have similarly struggled to give common cause, with the possible exception of Ulster Rugby winning the European Championship in 2000. There are a few shared days such as Halloween and May Day and some city and town based events such as the Carnival in Belfast. The utilisation of public space has changed but much of this could be said to be top down.

The NIHRC in its attempt to reflect the 'two communities' has also struggled to come to terms with the consociational nature of the Agreement. Its latest attempt at wording for a Bill of Rights for Northern Ireland argues that '[*G*]*overnment and public bodies shall, … adopt effective and appropriate measures to: …* (*b*) *preserve the essential elements of the identity of such persons, namely their nationality, traditions, religion, language and cultural heritage*'. The space for political creativity has remained minimal.

Chapter 6

Categorisation, Accounts and Motives: 'Letters-to-the-editor' and Devolution in Wales

Richard Fitzgerald and William Housley

Introduction

The establishment of a National Assembly for Wales has recently culminated in the opening of new award winning building now known as the Senedd located in Cardiff Bay. Whilst the initial process of devolution involved the granting of no tax raising powers and a limited portfolio in education, health, social justice, culture and economic development, the Assembly is now positioned to receive enhanced powers in the next few years as devolution unfolds and Welsh democracy matures.

With this backdrop our concern in this chapter is to explore how the operation and evolution of Welsh devolution is represented and discursively constituted within mediated public debate. In some respects the discussion builds on themes addressed during the course of previous work on the discourse of devolution in Wales (Housley and Fitzgerald, 2001, 2002b). However, a crucial difference here is that we explore materials gathered post devolution, as opposed to in the build up to the 1999 referendum. Our approach to this is informed by ethnomethodological approaches to situated action and 'dialogic networks' (Nekvapil and Leudar, 2002) within which newspaper accounts, talk and other interactional frames connect situated action into recognisable and 'stable' accounts of reality and events. We also draw upon notions of discourse derived from post-structuralist thinking which characterise discourses as circulating within the micro-capillaries of the social body and thus seek to locate the 'discourse of devolution' within concrete and observable materials that are manifest within a range of everyday, routine, social textual practices. The text(s) that we have chosen to examine consist of a selection of letters-to-the-editor of what is considered to be one of the national newspapers of Wales, *The Western Mail*.

Letters-to-the-editor represent a selection of responses and opinions filtered through an editorial agenda (Wahl-Jorgensen, 2002). On the one hand the correspondence must be deemed relevant for publication through satisfying various editorial criteria, such as geographic and temporal relevance, intelligibility and cultural capital, whilst on the other they must be intelligible to readers. For this they must be couched within recognisable and contestable contours of social, cultural, economic and political forms of category organisation. In this sense they display culture (including a political and 'public' culture) in-action. Furthermore, these category constructions appear within a context and task of public debate and are located within a textual manifestation that social scientists may describe as an aspect of the public sphere. Our purpose here is to analyse letters-to-the-editor as fragments and artefacts of public discourse whose organisation mirrors other orders of public space, voice and action in a fractal like fashion. Prior to exploring the method and materials examined during the course of this chapter we will provide some background and context to devolution and identity in Wales followed by a description of our method of analysis.

Wales, Nation, Devolution and Discourse

Nationalism and national identity in Wales has often been explored as a social construction where the activities of nationalist groups and organisations are seen in terms of the protection of monopolies in social and economic resources (Fevre *et al.*, 1997, Fevre and Thompson, 1999) and the relationship between configurations of Welsh identity and the challenge of 'inclusive politics' within new devolved political frameworks (Chaney and Fevre, 2002). Further work has explored the construction and negotiation of Welsh national identity within primary schooling and childhood where notions of national identity are related to an emerging devolved civic sphere in Wales (Scourfield *et al.*, 2003). Within this, the more mundane aspects of nationalism (Billig, 1995) and its interactional and situated characteristics in relation to Wales, Welsh identity and UK have been examined through political phone-in programmes (Housley and Fitzgerald, 2001, 2002b).

In this chapter we develop our interest in the textual and categorical vocabulary of devolution articulated in what might be seen as the public sphere. However, this is not specified as the public sphere in general terms but rather a particular fragment of public democratic activity, in this case letters-to-the-editor of *The Western Mail* newspaper. Our intention is to explore situated democratic action in relation to vocabularies of categorisation, accounts and ascribed motives in order to flesh out and render visible some of the cultural and political logics appropriated within public discourse in post-devolution wales (Blum and McHugh, 1971). As stated previously, letters-to-the-editor represent a traditional mechanism through which citizens have been seen to participate within the democratic public sphere (Wahl- Jorgensen, 2002). The primary method we use to carry out this analysis is Membership Categorisation Analysis, a method derived from ethnomethodology that provides an analytic apparatus to explore the organisation and use of social knowledge. It is to an explanation of the method and materials that we now turn.

Method and Materials Analysed in this Chapter

The methodological approach adopted in this chapter is Membership Categorisation Analysis (MCA). MCA, first developed by Harvey Sacks (1974, 1995), and developed by subsequent authors (McHoul and Watson 1984, Watson 1997, Hester and Eglin 1997, Jayyussi 1984, Fitzgerald and Housley 2002, Housley and Fitzgerald, 2002b), examines the way members construct their interaction and display their knowledge of the world through the complex but methodical organisation of social categories, devices and predicates mapped onto categories. It is this process of categorisation that Sacks demonstrates through his now famous example of the child's story 'The baby cried. The mommy picked it up'. The power of Sacks's descriptive apparatus is illuminated by the analytic consideration of how we hear and make sense of the story as one in which a mother picks up her baby in response to the baby crying. For Sacks, our understanding of this story is generated through recognising the social categories 'baby' and 'mommy' as related or tied to each other through the organisational device 'family'. Through this commonsense recognition procedure, a set of expectable attributes (predicates) may be associated with the categories (i.e., babies cry, mothers comfort their children) and linked together within the organisational device 'family'. This constitutes the actions as not only expected but also directed at each other, i.e., this baby's crying is for its mother and the mommy's action is because the baby is crying. Thus, the way we hear the story is that it is the mother of the baby who picks up the baby and she does so because her baby is crying, when in fact no such necessary connection is explicit in the sentences.

We make sense of the story through applying our commonsense knowledge about the way social categories act and interact to render the story intelligible. Accordingly, using this method, it is possible to approach an understanding and engagement with the life-world as through a commonsense organisation of categories and associated attributes that are made concrete *only in any particular location of their use.* Locating our understanding at the point of social action serves to maintain the necessary fluidity of social organisation and avoid the possibility of invoking prior assumptions preceding any analytic description (Hester and Eglin, 1997). Clearly there is no essential or *à priori* connection between descriptions of social categories, their behaviour or their interaction. Rather, baby and mommy in the example above are seen to belong together in this instance but may belong to other organisational devices at other times depending on the local specifics of their relevance. Social categories and their interactions are thus only rendered recognisable *in situ* (they are occasioned) drawing upon referentially adequate commonsense knowledge of the world and an assumed reciprocity of perspectives within the world (Sacks, 1995).

Developing this method further, Sacks describes two rules of application, the *economy rule* and the *consistency rule*, which work to under-labour the interpretation and understanding made. The economy rule, according to Sacks (1995: 221) refers to the practical process by which 'if a member uses a single category from any device than he/she can be recognised to be doing adequate reference to a person' whilst the 'consistency rule states that if a member of a given population has been categorised within a particular device then other members of that population can be categorised in terms of the same collection' (Sacks 1995). Sacks then derives a corollary known as the *hearer's maxim* which states 'if two or more categories are used to categorise two or more members of some population and those categories can be heard as categories from the same collection then: hear them that way' (1995: 221). The rules of application, therefore, work as practical registers that reinforce the observed or described actions of social categories, where such categories are collected within occasioned organisational devices which form a major part of the commonsensical framework of members' methods and recognisable capacities of practical sense making. Since Sacks's initial outline, the method has been developed in a number of ways (see Hester and Eglin, 1997, Housley and Fitzgerald, 2002b), one of which is to reveal through categorisation procedures a practical and occasioned moral schema though use of normative assessments which render actions accountable (Jayyusi, 1984).

As well as our interest in the practical reasoning displayed in the data, a further methodological consideration in this chapter is a commitment to a cumulative paradigm of social research (Silverman, 1998, Housley, 2002). The analysis that follows is a single case analysis. It does not represent an appeal to a statistical frame of validity or a counting of cases, although, clearly, such an approach in discourse studies is a valid line of enquiry. Rather, as suggested earlier, this chapter develops on previous exploratory research and thinking as a means of building upon a concern with moral categorisation, accountability and democratic discourse within inter-subjective instances and displays of concern within the 'letters-to-the-editor' section of what is considered to be one of the national newspapers of Wales, *The Western Mail*. The data were selected by a keyword search through an archived database of the letters-to-the-editor published in *The Western Mail*, post 1999, and complimented with a random examination of archived editions of the publication. The search identified 40 letters that were then whittled down to twelve 'case' examples that reflected different forms of textual 'account type'.

The analysis of letters-to-the-editor has a long history within the social sciences, although, for the main, this work has used quantitative approaches to explore the extent to which they represent the public demographics or whether they can be used as a political temperature gauge of public opinion (Buell, 1975, Sigelman and Walkosz, 1992, Hynds, 1994). Whilst this form of media remains a hazy barometer of public opinion and subject to editorial selection criteria, such practice can be understood in terms of the public sphere and democratic action (Habermas, 1989) as 'one of the few arenas for public discussion by regular citizens' (Wahl-Jorgensen, 2002:1). Letters-to-the-editor, then, occupies a site along with radio phone-ins where 'ordinary people', if not exactly given free rein, are at least seen to be having a say (Livingstone and Lunt, 1994, Fitzgerald and Housley, 2002) and may even conceive themselves as representing the public at large (Ross, 2004). The aim in this chapter is to further this focus of enquiry and complement current work and studies within a cumulative paradigm of research in which analyses of such public documents and materials contribute to an evolving understanding of the context, setting and phenomenon under investigation; in this case, the relationship between public discourse, language, and policy in the post-devolution period.

In the discussion that follows our intention is not to focus on identifying and analysing the topical organisation of the letters-to-the-editor page. This form of organisation within the current materials exhibits similar characteristics to those examined prior to devolution such as, bureaucracy and inefficiency, the Welsh language and Welsh identity, the relationship to Westminster and England (Housley and Fitzgerald 2001, 2002b). However, as a social and political process, devolution remains uncertain, fluid and open to competing claims and counter-claims concerning its success, shortcomings and future trajectory. As such, our interest here goes beyond highlighting topical organisation in favour of unpicking the levels of categorical organisation displayed in these texts and, in doing so, uncovering the ways in which these texts operate as accounts which ascribe political motive within frames of temporality. Consequently, our aim is to analyse the contours of various discourses that surround the process of devolution as it unfolds through time.

To this end we treat 'topic' within a collection of categorically ordered actions, events, assessments and summaries of the past and projections to the future as forming part of the practical sense-making that gives the constructed text its structure, direction and purpose; i.e. its social organisation. From examining the data as categorically ordered accounts we then move to a further level of organisation where the accounts are seen to involve ascribing various political and moral motives. Our interest here focuses on examples where the motives are ascribed to actions by an observer (the letter writer); thus, where the ascribed motive does not reveal the reason for the actual action described (that we or the letter writer cannot know), but rather reveals a grammar of motive ascription where an action is seen by the observer (letter writer) to contain the motive for the action. Ascribed motives are then a methodical product of the work of the observer's locally constructed description and accounting practices organised around assumed reciprocal knowledge and built within a perceived reciprocal framework, rather than a report of a factual state of affairs (Blum and McHugh, 1971). Through this, we seek to reveal the discursive contours and accounting practices within the normative and moral frame of social, cultural and political understandings and 'worldviews' in relation to the devolution process in Wales.

The Structure of Accounts

Accounts are understood as a primary interactional mechanism for justifying action and maintaining social organisation. Thus, accountable action is that which is recognisably sanctionable by other members. In the context of talk-in-interaction, this involves the elicitation of accounts that may inform others of a decision taken, a course decided or a diagnosis made. In one sense all utterances are 'accountable' (Garfinkel, 1967) in the sense that they reflexively constitute and display the sense of social organisation that is being locally accomplished by members on an ongoing 'no time out' basis. However, accounts can also be understood to refer to forms of talk that provide descriptions, explanations or justifications of activities, people, events and so forth. An account is not necessarily synonymous with a story. However, stories can often be understood to account, in terms of description, explanation and justification, for various matters or events. This process of 'accounting' is tied to the topical content of story type utterances and can therefore be understood to be primarily organised in terms of categories (Housley, 2000).

Accounts as normative assessments also involve an epistemological relevance through their description and accounts of 'reality'. Lynch and Bogen (1996: 280) note how certain moral entitlements are routinely accorded to the production of accounts in talk. These entitlements can be understood to be categorically organised and consist of a normative and moral set of inferences that are derived from the story and accorded to the teller. These may consist of the teller having lived through an experience or having a unique or privileged access to an event or occurrence. Furthermore, these moral entitlements are also routinely tied to the various occasioned activities that the production of stories may occur within. For example, stories may be used as vehicles to recount experiences central to a criminal investigation or cross-examination. They may also be elicited and deployed by members during activities in which matters relating to the truth and actual events are crucial (as in the Iran Contra Hearings elegantly analysed and explored by Lynch and Bogen, 1996). Accounts as utterances can therefore be understood to be deployed in a variety of settings during the course of a number of activities.

In the context of political communication and practice, accounts are crucial normative mechanisms for promoting one point of view as opposed to another or upgrading/downgrading different points of view (Housley and Fitzgerald, 2001). However, 'worldviews' and other similar orientating devices are not merely the 'assemblages of experience', but involve design in terms of understandings and categories that have purchase in the world; that are culturally recognisable and praxiologically relevant to the context of their production and potential audience(s). The structuring of accounts is, therefore, a reflexive component, mutually constitutive, expressing normative work within a specified field of relations. Thus a medical diagnosis and the predicated account/explanation to the patient possess certain contextual characteristics, as does the politician's answers to questions within public broadcasting settings (Clayman and Heritage, 2002, Housley, 2002, Housley and Fitzgerald, in press).

Letters-to-the-editor, as stated previously, represent particular forms of participation within a public broadcasting session. However, they are also understandable as accounts. As such, they include moral and cultural forms of categorisation and are also structures that are organised in fairly definite ways as a requirement of the context of public engagement and the display of views within the democratic sphere and the editorial context of newspapers (Wahl-Jorgensen, 2002). However, letters-to-the-editor also involve specific forms of categorical organisation and structure that are part of their 'design features'. We will now explore some features of their design in relation to examples from our collected materials.

Category Display, Structure and Organisation

One of the main observable 'design features' in the data is that the letters are often organised through a contrast structure whereby the action or event that prompts the correspondence is compared negatively or positively with other actions. In the example below the contrast is centred on the actions of the Conservative Party in Wales and their 'true' allegiance which lies in London. The 'reasonableness' of the argument about the assembly building is thus seen as a screen to their 'true' intentions.

Extract 1

Tuesday, 8 April, 2003
1.   SIR – The Conservative Party has patently failed to adapt to the
2.   new era of devolved government in Wales.
3.   Scratch the surface of many individuals in the party in Wales and
4.   they still look primarily to Westminster. They see the Assembly
5.   government in Cardiff as unnecessary and would do away with
6.   the system if only it were politically pragmatic to do so. Although
7.   I am no supporter of the Labour Party it must be credited with
8.   having a proper 'Welsh' identity.
9.   Carwyn Jones is often heard emphasising the need to make
10. devolution work. In contrast, Nick Bourne continually criticises
11. the plans for a new Assembly building, saying the money would
12. be better spent on public services.
13. This is a reasonable argument, but in reality it is a smokescreen
14. for the Tory true ambition of a return to central government, a
15. system that proved inadequate to Welsh needs for centuries.

Here, the writer constructs a categorical organisation in order to advance the argument that the Conservative Party in Wales is 'non-Welsh' and still primarily oriented toward Westminster (England). The construction of the contrast structure works through interpreting the first action of 'not being able to adapt to the new political reality in post devolution Wales' as part of the Conservative Party's continued orientation to Westminster, and by extension the English political leadership. This is contrasted with the view of the Labour Party as being a 'pro Welsh' party and so not looking over the border and hence adapted to post devolution Wales. Following on from this contrast device (anti-Wales Conservative and pro-Wales Labour), the actions of two individuals is introduced. The different actions of the individuals are interpreted as evidence of the initial contrast categories. What is of interest here is the way in which the writer builds his/her argument by transforming individual actions, or 'summative' actions, into group, or categorical, actions and in doing so shifts from inductive to inductive resistant accounting. The distinction between categorical and summative formulations is that:

> ... 'summative expressions' ... refer to a finite and nameable set of people, places, objects for example the 'minister for health' ... [They] establish commonsense grounds for testing the 'rightness' of statements such as 'the minister for health has resigned', whereas categorical [sic] uses such as 'politicians' and 'democrats' do not. ... [S]tatements such as 'democrats do X' are not proved wrong by the actions of a single democrat, instead 'what everyone knows ... about democrats can be used as a resource against which the individual in question becomes an exception or someone that requires further explanation. (Llewellyn, 2004: 950).

The accounting practices in the above example rely upon firstly creating a categorical context in which the Welsh Conservatives do not support devolution and 'really' look towards England. This is placed in a contrast position with the Labour Party predicated with having a 'proper Welsh identity'. Within this categorical context the summative actions of the two named individuals is introduced and transformed into categorical actions.

The actions, being rendered as categorical actions, means they become social actions, actions attributable through category membership, not personal identity, and so 'socially' accountable. So, although Nick Bourne calls for more money for better public services (a 'worthy action'), this action, tied to the category 'anti-Welsh' Conservative, renders the action accountable within the latent policy of undermining devolution and hence suspect. On the other hand calling for 'devolution to work' is treated as a document of support for devolution by Carwyn Jones and hence the 'pro-Welsh' Labour Party. In this case the 'Tory true' ambition of a return to central government is made to account for the action of the individual. Nick Bourne becomes subsumed with similar minded people (treated as a category) and the action becomes what 'anyone' (any member of that category) in that organisation (or 'device', 'the Conservative Party in Wales) would do. Thus his action is seen as part of, in light of, and underpinned by, the negative 'motives' towards devolution attributed to the Conservative Party. The move from summative to categorical action is also apparent in the next example although here a more complex organisation is woven together in order to build a further layer of categorisation involving a moral evaluation.

In the example below, the initial summative action that prompted the letter (the lack of a Welsh tick box in the 2001 census) is used as a category predicate through which to build a contrast device. Following the construction of this device, a second summative action is introduced. The second summative action (*The Western Mail*'s use of 'nation', 'national') is then built around a morally ordered temporal contrast between past, present and possible future actions.

Extract 2

1. SIR – In your editorial comment (May 25) you state, "the mystery
2. remains about why it was that the Government was obstinate in its
3. refusal to give Wales its tick box". I find it astonishing that you do not
4. realise why, because the reason is so blatantly obvious.
5. The sole reason is that the establishment in England, and their many
6. fellow-travellers in Wales, steadfastly refuse to acknowledge that the
7. people of Wales constitute a nation and that Wales is a country in its
8. own right. The process of undermining Welsh national identity has
9. continued unabated since the conquest in 1282, sometimes furtively
10. but often as a declared policy as with the Act of Union of 1536. All
11. large, imperial, conquering nations do this, the main methods being
12. linguistic oppression and allowing – even encouraging – unfettered
13. large scale immigration into the conquered territory. Witness the
14. Russian occupation of Latvia (1940-1991) which resulted in Russian
15. immigrants increasing from an insignificant number to 34pc of the
16. population. Likewise, since Tibet's conquest by China in 1950, Chinese
17. in-migration has reduced the Tibetan inhabitants from 100pc to 35pc in
18. eastern Tibet.
19. The tell-tale signs of this extreme reluctance to acknowledge Welsh
20. national identity are very much in evidence, not least in the media –
21. even in *The Western Mail.* In particular, your use of the words 'national'
22. and 'nation' is inconsistent. If you believed totally that Wales is a
23. nation these words would always refer to Wales. At present you
24. sometimes use them to relate to Wales, sometimes to Wales and
25. England, sometimes to Wales, England and Scotland, and at other
26. times to Wales, England, Scotland and Northern Ireland. Further
27. evidence of this is found in the readiness of many people – following the
28. deplorable example of Rhodri Morgan AM – to refer to The National
29. Assembly for Wales (its proper, official, statutory name) as the Welsh
30. Assembly, and its government as the Welsh Assembly Government.
31. Consistently using the correct shortened versions, The National
32. Assembly and The National Assembly Government, would repeatedly
33. assert the national identity of Wales, something that the London-based
34. political parties want to avoid at all costs. The French always refer to
35. their Assembly as 'L'Assemble Nationale de France' – never as
36. 'L'Assemble francais'!

In this example, the correspondent refers to a previous letter about the absence of a 'Welsh tick box' on the 2001 United Kingdom census. This had generated a degree of controversy particularly due to the fact that the categories of Scottish and Irish were to be included. The preface frames the 'mystery' of this omission as one that is 'obvious' and resoundingly clear. The first part of the account involves locating the elision of Welsh identity within the census form as one that is grounded within a systematic historical process; namely, the relentless subjugation and incorporation of Wales within a larger imperial-state apparatus. Here, as in the previous example, a summative action is made accountable by treating it as a predicate of a category, 'the English establishment and many fellow travellers in Wales', so rendering the action as categorical rather than an isolated instance. The category of the English establishment and Welsh fellow travellers is then brought into a device of 'all large imperial nations'.

Thus the initial action predicated to the category of the 'English establishment' and 'Welsh fellow travellers' is collected within the device of 'Imperial nations' where those actions are predicated to the new category collection with its own predicated actions, namely the subjugation of other nations through linguistic oppression and immigration. The predicates of large imperial nations are then given consistency (Sacks 1995) through examples of other large imperial nations, the categories selected being twentieth century Russia and China. In this way, the action of not having a Welsh tick box is predicated to England's historical relations with Wales, which in turn is made comparable with the asymmetrical relational pairs 'Soviet Union-Latvia' and 'China-Tibet'. What is also of interest here is that the categories are not allocated a hierarchical ordering within the device. Rather the absence of a Welsh tick box is equated without distinction to the actions of the Chinese Government in Tibet and Russian government policy towards her satellite states. Of course this does not mean that a hierarchy will not be read into the categories but that there is not one set up in the letter. In other words, the experience of Wales is one that is *unproblematically* framed within a collection of commensurable historical examples of modern state imperialism.

With the non hierarchal device established and fleshed out the author then moves to introduce the second summative action within this device.

Extract 3

(Repeated Section of Example 2).
19   The tell-tale signs of this extreme reluctance to acknowledge Welsh
20   national identity are very much in evidence, not least in the media –
21   even in *The Western Mail*. In particular, your use of the words
22   'national' and 'nation' is inconsistent. If you believed totally that
23   Wales is a nation these words would always refer to Wales. At present
24   you sometimes use them to relate to Wales, sometimes to Wales and
25   England, sometimes to Wales, England and Scotland, and at other
26   times to Wales, England, Scotland and Northern Ireland.

Following on from the initial constructed device of Imperial nations and the systematic subjugation of Wales, *The Western Mail* is then predicated with 'extreme reluctance' to acknowledge Welsh national identity. This is evidenced through the paper's inconsistent use of terms of reference 'nation' and 'national'. Again, the summative inconsistency when using these terms is transformed into a category predicate of being anti-Welsh. The negative attitude towards Welsh national identity now predicated to *The Western Mail* is also a predicate of the previous 'fellow travellers in Wales' thereby rendering *The Western Mail* as Welsh but not pro-Welsh, i.e., the 'paper' is a fellow traveller to the English. Thus the action is now connected with the English establishment (that includes London based politicians who may represent Welsh constituencies) who 'steadfastly refuse to acknowledge' Wales as a country and indeed commensurate with the actions of China and Soviet Russia. Within this, the writer also overlays a moral device organised around what has, what is and what should be happening.

By introducing the actions of *The Western Mail* into the contrast pair, a moral imperative is invoked where the actions of the newspaper are seen to document a disjunctive predicate to their category membership, or rather the category membership the newspaper *should* wish to belong to. By using the terms 'national' and 'nation' interchangeably the paper is seen to reveal its membership of the anti Welsh category whereas if *The Western Mail* did not want to belong to this category, if it 'believed totally', then it would use the terms 'correctly'. That is the terms are being understood to 'stand on behalf of' underlying motives concerning devolution and the aspirations of different Welsh public(s) in relation to Welsh national identity and its relationship with the British State and associated forms of political identity.

What is interesting is the way the argument is constructed through a separation of action and category (Jayyussi, 1984). Whereas previously the actions were predicated to other categories such that the actions documented membership of a category and hence made other actions accountable, here the action documents a category disjuncture. By unreflectively using the terms 'national' and 'nation' interchangeably, the newspaper is said to document its possible non-belief in Wales, although this could be changed by simply using the terms in the way the writer thinks they should be used in the future. This moral organisation uses a temporal distinction between the actions of the near present to which historical negative comparisons are made and the possible future where a change of action changes the category membership to the 'positive'. The underpinning force of the moral organisation is the assumed desire, wish, or need to improve or change the present and not continue or repeat the past. Here, then, the build of categories is designed to create a morally ordered evaluation of actions through a locally created, organised and contained device by which to allocate membership and non-membership.

Thus far in the discussion we have explored structure through a categorical organisation where a summative action is transformed into a categorical action. Transforming the action into a categorical one renders the individual or single action as accountable through a category reasoning, and possibly morally accountable. As such the account of the action becomes resistant to induction, collected within further category organisation renders the initial action as 'what everyone knows'. The move from summative to categorical accounts also allows a further level of category organisation to be invoked, that of motivation. By transforming the summative action into a categorical predicate, accounts can be constructed which not only create a context for the action as discussed above but also allow for the *ascription of motive* behind the action. In the next section we take up this theme and explore the way motive is ascribed to various actions within accounts.

The Motive of Accounts and Accounts of Motive

A further identifiable feature of letters-to-the-editor as accounts is the identification and ascription of motive to relevant agencies within some sort of temporal framing. The relationship between 'motives' and 'accounts' has an established pedigree within the social sciences (Scott and Lyman, 1968 and Blum and McHugh, 1971) and stems, in part, from Charles Wright Mills's exploration of situated action and vocabularies of motive (1978:904–13). In Scott and Lyman's description accounts are displays of intentions that can be utilised by the analysts as a means of uncovering motives. However, for Blum and McHugh (1971:106), the relationship between accounts and motives are far more complex than this 'surface' reading would suggest.

The idea of motives thus serves to formulate for members their interactions, insofar as they conceive interactions as experiences frames as events. Actors are thought by observers to have biographies and to engage the world with them. The grammar produces the link between the two. Motives are resources for connecting an event with a biography, and they generate the event as a member of the class of experiences owned by a body (as depicted in commonsense).

For Blum and McHugh, then, accounts form a complex method for ascribing moral and normative characteristics to an expanded matrix of agency within which institutions, organisations and individuals act. In terms of the accounts displayed in the letters-to-the-editor discussed in this Chapter, the interplay between account, motive and experience/perceptions is readily observable and thus provides artefacts (of one dimension of the public sphere) that can offer insight into some of the sociological characteristics and moral-political logic of devolution. As indicated above, the process of devolution is contested and debated through the provision of accounts which may represent different readings of the frame of devolution in Wales. In one sense they constitute fragments and resources that represent and display the distributed and situated character of the public sphere. It is a sphere within which members, institutions and organisations are morally and practically occasioned through text and categorisation.

Extract 4

1.   When devolution was first 'sold to us' in 1997 we were assured that it
2.   would bring 'Welsh solutions to Welsh problems' and allow us to at
3.   last take responsibility for our own affairs.
4.   It therefore seems remarkable that the most significant aspect of the
5.   current Assembly has been the total refusal of anyone at a ministerial
6.   level to take responsibility for anything.
7.   Transparency equals invisibility.

In the example above, motive is ascribed to an object; namely the devolved assembly and, more specifically, those who inhabit the higher levels of assembly government; in this case, the motive of refusal at 'ministerial level' to 'take responsibility for anything'. The grammar or 'descriptive conceptual apparatus' of ministers not taking responsibility is neither qualified nor elaborated as such. It is presented as a reasonable fact that 'anyone could know'. Indeed the rhetoric of transparent government is equated with its opposite 'invisibility'. This is heard not as an oxymoron, but as a normative pairing that constitutes an 'event' where one pair part follows the other (transparency → invisibility). Thus the inability of anyone to take responsibility when things go wrong is utilised as a motive for explaining this particular course of events within the recent life of the devolved assembly. Similar forms of moral and practical categorisation work can be discerned in the following extract.

Extract 5

1. J.T. Toner is right to attack the double standards ... whereby chief
2. executives and other highly paid local government officers accept
3. massive increases in salaries and allowances while preaching wage
4. restraint to those earning under 5 pounds per hour, often for
5. demanding and responsible work such as social and personal care to
6. the vulnerable in unsocial hours.
7. Quite frankly, if that is how they define the meaning and measure of
8. public service, perhaps they should leave now before any further
9. damage is done to the morale of those struggling on low wages to
10. actually deliver quality local services on the ground.
11. It is deeply disappointing that four years after devolution there has
12. been no radical or even discernible shift in the mind-sets of those
13. earning 45,000 pounds and 90,000 pounds plus. They continue to compare
14. themselves with counterparts in England or in the private sector
15. instead of identifying with the very great needs and aspirations of
16. people living in Wales.

In the example above, an event is described which depicts 'highly paid' local government officials calling for 'wage restraint' amongst the poorly paid who often carry out vital work for the public and social good. This act is seen as an inferential resource that displays a specific meaning and measure of public service that damages the morale of those 'working on the ground'. This 'event' in the local governmental structure in post-devolution Wales is ascribed to a specific motive, in a particular way within a particular contextual configuration (i.e. the letters-to-the-editor page). The highly paid agents of local government are in a state of comparison to 'counterparts in England' (where we may infer a more market led approach to local government is encouraged including higher salaries for local government 'executives') as opposed to identifying with the 'needs and aspirations of people living in Wales'.

Thus, the motive of an incommensurate mindset (that includes 'being like England) is identified as the motive for their high wages and lack of concern for the morale of important public service workers. Indeed, in this accounting of events the local government officials look to England rather than to Wales. The author is thus able to provide an account for the actions of Welsh government agents as not being in touch with the devolved realities of Wales today where the needs and aspiration of the Welsh people are seen as rising, in some way, to the democratic fore. Their motives are therefore not consistent with the category 'the Welsh people' and the associated predicates (e.g. needs). This inconsistency is read as a discrepancy between the normative pairing of local government representative and local democracy in devolved Wales. Here, then, motive is used as means of evaluating trust and questioning the moral grounding of the motives and 'true intentions' of some sections of the devolved 'government'.

In terms of the extracts discussed in this section (*Extracts 4* and *5*), it may be argued that letters-to-the-editor are situated forms of action that mobilise particular vocabularies of motive. More specifically, we suggest these accounts are not merely a means of revealing the intentions of actors or concerned citizens who have 'written in'. Rather, leading from Blum and McHugh (1971) we have attempted to highlight how, through processes of categorisation, letters-to-the-editor, as situated accounts, constitute and frame events in terms of inferred and ascribed 'motives'. The grammar of motives may involve the use of biographical material, temporal sequences and history as a means of ascribing motives to both personal and non-personal objects. Consequently, different agents and various forms of agency are imputed with motive as a means of 'explaining' relevant events within the unfolding moral drama of devolution in Wales. The explication and constitution of events as reasonable, explicable and understandable depends on both the categorical imputation and ascription of motive and its structuring within grammars or rhetorics of motive, cause and account. Indeed the structuring of these accounts is a reflexive component of the social organisation of the explanation of events and the ascription of motive. Both the structuring of these accounts and the logic of motive ascription are contextually driven in terms of the mutual interplay between the practical concerns of cultural recognisability and audience (recipient) design. This is necessary in order to achieve the clarity and 'sense' of a public discourse object (in this case a letter to the editor and having 'your say') and the editorial requirements and concern with 'generating debate'. Within the above discussion, this can be seen to involve the moral and political characteristics of the situated production of texts and vocabularies of motive concerning the flow of events within the political landscape of post-devolution Wales.

Conclusion

The current process of devolution in Wales serves as a perspicuous case study in which to examine the relationship between the public, media and political institutions, in part due to the fact that the process has been understood as an attempt to reinvigorate democratic participation. Consequently, discourse around devolution provides a window to explore how certain publics (in this case letter writers) make sense of and participate with an emerging Welsh public sphere and democratic identity. By approaching 'letters-to-the-editor' as 'fragments' of an 'imagined' public sphere our discussion has sought to describe the social organisational practices associated with promoting an opinion and world-view in relation to the devolution process in Wales. In doing this we have highlighted a set of social/normative practices that make practical use of the descriptive-conceptual-inferential apparatus of membership categorisation.

Within our discussion it is clear that the process of devolution, like the-run up to devolution, involves various arguments around identity and entitlement, configured around notions of inclusion and exclusion. However, whilst previously in our analysis the issue of identity and entitlement was largely organised around the perceived entitlement to vote and the future of Wales post referendum, the above discussion suggests that these topics have further dimensions within the process of devolution in which Welsh identity is predicated with obligation, moral entitlement and active participation. Here, being seen as Welsh and being pro-devolution can involve specified criteria, such as being from a particular political party, identifying with the Welsh people and describing Wales in a certain way, existing within a moral organisation and temporal obligation within the devolution process; and people, social categories and organisations are seen to 'reveal' and be judged on their 'true' alignment to, and belief in, the on-going project.

However, our discussion also engages with wider questions in an environment where it is argued that there is an increasing 'disconnect' between 'publics' and 'government'. This 'disconnection' takes place within a social landscape where fragmentation, distrust and uncertainty reign, to be replaced with a 'liquid modern' era where fleeting relations, individuation and the decline in the collective imagination and belief in the capacity of social institutions to effect change (Bauman, 2002) are coupled with a process of demoralisation and apathy (Fevre, 2000). Within this landscape, however, the media represents a space where discourses of democratic culture and public participation can be still found. The perceived inability of other institutions (e.g. the family, traditional politics, education) to change things has created a space that the media increasingly tries to fill, and part of this process is a conflation between viewer/listener and democratic citizen. One of the major consequences of this uncertainty is social anxiety (Bauman, 2002) within which the media, as ritual and ceremony, represents one of the main ways in which social anxiety is managed and processed and displayed. Whilst it is not our business to speculate on the character of certainty within current forms of social organisation and patterns of transformation, we suggest that the situated organisation of motives and accounts (in both text and talk) within the media often display ascribed characteristics of 'anxiety' through their topical display of despair, dismay and anger as recognisable design features.

These accounts, through the ascription of motive and explanation of events, also demand or entertain solutions to the identified cause and 'underlying' motive. For example, political interviewers utilise conversational procedure not only to hold politicians to account but also to elicit 'narratives of solution' within the interview ceremony. Narratives of 'anxiety' often follow identity work in radio call-ins. This is not only 'topic relevant categorisation' (Fitzgerald and Housley, 2002) where certain opinions are treated as tied to certain social categories but also displays privatised anxiety within the public realm of media discourse. Consequently, the relationship between media and public is not merely the business of generating accountability, processing experiences, ascribing motive, and allocating blame, but also of 'seeking solutions' and 'agents of solution' for these interactionally generated accounts (between public caller and media host or the motivated agent identified in letters-to-the-editor). Reflexively, these accounts are often editorially framed as 'public anxiety' within the democratic space of media discourse and public participation (Lunt and Stenner, 2005).

This, of course, represents the media doing 'collective work' in an age where other institutions are seen as ineffectual or in decline (see Bauman, 2002). It also does the work of connecting private experiences to public concerns (Mills, 1978). However, is this concrete or is it a ceremonial order through which 'uncertainty', 'social anxiety' and the 'identification of a solution' are 'performed' and enacted? Perhaps it is the case that 'ceremony', as categorisation work in 'letters-to-the-editor', contributes to the concretising of events and hence their intelligibility as objects in the world. In another sense, they act as a democratic laxative – a catharsis – an ideological ritual and performance or process of 'tension management and pattern maintenance', as Talcott Parsons may have described it. In more general terms, then, the above discussion might be seen as offering some situated documents that are to be found within organised performative rituals and practice that circulate within 'media-culture' and broadcast news. In turn, the analysis of these 'rituals' as practices may inform (in an empirical sense) wider questions of democracy and the decline of traditional social-political institutions on the one hand and reflections on the re-invigoration political institutions and public engagement on the other.

Chapter 7

'Fantasy Echo' and Modern Britishness: Commemoration and Identity in Northern Ireland

Carol-Ann Barnes and Arthur Aughey

Introduction

This chapter explores the connection between history, commemoration and identity. It does this by way of the intriguing, playful but suggestive phrase 'fantasy echo'. The phrase establishes the investigative framework for consideration of one recent event in Northern Ireland's history, the marking of the bicentenary of the Irish Act of Union. The study of this commemoration, in turn, provides a useful measure for influential academic reflections about public memory and the organization of public history. Furthermore, it permits critical reflection on the hopes for a 'new beginning' in relationships within Northern Ireland which some invested in the Belfast Agreement of 1998. The political investment by the Ulster Unionist leadership in the bicentenary of the Act of Union and the response by others to it is an interesting vignette of public life in Northern Ireland.

'Fantasy Echo'

In an article on history and the construction of identity, Joan W. Scott (2001) remarked upon an intriguing phrase she once came across when marking a student paper. That phrase was 'fantasy echo'. Only by following up the outline of the student's lecture schedule did she come to the conclusion that 'fantasy echo' was a misunderstanding of the French expression *fin de siècle*. However, Scott was struck by something imaginative and creative in the anglicised – and so, transformed – phrase. The words seemed to have a descriptive plausibility, 'offering a way of thinking not only about the significance of arbitrary temporal designations (decades, centuries, millennia) but also about how we appeal to and write history'. All sorts of historical references, she thought, appear to echo assessments of the past in terms of predictions about the future and the process itself was rather fantastic. The process involved both the repetition of something imagined and an imagined repetition. This, Scott argued, was the key to identity formation since retrospective identifications 'are imagined repetitions and repetitions of imagined resemblances'. When a person or a community claimed an historical identity, the 'echo is a fantasy, the fantasy an echo; the two are inextricably intertwined'.

On the one hand, 'fantasy is the means by which real relations of identity between past and present are discovered and/or forged'. It is that act of historical imagination, which imposes order on events and thereby 'contributes to the articulation of political identity'. On the other hand, echo connects past to present and present to past yet the 'return of partial phrases alters the original sense and comments on it as well'. While we can acknowledge the differences between historical experience and contemporary conditions, those differences are also familiar since they are echoes of *our* history, both positive and negative. Historical identification, according to Scott, operates as a fantasy echo, 'replaying in time and over generations the process that forms individuals as social and political actors' (Scott, 2001: 287–292). The value of this term is that it avoids both the essentialism of that sort of historical understanding which supposes an unchanging or timeless identity (fantasy) and also that sort of historical understanding which supposes that all identities are mere inventions or constructions (echo). Inextricably intertwined, continuity and change provide challenges for those charged with the institutionalisation of public memory.

How one commemorates an historical event is fraught with familiar difficulties. There is the need to present an entertaining collective story (fantasy) that resonates with public memory but also the professional requirement to present an interpretation of events that is consonant with current historical understanding (echo). The tension between the two is the tension between commemoration as a form of social cohesion and commemoration as an opportunity for social enlightenment. The tension is all the greater in Northern Ireland where public memory itself is divided and where historical interpretation is politically contentious. In this case, laying the blame for present discontents has become a vital popular pastime.

Indeed, one of the most acute divisions in Northern Ireland's public life has been identified within historical understanding itself, the interpretation of which comes as much from within an individual's socialisation as it does from his or her formal education. This 'informal' learning often impacts more deeply and significantly on attitudes and values than schooling (McBride, 1997, Stewart, 1977, Walker, 1996). The high-minded attempt to teach history as an aid to fostering reconciliation in divided societies has been framed within the wider context of the 'revisionist' debate, an acknowledgement that history is not about the truth so much as about a tentative effort to discover it (Boyce and O'Day, 1996: 1–14). If Irish history is the result of 'huge intersecting, and interacting, webs of circumstance' (Stewart, 2001: 6), then undoubtedly the past has shaped the present. What we choose to remember of that past is shaped by present day concerns, the commemoration of which becomes 'historical forces in their own right' (McBride, 2001: 2).

By contrast, professional historians try to shed present-day assumptions and immerse themselves in primary sources against a popular historical knowledge, which tends to be highly selective and 'shot through with present-day assumptions' (Tosh, 2002: 13). Tradition and nostalgia often provide the basic constituents of social memory, which answer a deep psychological need for security. This social need is believed to distort images of the past since it is based on belief, not enquiry. While some academic historians distance themselves from such distortions, it is not always possible to distinguish between history and social memory (*ibid*. 1–24). The very question of whose history it is has become an historical question itself. Its importance is based on the assumption, to which the French subscribed after 1789, that whoever teaches the nation its history, captures its soul (Gardiner, 1990: 4). The increasing demand for the 'popularisation' of history, conveyed through television, heritage sites, media, films and books, has significantly altered the environment in which it is both taught and understood, providing additional opportunities to re-evaluate traditional interpretations. If, as J.C.D. Clark notes, history is not just a set of techniques but rather 'an initiation into a culture by the transmission of heritage' (Clark, 1990: 35–43), then history becomes a battlefield in the contest for cultural hegemony as popularised versions determine how the story is told. By offering opportunities for the appropriation of the past, then, history-as-commemoration can become inherently political.

Public History and Commemorations

Public history is a distinctive cultural practice, its purpose being to enhance the audience's awareness of the value and uses of history. It is an interactive process between the academic historian's analysis of an object or event and the popular version held within a community. Since it seeks to reflect the history of the community it serves, so too is it shaped by the nuances of what is understood by that community as public history.

In *Commemorations: The Politics of National Identity*, for example, John Gillis notes the distinction between institutionalised memory, previously held by elites, and popular memory, increasingly claimed by urban middle and working classes in the late eighteenth century. The former marches steadily along a linear path, creating a consecutive account (or fantasy) in the process, while the later 'dances and leaps', and like an echo, leaves 'blanks' along the way (Gillis, 1994: 6). The democratisation of memory has become increasingly burdensome as we feel obliged to remember more and more but since the pace of modern society diminishes our sense of time and distance, ensuring that events of today are tomorrow's heritage, remembering less, we celebrate more. Thus public history depends on memory prompts, expressed through displays in a museum or popular commemorative rituals, which often display thematic as well as chronological 'leaps' (McBride, 2001: 1–42).

History, Heritage and Museums

Since history is interwoven with national culture, museums are especially suited to national purpose because they 'make manifest and tangible what is otherwise an abstract concept and they serve an important ontological function for the nation' providing cultural definition by telling its story to itself and others. Displays of public heritage as 'palimpsests of culture' function alongside the political sphere to shape and reshape national identities, thus setting the stage for future developments (Mason, 2004: 315–327). However, when history has the potential to be such a contentious issue, as in Northern Ireland, the presentation of historical events creates a major challenge for museum professionals, a challenge which has in the past, possibly, been more often avoided than accepted (Crooke, 2001: 120). While commemorative events are important in celebrating and sustaining cultural identities, they are undertaken at great risk because there is more than one 'history' in Northern Ireland and more than one method of remembering (and also forgetting) (Nic Craith, 2002: 41–45). As such, many commemorative events remain the source of antagonism. Since museums are in the process of 'memory making', shaped by their collection, display and interpretation, they are challenged to find their place within the spectrum of remembering and forgetting (Crooke, 2001: 122). Museum policy and the exhibitions they present can aid the transition to a more objective interpretation but whether they can ever be apolitical is questionable. Popular memory can be shaped by political myth-makers and it can also be appropriated by government. Museum professionals must be conscious of both possibilities. In professional commemoration, their task is to enable the audience to understand such myths and appropriations *historically*.

History, Culture and Populist Commemorations in Ireland

Populist commemorations have been crucial in formulating and sustaining identities in Northern Ireland. Therefore, these 'echoes' provide the potential for either reconciliation (common fantasy) or further antagonism (conflicting stories). Investigating Unionist identities between 1920 and 1960, Gillian McIntosh (1999: 2) notes:

> These large-scale public demonstrations and the political culture associated with them were an integral part of unionism, allowing the movement to appeal to and incorporate a diverse protestant community, gathering it into a coherent unit, defining its role in the union, and creating a particular identity for the Northern Irish state.

Similarly, Walker (2000). argues that during this period, commemorations symbolised identities inextricably linked to a particular community, displaying little tolerance for other historical views (Walker, 2000: 79–100). Religious divisions and disagreement over constitutional issues were compounded by circumstance.

> Both St Patrick's Day and Armistice Day had the potential to remind people of a shared history, of common interests and suffering. Instead they were used to emphasise differences and to develop more exclusive versions of identity and history (*ibid*. 100).

McBride supports this view and argues that the aftershocks issued and retrieved by both nationalist and unionist rituals were so potent that they, like Scott's *Fantasy Echo*, altered and simultaneously intensified identity-affirming allegories surrounding the 'grid of talismanic dates' (McBride, 2001: 2).

The way in which historical events and dates were marked, highlights the distinctiveness of public history, as history now becomes 'the small change of politicians interested in the upholding of special identities and traditions' (Furedi, 1992: 13). This has actually become part of a flourishing new cultural economy. The growth of heritage sites has not only precipitated the development of a burgeoning heritage industry but has also reduced the historical landscape 'to a series of free-floating tourist attractions' (McBride, 2001: 4) as 'blanks' left by academic history are filled in by popular historical and cultural groups (Crooke, 2001: 133–134). Populist commemorations can appear parochial to those who do not identify with them and are often regarded as exclusive and triumphalist in nature, thus reducing commemorative rituals to a case of 'one-upmanship' in the culture war. Can it be otherwise? Or is it, as A.T.Q. Stewart argues, that Northern Ireland's public memory reveals not a clash of cultures but a culture in itself (Stewart, 2001: 185). If Stewart is correct, the recounting of history provides little potential for reconciliation.

However, while certain aspects of culture (fantasy) may appear to have been claimed by 'one side' or 'the other', Mairead Nic Craith argues that the two traditions do share certain attributes. These 'symbolic resources' are not fixed but rather they change (echo) in the shifting context of British and Irish history thereby inferring the potential for alternative narratives (Nic Craith, 2002: 2–3). Jane Leonard's (1996) study of war remembrance ceremonies in Ireland since 1919 reveals one such changing context. Irish attitudes towards the Great War, both official and popular, have altered from one of hostility to a more empathetic recognition of those who participated, culminating in the 'Island of Ireland Peace Tower' on Messines Ridge in Belgium (Leonard, 1996: 4–24).

History, Culture and Reconciliation

That cultural heritage has the potential to play a significant part in conflict resolution in Northern Ireland has been expressed in statements on educational policy and local government programmes, thus drawing agencies, museums, libraries and heritage sites, as sources of information, into a public policy of mutual understanding and reconciliation. 'Parity of esteem' was at the heart of the Belfast Agreement of 10 April 1998 and in this respect it had the potential to alter profoundly the nature of the Northern Ireland 'conflict' by providing the very real *possibility* of moving from a position of 'either/or' to one of 'both/and' (Aughey, 2001: 131), even if to date, the politics of absolutes remains the *reality*. In Northern Ireland, then, 'cultural memories' create a tension between the necessity to resolve the political impasse and the wider social need to come to terms with the past. The importance of recognising memories and developing a process to deal with them has been acknowledged, but often recollections of such a traumatic and very personal nature merely serve to underscore and strengthen antagonistic identities, thus continuing the 'us and them' cultural war.

Literary critics have also addressed problems concerning the past and present and the attempt at reconciliation. Seamus Heaney (1993) agrees that certain images and symbols signify common loyalties, emblems of a symbolic past which also claim to be the historical past. For him, the potency of such echoes enhances the learning process, even when that process involves demystification and dismantling of the original image or *fantasy*. 'Breadth and refinement' challenge the narrow conception of loyalty and solidarity and are two of the most valuable effects of education. Sensitivity to the past enriches our lives. When flint spearheads and arrowheads were found during the Bann Drainage Scheme there was an immediate and real connection between present and past societies, the timescale of which creates a paradox of great closeness and great distance. Heaney interprets this as an analogy of the sectarian closeness and distance, which define that part of the country. Not suggesting that a sense of our Mesolithic ancestors will resolve the political problems of the Bann Valley, Heaney does propose that 'it could widen and clarify the lens through which we inspect the question of who we think we are (Heaney, 1993: 33–37). While the object of pluralism may be to 'extend genuine respect to fundamentally different cultures and value systems' (Clark, 2003: 14), endemic division and the desire to apportion blame ensure that popular memory-prompts remain paradoxical. This is the context in which Edna Longley (2001) speaks of the need for 'parity of disesteem'. In her view, '[c]ommemoration now functions as a contradictory site of conflict and conflict resolution. So does it provide homeopathic doses against violence, or keep the pot simmering until needed?' (Longley, 2001: 230). Since commemorative activity serves to sustain the echo effect by sending forth and picking up new resonance, it is likely that it does both things.

Reconciliation: The Role of the Museum

A former Director of the Ulster Folk and Transport Museum stated that museums should be used as a centre to '[E]nhance mutual respect for varying cultural traditions' and to provide a neutral space for such visits, where social discovery is 'safe'. In this context museums should become 'oases of calm' and a vision around which '… peoples of all persuasions could unite' (cited in Crooke, 2001: 127). Tentative engagements with political identities and symbols of division highlighted a new direction for museums and a reassessment of their purpose (Crooke, 2001: 135). In Northern Ireland, however, the role of the museum is complicated by difficulties of interpretation, representation and revisionism.

Trevor Parkhill (2002–2003) has addressed some of these issues: the need to incorporate revisionist history while at the same time make such revisions accessible to the general public; the extent to which an Outreach Programme could facilitate community groups to visit the exhibition to see their own side's role in the event, and to understand something of 'the other side's' version; the need for the museum to be seen by all communities as neutral territory where conventional versions of history may be challenged in a non-threatening atmosphere; the extent to which the curator's historical integrity remains intact when faced with the growing public expectation to mediate more directly than before with recent and divisive history.

For example, the exhibition to mark the bicentenary of the 1798 Rebellion tried to take an objective look at events while ensuring that the interpretation accommodated both unionism and nationalism, not by telling two sides of the same story but rather by handling historical matters sensitively. The museum consciously sought to provide 'a more informed understanding of the past' which would contribute to the 'positive steps towards political *rapprochement*' (Parkhill, 2002–2003: 37–38) that had been taking shape since the Belfast Agreement. There are obvious limits to this approach. In the most recent exhibition, *Conflict: The Irish at War* (2004), the museum stated that the ceasefires, far from generating mutual respect for victims of conflict, had been marked by repeated desecration of commemorative memorials.

One such controversial issue in Irish history has been the interpretation of the Act of Union of Great Britain and Ireland (1800). It has provoked a historiography which, until very recently, had been specifically written to sustain either unionist or nationalist worldviews and to confirm national identities, rather than as a dispassionate examination of its history. It presented a real challenge to those seeking to accommodate contradictory interpretations of the same story in a singular narrative (Kelly, 2003). Identities have been constructed around this event, a fantasy echo replaying across generations and helping to define individuals in political terms. The coincidence of its bicentennial and a new millennium (which as Scott notes is a pivotal point for appraisals of the past as well as predictions for the future) provided an opportunity to review its two hundred year history from the perspective of the 'new', post-Agreement Northern Ireland.

The Bicentennial Commemoration of the Act of Union

Although the Act of Union, the foundation of unionism itself, is an identity-affirming event, it had been – paradoxically – devoid of popular commemoration. If one accepts that the dearth of previous commemoration was because it was implicit in other events such as Remembrance Day or the Queen's Jubilee, then this would confirm McBride's contention that present day concerns determined that it was marked in 2001. Certainly, devolution throughout the United Kingdom harnessed contemporary debate about the future of the Union, while the tentative peace process focused global attention on developments in Northern Ireland. The Act of Union remains part of the legislative foundations under which people in Northern Ireland live. While one could argue that the Act itself is no more important today than it had been previously, symbolically, it *has* become much more significant. In that respect, to ignore the bicentenary in order to avoid upsetting the peace process could be seen as denying the constitutional foundation of Northern Ireland as well as insulting its unionist majority. Equally, to commemorate it could, under the new inclusive political dispensation, be seen as pandering to political triumphalism and insulting nationalists. When the Belfast Agreement institutionalised cultural matters in the newly created Department of Culture Arts and Leisure (DCAL), the Ulster Unionist Party availed itself of the opportunity to directly address a number of present day concerns, from reconciliation to cultural reassertion. The budget, meagre in comparison to either Health or Education, did not reflect the significance of the Ministry of Culture – its potential to influence cultural identity.

In February 2000, the then Minister for Culture, Arts and Leisure, Mr Michael McGimpsey MLA, set up an Act of Union Bicentenary working group. He invited a number of individuals with historical and archival interests to serve and all accepted. The composition of the group was as follows: Mr Gordon Lucy, Ulster Society (Chairman), Dr Arthur Aughey, University of Ulster at Jordanstown, Professor Paul Bew, Queen's University of Belfast, Professor Marianne Elliott, Director of the Institute of Irish Studies, Liverpool, Dr David Lammey, Senior Records Officer, PRONI (Secretary and Project co-ordinator), Councillor Dr Christopher McGimpsey, Belfast City Council, Dr Anthony Malcomson, former Chief Executive, PRONI, Mr Trevor Parkhill, Keeper of History, Museums and Galleries of Northern Ireland/ Ulster Museum and Dr Gerry Slater, Chief Executive, PRONI (Facilitator). A rolling programme of commemorative events was devised, with an exhibition as the central feature. These events included educational workshops for A-level students, a series of lectures, historical re-enactments, newspaper supplements, debates and a travelling exhibition. As a PRONI production, the main exhibition was based on documents, focusing on the pamphlet war, political cartoons and the key political players at that time. It was hoped that the 'original copy' of the Act of Union from Westminster and the Mace of the Irish House of Commons, neither of which had previously left their respective homes, would be central features of the exhibition. Its organization, however, was far from straightforward.

Cold Fish or Hot Potato? Reluctance at Westminster

When Lord Laird of Artigarvan asked the House of Lords what plans the Government had to commemorate the 200th anniversary of the creation of the United Kingdom, he was given a curt reply – 'none' (Hardman, 2000, G. Walker, 2000). Conservative chairman Michael Ancram attacked the Government's omission, saying it was typical of Labour's lack of respect for British history (McCartan, 2001, Sparrow, 2001). Indeed, Tony Blair had been accused of being unconcerned with historical issues, using them only for political expediency. Furthermore, one historian thought that although the Government claims that devolution has, in fact, strengthened the Union, their silence surrounding the birth of the United Kingdom of Great Britain and Northern Ireland suggested a subconscious belief to the contrary (Bew, 2001). Lord Laird's concern was that this lack of enthusiasm did not reflect historical ignorance or apathy but rather an acute awareness of the potential political heat that historical commemorations can generate in Northern Ireland. This was succinctly encapsulated and reflected in a phrase which originated in Westminster – 'archival Drumcree' (Gordon Lucy, in Barnes, 2004: 61). This inferred that any commemoration would be partisan and overtly triumphalist, infringing the notions of inclusion at the heart of the Belfast Agreement (*ibid.* 62, 78, 109). It is likely that Westminster 'remembers' history when it is convenient for it to do so and therefore, neither lack of historical awareness, nor apathy, account for the Government's lack of interest in marking the bicentenary. The most significant concern was undoubtedly political: mistrust of unionists not to make political capital out of the event.

A Sisyphean Task! Difficulties and Diplomacy

Westminster was not alone in its reluctance to accommodate an event that intimated political partisanship. David Trimble has been particularly scathing of local administrators who, he argues, are terrified of 'putting their heads anywhere near the parapet' when dealing with potentially politically sensitive issues (*ibid.* 109). Some unionists would go further and argue that notions of inclusion and the desire to redress an imbalance and appear impartial has, in fact, resulted in 'over compensation' against unionist culture by some public bodies (McCausland, n.d.). Before agreeing to the release of the Mace and other artefacts, diplomatic groundwork was required by the working group to assure the British and Irish authorities that the exhibition was 'sound' and that it was for 'people of any tradition to come to, to be informed and not offended' (David Lammey, in Barnes, 2004:73). Once assured, co-operation and encouragement were forthcoming, even if, on occasions, somewhat reluctantly. Initially, the National Trust displayed a similar reluctance when the working group requested the use of Mount Stewart, home of Lord Castlereagh, for the launch of the commemorations. Sensitive to the possibility of a 'bad press', the Board displayed 'timidity' towards history that could be perceived by the public as politically biased (*ibid.* 75 and 115). However, Ministerial negotiations resulted in Mount Stewart hosting the travelling exhibition, a series of lectures and *Living History* productions some eight months later.

Political sensitivity alone cannot account for the lack of public interest. The Ulster Museum genuinely believed that the story of the Act of Union had been sufficiently covered in the recent 1798 exhibition (*ibid.* 69, 90, 92), while other public institutions may have been unaware of the wealth of documentation available surrounding the legislation. The fact that the central feature of the commemoration was a piece of paper may also account for the lack of enthusiasm (*ibid.* 92). That the original legislative measure involved London and Dublin also implied a lack of local relevance (*ibid.* 79), a point contested by McGimpsey, who considered that the Act of Union was very much 'part two' of the 1798 story. Even within the unionist community, interest appeared limited. Whether this was merely from a lack of attentiveness to the technicalities of the legal structures or the fact that the Union now is not what it was in 1801 is not clear (*ibid.* 103 and 108). Certainly the key figure behind the commemoration was the Minister for Culture who saw culture as 'the golden thread that runs through everything'. But what was *his* motivation? Was it as apolitical as that of the working group?

Golden Thread or Golden Opportunity? Party Politics, Electioneering and Parity of Esteem

It could be argued that the bicentenary, falling as it did after the Belfast Agreement, provided a useful opportunity for promoting political self-confidence within unionism. It could symbolise that new, positive identity to which Trimble and the leadership of the Ulster Unionist Party aspired. Both Trimble and McGimpsey conceded that it served as a timely reminder of what unionism is all about (*ibid.* 109 and 117). There was also a cross-border dimension, through co-operation of government officials and institutions in Belfast and Dublin. The political significance and strategic thinking behind the involvement at Mount Stewart of Nicholas Robinson (the husband of a former Irish President), did not go amiss in Lammey's mind either (*ibid.* 75).

There were also wider political connotations. A survey showed that since the implementation of the Belfast Agreement in 1998 there had been a striking increase among Protestants who thought that their cultural tradition was increasingly under-represented and losing out to 'Catholic culture' – from 17 per cent in 1998 to 37 per cent in 2001 (Harbinson and Manwah Lo, 2004: 113). Only 30 per cent of Protestants considered their cultural tradition protected compared to 70 per cent of Catholics. Statistics from the 2001 *Northern Ireland Life and Times* survey noted that when interviewees were asked to describe what culture meant to them, 'the more controversial aspects of culture – such as marching on the Twelfth of July or Irish history – are mentioned by relatively few respondents'. Rather culture was considered to be visits to museums, attractions like theatres, community centres and cinemas (Heenan, 2004: 83–85). Therefore, if the population measures its affirmation of culture by the degree of representation accorded to them by public bodies, the survey implies that unionists consider their culture to be significantly under-represented. In this respect, the bicentenary commemorations, the central feature of which was to be displayed in a prominent cultural arena, the Ulster Museum, could be interpreted as unionist reimbursement for perceived investment in 'nationalist' culture.

In addition, the commemoration allowed unionism to respond to the charge that it possesses neither culture, nor ideology and that its historical awareness is entirely negative. Not only would unionism be presented in a more positive light, both in terms of having a culture and a proud history, but it could also be expressed in a non-triumphalist fashion, a point which Trimble saw as success enough. On the other hand, Trimble was eager to use the commemoration to remind those opposed to the Union of how its continued existence is 'an underlining too, of their failure' (in Barnes, 2004: 109). The language used by individuals was particularly revealing. Both Trimble and McGimpsey considered they were 'celebrating' the bicentenary (*ibid.* 109 and 114) and indeed a short press release, issued by McGimpsey's office to launch the programme of events, used the word 'celebrate' no less than five times.

Others considered the word 'mark' less likely to attract political criticism; even if the event was being celebrated, it could not be allowed to appear overtly so (*ibid.* 57 and 80). Paul Bew argued that if you concede the Act of Union did actually happen, then that allows for use of the word 'commemorate' (*ibid.* 102); David Lammey shared that view. The term 'commemorate' was actually used in the relevant literature.

By presenting the facts professionally and refusing to dodge contentious issues, a key aim of the working group was to demythologise much of the rhetoric surrounding the Act and to challenge preconceived ideas in the hope that renewed understanding could aid reconciliation. History symposiums in Belfast, Dublin and Wexford generated debate among academics and politicians, challenged narrow interpretations and brought to light new scholarly work. If the commemoration could present similar aspects to the wider public and challenge popular perceptions, there could be an increased awareness of historical understanding and contextual appreciation. Moreover, this could then be reflected in a corresponding sensitivity to the whole flow of Irish history, a *fin de siècle* revision of Northern Ireland's past. It was a fine line to tread between the academy and the Assembly, the historical and the political.

Thus, the repackaging of history to facilitate current political and economic agendas has seen historical memory 'recycled into [a] spectator sport and tourist attraction (Foster, 2001: 228). The extremes to which some present-minded thinking has been stretched, has caused considerable consternation among many historians, who increasingly see history as reflecting Lewis Namier's process of 'symmetry and repetition', where we imagine the past and remember the future (cited in *ibid.* 97; see also Barnes, 2004: 57, 59–60, 84). In this process, historical accuracy and objectivity can be misplaced; that it should not be so in the commemoration of the Act of Union bicentenary was the overriding concern of the working group (*ibid.* 59, 69–70, 83, 93, 97, 116). In this respect, it considered revisionism (in the sense of reassessing the evidence) as having the potential to aid the reconciliation process. But it felt that it could only make a worthy contribution if sources were properly subjected to historical scrutiny; if contentious issues such as bribery and Catholic emancipation were faced head on rather than avoided or excused (*ibid.* 59) and if events were displayed as not always being black and white, but recognizing that shades of grey highlighted the complexities of the situation (David Lammey, *ibid.* 70). This was reflected in their mission statement:

> To promote understanding of the passing of the Act of Union as an historical event, and of the personalities and the social, political and economic implications.
> (Act of Union Bicentenary Working Group, Minutes, 29 March, 2000).

Since any commemoration of the Act of Union would be seen by some as purely political, the need for objectivity was paramount. Rather than *Telling tales and making it up in Ireland*, the bicentenary working group was determined to tell the tale and get it right, 'whether we liked it or not, [we were] going to get the historically accurate picture' (Michael McGimpsey, in Barnes, 2004: 116). For Trimble, it appeared that the commemoration itself was a sufficient political success and a measure of the Unionist Party's new influence in public life (*ibid.* 111).

Exhibition and Reaction

The working committee contributed heavily to the *Belfast News Letter* supplement of 22 January 2001 and achieved their aims of being educative and inoffensive as well as entertaining. The articles were factual and could not be considered in any way triumphalist, except by those who would never see the Act of Union itself in any other light. The supplement had been published to coincide with the launch of the bicentenary programme of events at Market House, the Town Hall in Newtownards. An article in the main body of the *News Letter* took the opportunity to draw an analogy between the bicentennial of the Act of Union and the potential generated by the Belfast Agreement to create a new 'Union' under which we could all live (McKeown, 2001).

Sinn Fein, however, considered the commemorations to be 'deeply offensive to all democrats as well as nationalists and republicans'. Sinn Fein's Mary Nelis, deputy chair of the Northern Ireland Assembly's Culture Committee, commented that she would welcome a 'critical examination' of the Act, but objected to the use of public money for celebrations, believing that 'celebrating the Act of Union is not about promoting inclusion, equality or cultural diversity. It is about celebrating political domination' (Thornton, 2001). McGimpsey contests Bew's assessment that her view is extreme, even within Sinn Fein, but rather considers it 'not atypical' of republican reaction (in Barnes, 2004: 105 and 114). Perhaps she considered the Minister's lapse into the politically incorrect terminology, 'celebrate', at the opening event in Newtownards as justifying the accusation. Further criticism was limited to the expenditure involved (*ibid.* 76 and 114), which may confirm McGimpsey's analysis of the republican predicament: that to denounce the events in an overtly political manner would only reveal republican intolerance. However, there may also have been a strategic determination on Sinn Fein's part to ignore the bicentenary, thereby limiting the attention it received. The old historical narrative of the Union's imposition and corruption was more suited to the republican agenda. To engage with any historical challenge to that narrative would concede to it a legitimacy which republicans denied anyway. This may have been politically astute but it hardly signalled a 'new beginning' in Northern Ireland.

The bicentenary exhibition itself could be said to reflect the popular image of unionism. It was approached in the way in which Eoghan Harris suggests unionists approach politics – as lawyers rather than as dramatists. It was a 'black box' exhibition, sober and factual, mirroring the puritanism that remains in Ulster Protestantism itself. While nationalist history has primarily been based on the concept of struggle, unionism has centred on legalities and the constitution. That events and artefacts presented in the exhibition were document-based, a petition not a struggle, confirms this assertion. It was a focused exhibition; like Dean Godson's conception of David Trimble as a 'minimalist' Unionist, it dispensed with the 'clutter' of flags and banners, as well as the myths surrounding the Act. Even review of the impact of the museum exhibition was minimalist.

No official evaluation of the exhibition was undertaken even though visitors to the Ulster Museum were asked to fill out cards stating their impressions. There may be several reasons for this. The quality and quantity of the cards provided a limited amount of information; the importance of comprehensive evaluation was in an early stage, while constraint of time and staff ensured attention was quickly redirected to the next project. What the comment cards did reveal was that not only does nationality remain an integral part of an individual's identity but also the Act of Union itself continues to be a measure of it, as illustrated in the following comments received by the Museum (cited in Barnes, 2004: 48–49):

> An excellent representation of a somewhat important but forgotten part of our national identity and history.

> At last, an exhibition which is not neglecting this important part of our identity. The Act of Union must not be lost in nationalist romanticism.

> Insulting. Will always be Irish and proud of it.

> Crap, this is free Ireland.

That some of the comments were written in Irish was a point in itself. Other cards reflected on how the event was portrayed:

> Although I found the Bicentenary Act of Union well done, I must say it was appallingly one-sided and extremely prejudiced against the catholic population of Ireland. It is sad that the museum still opposes catholic emancipation in its truest form to this day.

> Good to see the Act of Union's bicentenary has not gone unmarked. A bit dry in spots, as one would expect from dependence on written evidence. I enjoyed the objective way the 'Act' has been presented.

> Very informative – a different perspective on the Catholic attitude to the Union, from the view taught to us in the 1950s history lessons at school. Well done a great exhibition.

> Excellent exhibition. This is precisely the sort of exhibition that the Ulster Museum ought to have on a permanent basis. All too often our political history has been neglected out of modern day expediency.

The most striking aspect of the comment cards is how they underscore the inextricable links between history, identity and culture and how culture has remained politicised. In turn, its institutionalisation, through DCAL, allowed unionists to send a number of messages: a reclamation of cultural space to help counterbalance a flourishing, self-assured nationalist culture; an assertion of both its distinctive and representative characteristics, ensuring that not only would others see unionism more clearly but that unionists could see themselves more clearly as well; and a successfully repackaged, non-triumphalist unionism which could broaden its appeal locally, nationally and internationally.

Conclusion

Marking the bicentenary of the Act of Union in 2001 exemplified how the commemoration of history can be used to address present day concerns and in doing so provides a new basis against which all future enquiry takes place. Appropriation and interpretation of the past continues to provide the potential for both reconciliation and further division. McGimpsey himself unconsciously employed Scott's concept of fantasy echo; to 'elide historical differences and create apparent continuities' (Scott, 2001: 304) when he proposed that:

> I never saw it as a zero-sum game; I always saw it as a shared thing, even if there were parts of it that you didn't agree with, or parts that you wished had been different but whatever it was, this is your lot, this is your legacy (in Barnes, 2004: 118).

The commemoration of the bicentenary of the Act of Union revealed all those ambiguities of political culture in Northern Ireland. Indeed, it illustrated the way in which all public events involve a mix of motives and objectives. On the one hand, the working group strove to deliver events that were as true to the historical evidence as possible. On the other hand, these events themselves were also invested with a political significance by the Ulster Unionist Party. In some ways this also involved its own ambiguity. The way in which the bicentenary would be commemorated was not only designed to boost morale but also to show the extent to which unionism was no longer triumphalist or sectarian. Here was the intersection of professionalism, political expediency and public service and all elements contributed to the commemoration of the Act of Union.

Similarly, the nationalist response to the commemoration was also ambiguous. On the one hand, there was the acknowledgement that the Act of Union was an important event in Irish history. In the supposedly more accommodating atmosphere of post-Agreement Northern Ireland it was impolitic to deny it a place on the heritage calendar. On the other hand, there was a general reluctance (with some exceptions) to engage with any evidence that would challenge the nationalist fantasy that the Act was an unmitigated disaster for Ireland. The Union could only be admitted as an echo of past wrongdoing and its Act could not be re-imagined as anything else. What was important was not winning or losing the argument about whether the Act should be commemorated but ensuring that the laying of historical blame remained unchallenged. This specific Northern Ireland territory would be familiar to philosophers and practitioners of history.

In *The Idea of History*, Collingwood (1961) noted Rousseau's view that rulers could only give people what the people themselves were ready to accept (Collingwood, 1961: 86).

The compulsion which the devil-haunted mountains exercise on the man who would cross them consists in the fact that he cannot help believing in the devils (*ibid.* 316–7).

For Collingwood, the philosopher, to cross those 'devil-haunted mountains' of history involves facing the demons head-on and telling history as accurately and objectively as possible. For Stewart, the historian, the public effect of this in the Northern Ireland case would always be limited since traditional narratives continue to hold some adherents with mesmeric force (Stewart, 2001). For Stewart, historians are unlikely to exert any real influence on a nation's view of its past. He uses a Raymond Chandler quotation to illustrate how their work is 'not so much disputed as simply ignored'. '"There are two kinds of truth", wrote Chandler, "the truth that lights the way and the truth that warms the heart"'. (Stewart, 2001: 185). There may indeed only be *one* history (fantasy) but there will always remain more than one echo since, as Joan Scott concluded, identity is only secured by 'filling the empty categories of self and other' (Scott, 2001: 292) with the echoes of *our* history.

Chapter 8

Engendering Devolution

Carmel Roulston

Introduction: Women's Movements and Women's Inclusion in Devolution Politics

Constitutions have for the most part been constructed by men and have reflected (dominant) male perspectives on power, politics and citizenship. The interests of women have often been neglected, as women have seldom been party to the drafting of constitutions. When they have had an input, it has tended to be as a minority, seldom claiming a right to be there as women, but rather as 'citizens who happen to be women'. Constitutions are the frameworks which aim to determine 'who gets what, when and how'. They will often include an expression of a set of values and aspirations for the society, incorporating concepts such as fairness, respect, equal treatment. Feminist writers have more than adequately established that the models of citizenship which have become established from the seventeenth Century onwards have been based on aspects of behaviour or images associated with men: the warrior, the self-reliant, independent and rational individual. Women in European cultures, as Pateman (1990) points out, were granted citizenship in recognition of their domestic heroism. In recent times, women have been expected to assimilate to a masculine model or accept lesser status. Recognising difference has meant accepting exclusion from a masculine public world of politics.

More recently, writers such as Ruth Lister (1997) have aspired to new conceptions of citizenship based upon the principle of 'differentiated universalism'. This implies changing the gendered meanings attached to the public and private spheres, incorporating the values of care into the image of the citizen (male and female), and using the levers of public policy to achieve a fairer division of domestic labour. Above all, the concept of citizenship should be cleaned of all connotations of worth based on autonomy and independence, the fictions which render 'women's work' invisible. Citizenship should remind us, says Uma Narayan, (1997: 65), that we all have 'a collective as well as individual stake in the decency and humaneness of our policies and public arrangements'. The 'social-welfare' states of Scandinavia have achieved a redistribution of power, resources and influence which has brought women into mainstream political influence. In other liberal-democracies, it has proven more difficult for women to gain admittance to the political mainstream, and to challenge the processes which reproduce their exclusion.

Periods of constitutional change can afford the opportunities for previously excluded groups to achieve shifts in the balance of power and influence. Women in Northern Ireland, Scotland and Wales were quick to see the potential for radical change in the processes of creating new political settlements in those countries. Organised groups of women were prominent in support of new political arrangements, while at the same time asserting the need to include 'women's perspectives and concerns' in negotiations aiming to create new institutional frameworks. In each country, there were high hopes that the new institutions would be based on a fairer distribution of political power and influence between men and women. The outcomes have been different in each of the three new devolution regimes. The factors influencing the different outcomes are many and complex, relating to the nature of the campaigns for gender equality, the pre-existing political contexts and the extent to which divisions among the women themselves had a significant impact.

Northern Ireland: Women's Place in Conflict and Change

Traditionally academic work on identities in Northern Ireland has been dominated by investigations into the constitution and interaction of antagonistic ethnic identities. Much of this research has been characterised by an inattention to gender identity, with researchers concerned with understanding and resolving the constitutional question tending to ignore the gendered dimensions of ethno-nationalist conflict and other feminist concerns. In the 1990s, a limited, yet significant body of feminist research seeking to investigate the relationship between ethnicity and gender in the constitution of political identity and subjectivity within Northern Ireland (see Cockburn, 1998, Miller and Wilford, 1998, Porter, 1998, Roulston and Davies, 2000, Sales, 1997) emerged. However during the current crucial period of conflict resolution there has again been a tendency to ignore or reify out of existence developments in the dynamics of gender politics within Northern Irish society.

Contemporary feminist theory renounces the idea that any singular definition of female identity is possible or desirable and has revealed women's identity as a web of overlapping, shifting and often conflicting subjective interrelations. The multi-faceted nature of identity and its implications for gender politics has been documented by feminists interested in Northern Irish society. In particular it has been noted how nationalist identities in the form of Unionism and Irish republicanism have prevented the emergence of a stronger more unified women's movement (Roulston, 1997). The emergence of feminism produced new allegiances and divisions even as it changed and displaced traditional ones. The spectrum of responses from women with feminist identification to the Northern Ireland Women's Coalition – from strongly welcoming to very hostile – demonstrates the sensitivities to representation claims. It also relates to a division between macro- and micro-level forms of political activism which holds opportunities and risks for women. At the micro-level, we find many women-focused activities, often arising from the immediate difficulties that political conflict causes for women. These activists frequently resist the 'peace and reconciliation' discourses often expected of women's groups. Conflict, including conflict between women, is part of political life.

At the time of writing, Northern Ireland is still experiencing a lengthy suspension of progress to genuinely inclusive and sustainable democratic governance. This present stalemate has coincided with a stalling of progress towards the inclusion of women. This may have particularly serious consequences for a large section of the female population whose inclusion has so far not been by feminist campaigns and analyses. These women may also be the least likely to find other agents to facilitate or assist their entry into effective political life. One part of the process of negotiating the Good Friday Agreement was to open new 'discursive spaces' for campaigns about exclusion of women. Have these spaces been receptive to some women at the expense of others?

Equality and Difference in the NI Women's Movement

The extent to which women's voices – and feminist issues – were heard in the peace talks process was a result of the campaigning by a multitude of women's groups over twenty years in Northern Ireland. Despite long-standing suspicions about 'feminism' (discussed in Miller *et al.*, 1996), the feminist strand of the women's movement proved more influential than might have seemed possible in the 1970s.

The experiences of feminist campaigning in Northern Ireland have given rise to reflection and theory in recent years; for the most part in the 1970s and 1980s, debates were characterised by practical issues of strategy and policy, adapting 'off the peg' theories and concepts imported from elsewhere. As in the US and elsewhere in the English-speaking world, Northern Ireland feminists faced the dilemmas of equality and difference, hoping to achieve genuinely 'equal citizenship rights with men' to 'enable them to participate as their equals in the public sphere'. At other points, the stress was placed on women's particular concerns and values (Lister, 1997: 92–93).

In Northern Ireland, the equality perspective was dominant in the 1970s, especially in the Northern Ireland Women's Rights Movement (NIWRM), founded in 1975, a function of both the origins of the movement in the experiences of women from civil rights, trade-unionist and broad left backgrounds and of the considerable levels of disadvantage faced by women. It was a dominant but not exclusive perspective as conflicts within the NIWRM revealed. It would not be accurate to simply assign the NIWRM to the 'equality' side of an axis; this was a 'coalition' including trade union women, socialist feminists, liberal feminists, civil right campaigners, radical and lesbian feminists and community activists. It would be fair to say that it was on the equality end of a spectrum, with other, later groups, such as the Belfast Women's Collective more clearly focused on 'difference(s)'.

One feature of NIWRM campaigns was that the stress on attaining equality of women with men went hand in hand with maintaining that differences among women should be emphasised as little as possible. That is to say, there was a perception that it was the 'gender' part of women which led to their receiving unfair treatment. Overturning this required women to 'abstract from' other oppressions or exclusions; these could be addressed in other contexts. There was both good sense and disingenuousness in this. Good sense in so far as the experience of women campaigners for over half a century had been that the leaders of nationalist movements would happily disrupt women's unity. Disingenuousness in so far as there was a masked awareness that these 'other' disruptive identities were related to privilege and disadvantage among women. Despite the attempts to minimise conflict in the name of feminist solidarity, this ideal of a cross-community movement of Catholic and Protestant women was regarded by other feminists as a denial and suppression of differences (Roulston, 1997) and there were numerous splits and regroupings. The difference approach came more to the fore among NI feminists in the 1980s, with a greater focus on the different needs and values of women. Coinciding with this, organised feminism became more diverse, fragmented and divided, with overt hostility emerging over attitudes to the NI conflict, and feminists on both sides of the divide claiming to be closer to 'genuine' feminist values and goals.

Divisions over the 'national question' also overlapped with class differences. A substantial proportion of 'women's activism' involved women from working-class communities engaged in a variety of campaigns, including nationalist, community-based and peace-oriented. Women's participation in politics in this era was largely in the voluntary NGO sector or in grassroots, community-based organisations. The latter, widely referred to as 'the mainstay' or 'the backbone' of community life in NI, became linked to a stereotype of women as not only more peaceful, but also imbued with more practical wisdom and altruism than males engaged in 'macro-level' party politics.

Women's community activism was constrained by the structure of 'parallel universes' (Galligan and Wilford, 1999: 168) that characterised social life in Northern Ireland. Women often mobilised in support of their national or religious communities against actual or perceived threats or oppression. Women were centrally involved in the civil rights protests over discrimination against Catholics by local councils and other authorities. The Northern Ireland Civil Rights Association, established in 1967 to campaign against discrimination in law, policy and employment also contained many women among its members. As inter-communal violence escalated in the early 1970s, the impact of security policies on predominantly working-class Catholic communities brought a strong resistance which women were to the fore in mobilising and sustaining. Women in Protestant areas were also drawn into community based movements of solidarity. In both communities, women were to the fore in the creation of support groups for those imprisoned for paramilitary violence and their families, as well as campaigns for special status for such prisoners (Sales, 1997).

The parallel universe pattern did not, however, encompass all social and political engagement. Even during the worst years of the Troubles, women in Northern Ireland organised actions for improvements in social, welfare and environmental policies, often motivated by concern for the health and well-being of their families (Porter, 1998). Groups of women displayed great imagination, capturing attention despite having few resources. The 1970s saw the emergence of many such local and often short-lived groups, as well as the development of larger campaigns and networks.

Commentators have often noted the extent to which women from both the unionist and nationalist communities were trying to attract the attention of policy makers to a similar set of problems. Unemployment, poverty, poor provision of services, social exclusion and violence (from the security forces as well as paramilitaries) affected both communities.

Such commonalities did not always result in united, cross-community movements of women, although, in spite of many obstacles, some have been created. Women, for example, were to the forefront in the creation of 'peace movements' and of networks which crossed community divisions. Women in peace movements did not always adhere to a feminist agenda, though we find some overlaps with the 'difference' perspective that women are likely to value peace and reconciliation more than conflict. In Northern Ireland in the late 1970s and 80s, the peace activities of women on larger (the Peace People, with its Nobel Prize-winning founders) or smaller (local women's peace groups) scales became an arena of activism for women which was broadly approved of in theory, though sidelined in practice by government and community leaders. Peace became a politically contentious issue. It became important to distinguish 'peace as merely non-violence' – which would leave fundamental social and political inequalities in place – to 'peace with justice', which would imply that the fundamental causes of the conflict had been resolved. For this reason, women's peace activism was controversial within the broader feminist and women's sectors.

As Sales (1997) and others have noted, there has been a stronger tradition of a community-based oppositional politics among the Catholic/nationalist population in Northern Ireland, because of its alienated relationship to the state. While voluntary organisations and pressure group activity has also had its place among the Protestant population, radical politics was more likely to take the form of trade unionism or left wing or radical party politics. By the late 1980s, however, various influences had led to a reduction in this divergence, especially where women's involvement was concerned. A growing sense of alienation based on fear of betrayal by the British state among sections of the Protestant population and the effects of Conservative government welfare policies on the fabric of social life produced a new style of political engagement which brought more women into action. They too were demanding, among other things, better housing, education resources and fairer treatment for young people (Porter, 1998). It is worth noting how much was expected of the women's sector by mainstream policy makers as well as by other community leaders. They were – with minimal resources – expected to provide support networks for their communities and contribute to social stability. Some funding bodies expected to see some evidence of 'cross-community activity' (which could often be risky for the women concerned) while others required women's groups to meet targets for results of educational programmes.

Women's involvement in campaigning did not necessarily produce a commitment to feminist ideas or strategies. Indeed, as Miller *et al.* (1996) and Cockburn (1998) observed, the majority of women involved in community politics were unlikely to identify as feminist. The feminist and community sectors were not, however, completely separate. Feminists were to the fore in the creation of women's centres, for example, and there were numerous campaigns which traversed the feminist/community women divide. The Northern Ireland Women's Aid Federation, which has gone from strength to strength, was founded at this time. Trade union campaigns for equal pay for women and to extend the Sex Discrimination Act to Northern Ireland have had long term effects (Evason, 1991). The EOCNI has been a most effective advocate on all women's issues and has forged links between the different strands of women's community politics. Of great importance in the building of inclusive campaigns was the women's section of the WEA, which, in 1992, convened a multi-stranded conference which allowed for the expression and discussion of difference in ways that had not previously been experienced. In addition, groups such as the Women's Research and Development Agency, which operated as a 'think-tank' and facilitator for women's groups of all kinds, were able to link the different strands of activism effectively.

There were certainly tensions between 'feminists' and 'community-based women' which were due in part to differences of life experiences and interpretations of events and experiences. Some feminist campaigns and demands were perceived to have less relevance to the lives of community-based activists. Nevertheless, despite such tensions and lack of resources, this multi-stranded women's sector survived and even flourished. Three possible explanations may be offered for this survival. Firstly, there was determination and commitment on the part of many activists from all sectors. Secondly, European (and UN) legislation and campaigns promoting women's rights provided inspiration and sometimes resources. Finally, the policy process during direct rule, which (especially during Labour administrations) allowed some opportunities for women to influence policy which would have been more difficult to achieve in a devolved assembly dominated by local parties. This must not be exaggerated. Access for the majority of women (and other excluded groups) was very constrained (Cockburn, 1998: 58) and many argued that the processes lacked transparency. But, on occasions, most significantly in the build up to the peace process in the 1990s, policy-makers (both civil service and party political) in the Northern Ireland Office and the NI Civil Service actively sought women's input. An important influence was the report produced by the independent Opsahl Commission (1993), which researched citizens' ideas about ending the conflict and creating a new society. The importance of women's work in community groups was particularly highlighted in the report of the Commission, whose members were profoundly impressed by the carefully prepared and presented statements from groups and activists. No doubt policy-makers were guided by an instrumental view of the value of women's commitment to their communities, which was not motivated by the agendas or aspirations of the majority of women activists. The latter, however, were able to avail of the opportunities presented on occasions, however limited they might have been.

Women's Inclusion in Democracy and Peace Building

In the late 1990s, the emerging peace process brought protests about the predicted absence of women from the proposed all-party talks. The creation of stable democratic institutions in the post conflict era, with parallel projects to define citizenship and draft constitutions has often seemed to offer openings for women to shift the traditional balance of power more in their favour. In reality, as Miller and others note, women are often 'eased out of the public sphere towards the end of the transition process' (Miller, 1998).

Concerns about the exclusion of women from the emerging peace process were voiced at a Conference (Clár na mBan) convened by a group of republican feminist community and political activists in 1994. The Conference report called for more transparency on the process and expressed a strong claim for the inclusion of women on both sides of the 'constitutional divide' in political decision-making. In 1995, a network of women with a substantial record of activism, led by Monica McWilliams, convened a bigger conference on the theme of Women's Inclusion and Ways Forward. This gathering, which was partly funded by the NIO, brought together representatives from almost 200 groups and laid much of the ground work for women's inputs to the peace process. The conference report (Fearon and McWilliams, 2000) recommended that a broad commitment to improving the status of women in politics was no longer sufficient. A clear strategy for the support and development of women's participation should be devised, including the matter of setting targets for women at local, regional and parliamentary level. In particular, the Conference concluded that specific 'mechanisms for women to become involved in Constitutional talks are needed'.

The Irish and British governments issued a Joint Communiqué on February 28, 1996, proposing that elections be held to choose the delegates to the forthcoming Peace Talks and inviting parties to present their views on the electoral system. Voluntary organisations were not specifically invited to respond, but many did so, including the Northern Ireland Women's European Platform (NIWEP), which advocated the adoption of an electoral system which would maximise the number of successful women candidates. They referred to the beneficial effects of women's civil society activism, which would not be reflected in a Talks process involving only the bigger mainstream parties.

When the British government published proposals for the election which recommended a hybrid, two-tiered list system of proportional representation that would elect 110 delegates to a Forum for Political Understanding and Dialogue, the Nationalist and Republican parties were dismayed by what seemed to be a concession to Unionism built into the framework of the process. A partnership of organisations including NIWEP, issued invitations to over 200 groups of women to attend a meeting to discuss what should be done to ensure that women were represented at the Talks Table. Recognising the concerns of nationalists, they nevertheless identified an opportunity for women in the electoral system and decided that this was worth pursuing. Over the course of the following week, NIWEP and others lobbied both governments on the issue of a women's network contesting the election. To many women's surprise, civil servants responsible for the election process responded by indicating that a woman's party could be registered. Further meetings and agonised discussions followed, the outcome of which was the creation of a Women's Coalition (henceforth NIWC) to include women from all communities and classes, and to attempt to win seats for women in the proposed process of talks. This was a radical move towards bridging the gap between women's micro activism and mainstream politics.

The justifications for women's inclusion deployed a rhetoric which stressed the particular contribution which women would make, but attempted to avoid the 'essentialism' of an appeal to women's more peaceful nature. Instead, the argument was based around NI women's particular experiences of what Porter has called 'a situated politics of everyday life' and their understanding of how to accommodate and manage differences learned in grass-roots movements. The theory underpinning the proposal incorporated aspects of feminist ethics and moral theory – with its emphasis on 'care' and 'responsibility for others' as core elements of citizenship – and Iris Young's (1990) theories of justice as recognition. These were drawn together in adaptations of the principle of transversal dialogue across difference, a set of practices which became templates for feminist inspired peace-building action. Such justifications did not appeal to all feminists or community-based women activists, to say nothing of women already in political parties or movements. This was especially the case for women who were opposed to the process and the subsequent Agreement, who viewed the mechanism by which women's inclusion was achieved with great suspicion.

Women activists (including feminists) from republican and loyalist traditions expressed strong reservations about the NIWC project. A central concern was that the unity around the demand for women's presence in the political talks would crumble as soon as any specific political outcome had to be chosen. In fact, the unity within the NIWC survived to make a major contribution to the success of the peace process, and to play a significant part in the first Assembly, despite the considerable diversity of identities and viewpoints contained within it. The key factors ensuring success were the continual practice of seeking dialogue across the differences within the Coalition, and the firm resolve to apply the core principles of justice, equity and human rights to all new political tasks and challenges (Fearon, 1999).

The NIWC highlighted the potential for women to make a difference, and opened a discursive space which allowed the absence of women from mainstream politics to be noticed and discussed. The party also acted as a catalyst for general discussions about the under-representation of women in public life, and allowed discussion to develop about the positive effects of women's inclusion. In addition, of course, the policy proposals put forward by the NIWC resulted in more gender sensitivity than would otherwise have been the case.

The NIWC had always stressed the importance of incorporating civil society in the process and attempted to consult NGOs and grass-roots groups on key policy proposals. As a result, the NIWC lobbied and argued successfully for the introduction of policies which might not have been there otherwise. These included a strong Equal Rights agenda, with a commitment to 'equality proofing' of legislation. Related to this, they strongly advocated the introduction of a Bill of Rights, which was a radical departure from British constitutional tradition. The Bill was to be drafted by an inclusive Human Rights commission after the successful completion of the process. The longer-term inclusion of civil society organisations in policy-making was secured through the creation of a Civic Forum which could advise the elected Assembly about the impact of legislation on various social groups including business, trade unions, churches, the unemployed, rural communities as well as women. As noted elsewhere, the incorporation of civil society organisations was a particular feature of the Northern Ireland peace process, generally viewed as important to the (at least partial) success in 1998.

> At least four of the political parties involved in negotiating the Good Friday Agreement (were) substantially influenced by community sector politics. ... Perhaps the most obvious of these is the NIWC, whose members have been substantially drawn from the NGO sector (and which) ... attempted to infuse the political process with the NGO values of inclusiveness, dialogue, and tolerance. There is tangible evidence that the ideas and ethos promoted by the NGO sector have impacted directly on the political structures of Northern Ireland (Cochrane, 2001: 151).

The NIWC represented a daring and ambitious attempt to link the aspirations towards better representation for women and inclusive, peaceful politics in general. The balance sheet of the first Assembly shows that neither of these aims was fully realised. As one analyst notes, gender issues which are controversial in many societies 'are even more divisive in Northern Ireland' (Cowell-Meyers, 2003: 89). Despite many attempts, it proved difficult to achieve cross-party caucuses of women Assembly members, and there was no substantial increase in the numbers of women selected for the second (postponed) elections to the Assembly. Equally significant for women, perhaps, has been the lack of interest in, and resources devoted to, the Civic Forum, which might have allowed women access to influence from their civil society locations.

Women Still on the Margins?

The success of the peace process has, to date only been partial. Governance in Northern Ireland is currently in a state of uneasy balance between the Assembly and a number of 'public bodies', which operate as they did during the period of direct rule, when we were not capable of agreeing on a fair system of balancing resources and values. Equally unacceptable has been the failure to include women in key institutions such as the Policing Board.

The Assembly elections of December 2003 indicate that progress towards full inclusion of women in mainstream politics has also been partial. There are more women in the Assembly, but apparently less hope of a women's caucus, as all the Unionist women are anti-Agreement. Although the 'big' division over ultimate national identity has been re-cast somewhat, women are to be found on all sides of the axes of difference – nationalist anti- and pro-agreement, unionist anti- and pro-agreement, feminist pro- and anti-agreement. In the polarised atmosphere prevailing during the elections, the NIWC elected representatives narrowly failed to hold their

Assembly seats; nationalist identities still have more political weight than gender identities. Nevertheless, the pressure to include women has had some success, with three women now holding Westminster seats. Against the trend for local elections, two of the three are from Unionist parties.

At the micro-level, there are still many women active in community/voluntary activities, often arising from the immediate difficulties that political conflict causes for their neighbourhoods and families. Many of them resist being categorised as part of a 'women's movement', or being associated with women's rights discourses. There are two sometimes overlapping reasons for this. Firstly, the predominant allegiances are to ethno-nationality and class. Introducing a gender dimension can be threatening to the unity of 'beleaguered' communities. Secondly, attachment to women's issues can result in women being sidelined; women's issues are still perceived as not 'real issues'. Many women activists currently also frequently resist the 'peace and reconciliation' discourses often expected of women's groups. While this is understandable – after all conflict, including conflict between women, is part of political life and women should not be required to be more peace loving than men – it tends to limit the potential for women to resist the sidelining of women's issues and perspectives. It seems imperative now for some research to chart and understand more fully the operation and effects of such polarisation of women at community as well as political party levels. Perhaps, in contrast to the NIWC stress on the linkage between women's inclusion and the success of the peace process, it is now time to highlight the importance of the inclusion of the widest possible spectrum of women's voices.

The evidence from recent Northern Ireland Life and Times (NILT) surveys shows that there has been a growing acceptance among both men and women that women have a right to be in politics. The continued popularity of education and training programmes such as 'Women into Politics' shows that women are willing to make extra efforts to show that they are able to act effectively as representatives. The major parties are still reluctant to make the extra effort to increase women's chances of electoral success, with none taking up the opportunity to adopt positive measures offered by the Selection of Candidates Order.

The dimension which now needs attention is how mainstream political institutions can finally be brought to introduce – and implement existing – policies to make it possible for women to take their rightful place at the centre of political life. Too often in Northern Ireland the responsibility for change and progress has been passed to those least well placed to achieve it. Women have done more than enough to show the injustice of perceptions that they are somehow not quite 'good enough' yet to be in politics. At this stage, it is those who occupy the centre who should change their ways. Frustratingly, it will certainly take further initiatives from women before this can be achieved. During the current review of the Northern Ireland Agreement, the complex proportional voting system for allocation places in the Assembly's Executive will come under review. A more generally beneficial review would be of the electoral system for the Assembly itself. Had an Additional Member system, of the type applied in Scotland, been adopted for Northern Ireland, not only would the NIWC have had a stronger base but the smaller Loyalist parties would also have been assured of better representation. This system was discussed in 1998, but was rejected largely because it was associated with the highly disproportional system adopted for the Forum elections, which had little credibility with the wider public. In addition, the largest parties in the Talks were hostile to any new electoral system (though there is reason to believe that Additional Member system would have benefited some of them).

Lobbying to introduce such a change would now be opportune. It also seems that a Political Forum for women which would aim to achieve a sharing of experiences and to campaign for the implementation at the political level of the stipulations on gender equality of Section 75 of the Government of Northern Ireland Act (1998). Equality-proofing the political process is somewhat overdue. Prospects for the inclusion of women – in all their diversity – would be enhanced by a review of the Civic Forum which enabled that body to become a genuine force for change, development and inclusive governance. Finally, the women's voluntary and community sector is seriously under-resourced. While there has been some funding allocated for the 'social care' or educational dimensions of their work, the campaigning and research groups are dependent on precarious and short-term funding. Given the contribution such groups have made to maintaining a community infrastructure before, during and after the Good Friday Agreement, this is a poor reward.

Scotland: Civil Society in a Peaceful Transition

A long campaign was waged to achieve greater autonomy for Scotland within the UK. In 1978/9, a proposal for devolution of powers from Westminster to Edinburgh was defeated in a referendum. The campaign gathered strength again in the late 1980s as alienation from central government in London was intensified as a result of Conservative policies. Having learned from the (narrow) defeat in the 1970s, pro-devolution campaigners attempted to build a broad consensus for change, even before legislation was prepared. A Scottish Constitutional Convention (SCC), a coalition of pro-autonomy political parties and pressure groups was convened, which aimed to convince the electorate that there would be great benefits to Scotland if devolution could be achieved. There was a significant mobilisation of women – across Party divisions – in the Women's Co-ordination Group, who argued that a new Parliament for Scotland must be radically different from the 'Westminster model' of adversarial two-party politics. This could be achieved – among other proposals – by bringing more women into political life.

These and other proposals were reflected in the reports of the Consultative Steering Group, which attempted to incorporate into the structures of the new Parliament the principles of power-sharing, accountability, accessibility and equal opportunities. The model is of a partnership between citizens and parliament which will open the gateways to decision-making processes for 'ordinary people'. They were included in the Bill, which initiated a new referendum, and was overwhelmingly accepted by the electorate in 1998 (Brown, 1998).

The report of the SCC (1995) included an electoral contract, signed by two major (in Scottish and UK terms) political parties (Labour and Liberal-Democrats), which committed them to achieving equal numbers of men and women in the first Scottish Parliament. In the end, a proportional electoral system was adopted which included a 'party-list' element. The Scottish Parliament, first elected in May 1999, has seventy-three constituency members elected by first-past-the-post, and fifty-six chosen from party top-up lists to represent eight regions. These additional regional members ensure that the parliament's party balance reflects the popular vote by giving extra seats to parties whose number of constituency seats is proportionately less than their share of votes. Most women MSPs are constituency members, though the Scottish National Party relied on the regional list system to facilitate women's election by placing them near the top of its lists in 1999. Labour used a system of twinning, whereby neighbouring constituency associations would each nominate one woman and one man as candidates, to increase the number of women elected.

The Labour Party and the Scottish National Party (which regards the current devolution arrangements as unsatisfactory, preferring complete independence) put forward significant numbers of women candidates in the 1999 elections. For Labour, 50 per cent of members elected were women, with almost 43 per cent of SNP seats going to women. In all 37.2 per cent of members were female, a great success in the UK context and even compared with other European states. Indeed, this is the figure thought to be a 'critical mass', sufficient for women to have a substantial influence on policy (Brown *et al.*, 2002). As Arthur Aughey points out (2003), expectations 'were high that devolution would be a qualitatively different and not just organisationally distinct approach to politics'. The new arrangements in Scotland took some time to settle in, and there was early disappointment that the 'new politics' had not yet arrived. There have been accusations of 'sleaze' and that the Parliament is still a 'boys' club'. Nevertheless, women's issues have remained high on the agenda and hopes remained high that it would become the place where fewer obstacles stand 'in the way of women' (Mackay, 2001).

As in Northern Ireland, there has been a strong focus on equality issues, with the creation of an Equal Opportunities Commission in the Parliament and an Equality Unit set up by the Executive. An important element of the new style politics has been the establishment of channels of influence for non-governmental organisations, through the mediums of a Civic Forum, regular consultations and in the portfolio of the Minister of Communities (which has responsibility for the equality strategy). This has resulted in a general trend towards socially inclusive legislation, with better care for pensioners, support for students, action on child poverty and community regeneration all on the policy agenda. Many of these measures directly or indirectly are of interest and of benefit to women, and have been on the agenda of women's groups for many years.

There has been some disappointment with progress towards equality for women in the new Scotland. 'Increased access and "voice" have not resulted in increased influence' (Mackay, 2004: 92) and there are fears that ministers believe that gender equality issues have been 'sorted' and are now giving them a lower priority

(Fitzgerald, 2004: 77). In contrast to Northern Ireland, however, a fund to support women's organisations has been created, and funding has been allocated to help create a Scottish Women's Convention. A working group to develop a multi-stranded action programme for women, in consultation with women's organisations has also been set up. There have been success stories; taking action on domestic violence has moved higher up the policy agenda than previously. In addition, the Parliament has taken seriously the process of 'gender-budgeting', that is, analysing the differential impact of policies and resource-allocation on men and women. Campaigners on women's issues believe that there is still a long way to go, and are concerned to ensure that the diversity of women is reflected in future policy action.

Wales: Inclusive Governance?

Before devolution, politics in Wales appeared to be almost as unwelcoming to women as in Northern Ireland. The political parties and mainstream institutions were male-dominated. There had been only four women members returned to Westminster before 1997, and local government was also overwhelmingly male. The road to devolution in Wales was more problematic than in Scotland, with the country divided into two equal camps, sharply opposed on whether devolved government was desirable. The referendum was won by the pro-devolution side with the narrowest of margins (50.3 per cent for) on a low turn-out (51.3 per cent). As in Scotland and Northern Ireland, the prospect of new institutions being created opened a debate about participation and representation which resulted in the adoption of a more inclusive electoral system. In Wales, the campaign for women's inclusion was much more low-key, but again a key event provided an opportunity to assert a strong claim that the new arrangements be more inclusive than the old. In 1994, after the Parliament for Wales Campaign's democracy conference, a clause on gender equality was added to the Draft Democracy Declaration (which had previously made no reference to gender in politics).

As in Scotland, women's rights campaigners persuaded the Labour party in Wales, to use a system of twinning, whereby neighbouring constituency associations nominated one woman and one man as candidates. Plaid Cymru also increased the number of women candidates, with the result that after the first Assembly elections, 40 per cent of Assembly members were women. The electoral system in Wales as in Scotland was chosen because it favoured the inclusion of previously under-represented groups and parties. In both countries, contrary to expectation, the increase in the numbers of women elected was due to a greater extent to positive action in candidate selection for constituencies than to the benefits of the list system for producing a better balance among the 'additional members'. In the second elections in 2003, the Labour party did not use twinning, but had women-only short lists in six constituencies. Plaid Cymru used the list system to promote women candidates, with the result that the percentage of women members increased to fifty percent (Squires, 2004). The Welsh Assembly now leads the world with women's representation being equal with men. Whereas Scotland had enjoyed a greater measure of autonomy prior to 1997, in Wales, as in Northern Ireland, there was perceived to be a democratic deficit, with the Welsh Office ruling in a very centrist fashion. The new political arrangements promised greater access and influence to interest groups and non-governmental organisations in policy consultation. As in Scotland and Northern Ireland, a statutory requirement to promote equality in all areas of work and policy was built into the principles for government for the new Assembly.

Despite some initial scepticism, based on the limitation of powers for the Assembly – which cannot introduce primary legislation – there is clear evidence that 'gender equality activists have successfully used the opportunities presented by constitutional change' (Chaney, 2003). In both Scotland and Wales there is frustration that legislating in some social policy areas is still dependant on initiatives from Westminster (where the gender balance has become slightly less equal in the 2005 election). In Wales, progress has been made largely in policies and practices relating to the public sector, with equal pay and fair treatment practices in public sector bodies and the civil service being enhanced. The influence of civil society lobbying has resulted in discussion of policies addressing social and economic inequalities.

Nevertheless, gender equality remains a contested issue. Local government is still an influential arena in which males dominate. In the 2005 Westminster election, a disaffected Labour party member who believed he had been disadvantaged by the positive action policy stood as an independent candidate and won easily. Progress towards gender equality may be one of the successes of Welsh devolution, but there are many policy battles to be fought and changing attitudes remains an uphill task.

Conclusion

A number of factors combined to allow women to take advantage of the 'window of opportunity' presented by the creation of new political arrangements. The mobilisation of civil society and non-governmental organisations – in different ways – in support of the processes in all three countries meant that women's movements were centrally involved. Women's organisations in the three countries exchanged knowledge and experience, learning from each other and from the experience of campaigns elsewhere. The effective campaigning by women in the South African peace process for fair representation was a particularly inspiring example for women in Northern Ireland, and by extension the other two countries. The choice of electoral system was important as well, although in Northern Ireland the major parties could not in 1998 bring themselves to accept the more proportional system applied in Scotland and Wales. In the final analysis, however, it was women's willingness to take the chance, to demand fair and equal participation in determining the future of their countries that made the difference.

Chapter 9

Marketing Identities in Devolved Regions: The Role of Global Corporate Culture in Scotland and Wallonia

Sharon Millar

Introduction

Recently I saw an advertisement on BBC World for 'Wallonia, Belgium' (the French-speaking, autonomous region in the south of the country), which was obviously aimed at the global marketplace, with well-dressed, good-looking business folk surrounded by hi-tech offices and buildings, impressive infrastructure and pleasant scenery. That countries, regions, or cities are products to be marketed should come as no surprise; that has long been the case, for instance, in the tourist industry. As Beckerson (2002: 133) notes in relation to Britain, 'marketing and place promotion have become important areas of local and regional government policy', reflecting Britain's transformation from a manufacturing to service economy. Consumer culture too has affected our individual identities in terms of the range of 'personalised' or 'off the peg' identities available for us to buy into, and the global context is seen as having effects on the shape of national and cultural identities (Morley and Robins, 2001: 10).

This chapter will take a marketing perspective as its starting point to explore identity-making and representation in the context of devolution in the UK and regionalisation in Europe. This marketing perspective should be understood in a literal rather than metaphorical sense; the approach is not that of Bourdieu (1991) with his concepts of linguistic market, cultural and symbolic capital and anticipation of profits. Rather marketing is understood, following the definition of the *American Marketing Association*, as 'an organizational function and a set of processes for creating, communicating and delivering value to customers and for managing customer relationships in ways that benefit the organization and its stakeholders'.[1] Hence, the focus is primarily on the macro-level of state institutions and their representations of organisational self, region and people, rather than the

---

[1] www.marketingpower.com/live/content21257.php.

micro-level of individual interaction and the localised, lived experience of regional identity. My argument is that since processes of localisation, be these devolution or regionalisation, have taken place, or are being maintained, in a global context characterised by global market concerns and electronic communications, corporate and consumer culture is likely to impact on the representation of regional identity at the macro-level. To explore this argument, the Chapter will consider the websites of relevant institutional bodies in Wallonia and Scotland to see if and what identities are being marketed. Scotland will then be taken as a case study where contemporary contexts in relation to Scottish identity will be examined. Such institutional websites form part of e-government, itself a manifestation of wider trends, such as globalisation, rapid developments in information and communication technologies, new perspectives on organisational management and changing perceptions of what government at whatever level should be (Drükne, 2005). The websites can also be seen from the perspective of paradiplomacy, that is the international activities of regional or subnational institutions, a phenomenon often ascribed to the same wider trends noted above in relation to e-governance (Keating, 1999).

The Chapter is not intended as a comparison of Wallonia and Scotland, although this will be done when relevant, but as an investigation of how corporate and consumer culture is being applied in both an established, autonomous European region (Wallonia was recognised as an economic region in 1970 and granted regional autonomy in 1980) and a more recently devolved region in the British Isles (Scotland was granted devolved powers in 1998). The specific choice of Wallonia and Scotland, as opposed to, for example, Catelonia and Wales, is due partly to linguistic abilities and partly to my own Scottish roots.

Institutions on the Internet

The Walloon Region

Wallonia is one of the three federal regions of Belgium, the other two being Flanders and Brussels, and overlaps with two of the country's four linguistic communities, namely the French-speaking and the German-speaking. The state also recognises four regional languages in Wallonia: Champenois, Gaumais, Picard and Walloon. As Belgian politics has long been characterised by division and struggle, Wallonian representations and marketing of identity can only be understood in the context of the more numerous Flemish-speaking community and the more prosperous region of Flanders. Hence the Flemish dimension will be referred to when relevant. The Walloon region has a Parliament and an executive with wide-ranging political and economic powers. There are two main websites, that of the Parliament and that of the region. The parliamentary website[2] contains information in French only about parliamentary structure, functions, agendas and publications as well as practical information regarding access and group visits. Each page has the Wallonian emblem

---

[2]   http://parlement.wallonie.be/content/.

at the top, a red cockerel, placed within the letter 'P' and exterior and interior shots of the Parliament building. The website of the region (*la Région wallonne*) – the *site Carrefour* ('crossroads site') – operates as a portal and will be focused on in detail here. In addition to general information about institutions (Parliament, government), its homepage[3] provides four overarching, colour-coded links: *citoyens* (information for citizens); *enterprises* (information about how to start and run businesses); *thèmes* (list of topics selected by the Wallonian government as *les centers d'interêt des utilisateurs* [centres of interest for users], e.g. agriculture, tourism, Europe); and *découvrir la Wallonie* ('Discover Wallonia', tourist information). Every page on the website comes with the regional logo, a red 'W' where the final stroke ends in an arrow pointing upwards. There are live links to five other languages (German, Dutch, English, Italian and Spanish) on the homepage and on the web pages of the 'Discover Wallonia' link. As on the Parliamentary website, the Walloon language makes an appearance in the form of a sub-link to the regional anthem.

Accepting that there are clear marketing dimensions to the homepage (most obviously the logo and tourist information link), the question is what audience does the Walloon region have in mind? The homepage uses several instances of the second person pronoun *vous* and *votre*, the latter clearly the polite form and the former either the singular, polite form or plural. Pronoun use is a well-recognised feature in the construction of self, groups and audiences in all forms of discourse and, regardless of theoretical approach, is often a feature of analysis. It is difficult here, however, to ascertain precisely the referent of these pronouns, except in the link to citizens, where 'you' means 'you the citizen'. Elsewhere, the second person reference could be to citizens, would-be citizens, tourists, outside investors, essentially any 'you' that visits the site. What is certain, however, is that 'you' must be able to understand French as links to all of the other languages only translate general headings and not content, except in the 'Discover Wallonia' web pages. Note too that German is given no special treatment despite the fact that the region houses the Belgian German-speaking community within its borders. Chilton (2004) notes that, in political discourse, choice of language serves an indexical function, one means of indicating political distinctions, distance and solidarity. Given that Wallonia strongly identifies with the Francophone community in Belgium (Keating, 2001), the dominance of French on its regional website is neither surprising nor accidental, although the availability of multilingual options may also be determined by time and money considerations.

Turning to the link to *citoyens*,[4] we are told that this link has been 'inspired by the major steps you will accomplish in the course of your life. It will direct you to the competent body, the website or the resource area which will respond to your questions, your expectations!' (*s'est inspirée des grandes démarches que vous accomplissez au fil de votre vie. Elle vous orientera vers l'organisme compétent, le site Internet ou l'espace ressource qui répondra à vos questions, à vos attentes!*).

---

3   www.wallonie.be/index.shtml.
4   www.wallonie.be/fr/citoyens/home.shtml.

Sub-links include work, health, family life, pensions, leisure, arts and culture. Also available for citizens is *Belgopocket*, a book of information based on the questions most frequently asked by citizens. In addition, there are links to current events and news, including, for example, a role-play game open to associations, e.g. sportsclub, youth group, or institutions, e.g. prison, where the ideal 'citizen village' (*village citoyen*) is to be constructed, hence giving players an insight into the workings of a local council and the realities of local politics. All of this typifies e-governance with its concerns with 'higher quality services, greater engagement with citizens' (OECD 2003: 12).

It is not, however, made explicit who *citoyens* are, i.e. people with Belgian passports or people who simply live in Wallonia; rather the link defines what *citoyens* need to know and might be interested in. There is an assumption of citizens as active and participatory: people who will be seeking information, who will have questions and expectations. The website is designed to cater for these, keeping the citizen/customer not only informed, but involved and satisfied, with options for asynchronic interaction via email using a *poser une question* link ('ask a question').

How the region views itself and its citizens is best revealed in the link to *Le contrat d'Avenir*[5] ('the contract for the future'), which presents a strategic development plan to renew the region and to boost confidence. Wallonia has for many decades been in serious economic decline, due partly to the region's traditional reliance on heavy industry such as mining and steel, and is very much the poor relation when compared to Flanders (Fitzmaurice, 1996). In a sub-link called *Osons rêver* ('let's dare to dream'), in a section entitled *Rêvons d'une Wallonie forte de ses valeurs* ('let's dream of a Wallonia strong in its values'), we are told that:

La Wallonie est une société, démocratique et participative qui satisfait les aspirations individuelles et collectives de ses habitants. Liberté et sécurité, initiative et protection, égalité et différence, ambition et rêve, avantages concrets et vision collective y sont garantis et stimulées. Les Wallonnes et les Wallons sont conscients de leurs droits comme de leurs devoirs. Ils éprouvent un fort sentiment d'appartenance à leur ville ou leur village et davantage encore à leur Région.

De leur latinité, ils tirent et cultivent leur indépendance d'esprit, leur audace visionnaire, leur convivialité et leur sens de l'accueil. Les Wallonnes et les Wallons sont unis par des liens sociaux et de cordialité puissants et partagent un socle de valeurs communes, pétries d'humanisme.

(Wallonia is a democratic and participatory society which satisfies the individual and collective aspirations of its inhabitants. Liberty and security, initiative and protection, equality and difference, ambition and dream, concrete advantages and a collective vision are guaranteed and stimulated there. The Walloons are aware of their rights as well as their duties. They feel a strong sense of belonging to their town or their village and even more to their Region.

---

5   http://contratdavenir.wallonie.be/apps/spip/.

From their Latinity, they derive and cultivate their independence of spirit, their visionary audacity, their conviviality and their sense of hospitality. The Walloons are united by social ties and powerful cordiality and share a base of common values, shaped by humanism).

Here is identity-making of the region, mostly in general 'civil' terms (democracy, liberty, equality etc.), and its people, mostly in group solidarity terms where again the 'civil' appears (humanist values), but ethnicity too creeps in with the reference to Latinity, seen as the source of specific group personality traits (independence, hospitality etc.). Throughout the text of the *contrat d'Avenir*, the emphasis is on citizenship and the positive, personal characteristics of the Walloons as a group. So for example, Walloon citizenship is described as *active et solidaire* ('active and solidary') and neighbours envy *notre modèle de concertation sociale, notre dynamisme, notre modernité* ('our model of social agreement, our dynamism, our modernity') (under *osons rêver* link, and subtitle *intégrée dans l'Europe et solidaire du monde*). This type of rhetoric has roots in earlier initiatives, such as *La Wallonie au futur* (Wallonia in the future) from 1987 where intellectuals defined a 'project for society', based not on nationalism but more universal, humanistic values (Destatte, 1998). Similarly, Van Dam (1997) in an interview study of identity among the professional classes in Flanders and Wallonia identified characteristic types, one of which *le creatif et le tolerant* ('the creative and the tolerant') was more typical of Wallonian conceptualisations, with an emphasis on *l'invention* ('invention'), *un goût pour la liberté* (a taste for liberty), *la démocratie* ('democracy'), *la solidarité* ('solidarity'). As in the *contrat d'Avenir,* some of the interviewees attributed these qualities to cultural influences, i.e. French or Latin vs. German or Germanic:

Par rapport à l'esprit creatif, on a toujours dit que le Français a l'esprit pétillant de son champagne et que l'Allemand a la lourdeur de son organisation (chef d'entreprise wallon) (Van Dam, 1997: 118).

(In relation to the creative spirit, it has always been said that the Frenchman has the sparkling spirit of his champagne and that the German has the ponderousness of his organisation (head of Wallonian company)).

Il y a un esprit d'indépendance en Wallonie, il y a moins cette tendance de se regrouper comme en Flandre. Sur le plan culturel, les Français sont plus indépendants que les Allemands. Les Allemands sont toujours en groupe, toujours ensemble, toujours chacun pour son groupe. Et la Wallonie est plus latine (Van Dam, 1997: 119).

(There is a spirit of independence in Wallonia, there is less of this tendency to regroup oneself as in Flanders. On the cultural level, the French are more independent than the Germans. The Germans are always in a group, always together, always each to his group. And Wallonia is more latin) (director of Wallonian company).

What is noticeable throughout the text of the *contrat d'Avenir* is the variable use of person, be this shown by verbal morphology or pronouns. The first person plural is used primarily in the headings ('let us dream'), where it has inclusive reference (you and I); when used in the text, it has variably inclusive ('our recovery') and exclusive reference ('we have taken') as in 'we have taken the necessary measures to make our recovery a success' (*nous avons pris les mesures nécessaires pour réussir notre rebond*) (from *Introduction* link). The body of the text, however, uses primarily the third person, singular and plural, resulting in a rather neutral text, suggesting distance between the authors and the audience and lacking the pathos often found in the rhetoric of politicians when trying to construct solidarity (e.g. 'We Walloons are aware of our rights'). The question is can the *contrat d'Avenir* be seen in marketing terms? I would suggest yes. The very label *contrat d'Avenir* not only connotes the business arena, but hints of advertising rhetoric; a label such as *plan stratégique de développement* ('strategic development plan') presumably lacks the required panache. The contract is between the region and its citizens, and hence advocates joint responsibility for the future. In a sense then, it is casting citizens into the role of stakeholders in the region and not just consumers of services: *Chaque Wallonne et chaque Wallon sera associé et responsabilisé dans la création de son avenir et de celui de ses enfants* ('Every Walloon will be associated with and given responsibility for the creation of their future and those of their children'); *Le Contrat d'Avenir, c'est la mobilisation. Soyons toutes et tous acteurs du renouveau wallon* ('The contract for the future is mobilisation. Let us all be players in the Walloon renewal') (from *Introduction* link).

To some extent, the Walloon region has something of a problem. It admits to a 40-year period of decline, which they claim has now been arrested; but since the region has been autonomous for 25 years, this means that its entire history as a federalised unit is coloured by a lack of economic success. Little surprise then that advantages of regional legislative powers are mentioned in the *contrat d'Avenir*; this is done in terms of internal and external advantages. Within the region, legislative powers allow for direct implementation of policies 'for our development and adapted to our specifications. We have the means for our ambitions' (*pour notre développement et adaptées à nos spécificités. Nous avons les moyens de nos ambitions*) (from the *Introduction* link). Externally, regional legislative powers have meant a pivotal role for Wallonia in cooperation between regions in Europe.

> *Grâce à son statut de région à pouvoir législatif, elle se distingue en jouant un rôle moteur dans la coopération entre les régions d'Europe et au sein des instances décisionnelles de l'Union Européenne.*

> (Thanks to its regional statute with legislative power, it distinguishes itself in playing a driving role in the cooperation between the regions of Europe and in the midst of decision-making bodies of the European Union).
>   (From *Osons rêver* link, under *intégrée dans l'Europe et solidaire du monde*).

Generally, comparisions are made with regions, and not countries. For instance, in the *Osons rêver* link, under *Rêvons d'une Wallonie confiante dans l'avenir*, it is stated that Wallonia 'has regained the standard of living of the majority of the regions in

Northern Europe' (*a retrouvé le niveau de vie de la plupart des régions d'Europe du Nord*). Similarly Belgium is seen as a network of regions, making a federal state:

> Au sein d'un Etat fédéral enfin arrivé à maturité, la Wallonie tient solidement sa place dans les échanges équilibrés et sereins qui l'unissent aux autres Régions et Communautés du pays. Reconnue comme une entité de référence par les opérateurs économiques et sociaux, elle offre un cadre adapté pour appréhender efficacement et humainement la mondialisation.

> (In the midst of a federal state finally having reached maturity, Wallonia solidly holds its place in the balanced and lucid exchanges which unite it to the other regions and communities of the country. Recognised as a unit of reference by economic and social operators, it offers a framework adapted for apprehending efficiently and humanely globalisation).

There is little sign of the national in the *contrat d'Avenir* (indeed the words 'Belgium' and 'Belgian' appear very infrequently on the Walloon region website as a whole). Rather glocalisation is a more prominent theme: Wallonia is a region now comparable to other regions in Europe, at the leading edge of communicating with these regions and the EU and communicating well with the other regions that make up the federal state of Belgium. Arguably the region via its website is trying to develop for its citizens a framework for regional identity, which lags behind both national and local identities; for example a survey from 1999 indicates that in Wallonia 14.9 per cent identified with the region vs. 34.4 per cent who identified with Belgium and 29.7 per cent who identified with their locality (Keating, 2001:87).

The Scottish Executive and The Scottish Parliament

Unlike Wallonia, Scotland is not a unit within a federal state. The United Kingdom currently have two devolved regions, Scotland and Wales; the devolved status of Northern Ireland tends to be unstable given the political circumstances. England as such does not have its own exclusively English Parliament or government. The Scottish equivalent to the Wallonian websites are those of the two devolved government bodies, the Scottish Parliament (SP)[6] and the Scottish Executive.[7] The homepage of the Scottish Parliament focuses on links to, for instance, parliamentary business, news and events, visiting Parliament, and exploits shades of the characteristic blue colour of the Scottish flag. The logo of the Parliament is the cross of St. Andrew (the Scottish flag) topped by a crown, but visual symbolism is relatively limited. The business/marketing aspects of the SP, however, are obvious. It sees itself as a corporate organisation, having a parliamentary corporate body, and providing corporate publications such as annual reports and accounts. In addition, it is also a tourist attraction with cafés and off- and online gift shops, selling general

---

[6]   www.scottish.parliament.uk/home.htm.

[7]   www.scotland.gov.uk/Home.

gifts as well as souvenirs, such as a teddy bear with a Scottish Parliament jumper. It has branded 'Holyrood Scotland' for its merchandise from the gift shop, the logo consisting of a detail from one of the windows in the Parliament building.[8] Place and country branding is now common practice; we need only think of New Labour's re-branding of Britain in the late 1990's as 'Cool Britannia' (Leonard, 1997). Most recently Edinburgh has joined the ranks of the branded, the soberly-named 'Edinburgh City Regional Brand' being launched in 2005 by a partnership between public and private bodies'.[9]

The homepage of the Scottish Executive (SE) plays with visual, national symbolism to a much greater degree than that of the Parliament. It is visually unmistakably Scottish: the blue and white cross of St. Andrew flies at the top and appears as iconic links on several occasions; there is a pale-blue silhouette of the country's land mass; there is a fairly prominent photograph of scenes Scottish, which changes frequently (e.g. a scuba diver in a presumably highland Scottish loch, an historical building); a smaller, unchanging photograph of a sunset over a loch with hills and castle ruins; the predominant colours are various shades of blue and white. Compare this to the homepage of the United Kingdom government,[10] where no national visual symbolism is apparent, with the notable exception of the link to Scotland, Wales and Northern Ireland which, most significantly, is accompanied by the Union Jack. Similarly, the homepage of the Welsh Assembly Government[11] is modest with its visual national symbolism, using only a line drawing in grey of the dragon crest.

In terms of content, the SE homepage has sections on, for example, news, topics (e.g. agriculture, arts and culture, fisheries, justice, sport, tourism), publications, consultations, job vacancies, about the SE, InfoScotland (which deals with current publicity campaigns), Scotland is the place (which gives information and advice for people coming to live and work in Scotland), and European Union. There is also a link to Gaelic, which brings you under the topic of 'Arts and Culture', where it is explained (in the English version of the Gaelic pages) that despite decline Gaelic 'is still alive and an official language of Scotland, as well as a priceless part of our nation's living, diverse culture'. However, there are no 'other language' versions of the SE website, be this Gaelic or Scots. This contrasts with the Scottish Parliament (SP) website, which gives a choice of 12 languages other than English, including Gaelic, Scots, Catalan, Bengali, Urdu, Arabic and Chinese, although these non-English versions, with the exception of Gaelic, are not direct copies of the English web pages; more limited information comes in multilingual format. The languages chosen seem to reflect the ethnic composition of Scotland (e.g. south-east Asian languages) and major languages of the EU and beyond; the inclusion of Catalan is no doubt due to the official links, as of 2002, between the Scottish and Catalan Parliaments. One

---

[8]   www.graphicpartners.co.uk/pressandnews/article1.htm.
[9]   www.edinburghbrand.com.
[10] www.direct.gov.uk/Homepage/fs/en.
[11] www.wales.gov.uk/wag/wag.htm.

explanation as to why the SE does not give multilingual options, while the SP does, may lie partially in a crucial difference between the two: the SP is more tangible and its proceedings more public, being not just a body of people, but a building, and thus, like its southern sister, a marketable tourist attraction. Interestingly from a corporate and consumer perspective, the website of the Westminster Parliament has no multilingual links.

In terms of identity marketing, the SE is clearly presenting Scotland as multicultural, but this is done differently depending on the link followed. For instance, 'InfoScotland' gives information about a current campaign, 'One Scotland: No Place for Racism', which aims to combat racial discrimination, which is explicitly acknowledged (under the 'racism in Scotland' link): 'Scotland prides itself on being a friendly country, welcoming of strangers. In reality however, alongside this culture of hospitality, there has also existed a long history of racism in Scotland'. In a 'what are we doing' link, the SE declares its commitment to 'tackling racism and discrimination, and encouraging respect for the diversity of the people of Scotland'. Classic marketing techniques are used to raise awareness of the problem, such as a series of advertisements for TV, cinema and transport outlets and a 'Scotland's many faces' exhibition, consisting of a mosaic of over one thousand Polaroid pictures of the diverse population of Scotland (sponsored by Polaroid). On the website ('One Scotland', under 'tell your story' link), people are encouraged to submit their own stories and a number of both negative and positive stories from people from varied national and ethnic backgrounds are given, e.g. Bangladeshi, African, Jewish, English, Scottish, Asian Scottish, Scottish traveller.

Not surprisingly, such frankness about racism is avoided in a different link on the website, 'Scotland is the place', which brings you to a non-governmental website, dealing with moving to and finding work in Scotland. Here the process of marketing multicultural identity uses exclusively positive rhetoric and adds a historical dimension to Scotland's welcoming of multiculturalism:

> Scotland is a multicultural society of just over 5 million. People have been coming to live here from all over the world for centuries, so you can be sure of a warm welcome. And of course, Scottish people are famously friendly …

> Now Scotland is actively seeking a flow of Fresh Talent to flourish alongside native-born Scots and secure its place as an essential part of the global economy. Scots have always had an international outlook. Now in the twenty-first century, Scotland wants to attract New Scots who will make this their home.

The potential new arrivals are not 'immigrants' or 'foreigners' but 'New Scots', people who will become 'Scots' by virtue of arriving in the country. This site, too, provides stories from people who have settled in Scotland, but these are all upbeat and enthusiastic. This is marketing Scotland in the global context to (educated and skilled) immigrants; mentioning racism is obviously not an ideal advertising strategy. In contrast, the SE is trying to market within the country the idea of diversity, the idea that Scotland is in fact multicultural and that the people of Scotland come in different shapes, sizes, colours, dress and languages. In a sense the SE is selling to the people of Scotland the image that is already being marketed globally. That this is needed is suggested by a Centre for Human Ecology (CHE) report on research carried out in 1999. Entitled *Embracing Multicultural Scotland: The People Speak*, this involved groups of people from ethnic minorities who were interviewed about identity, multiculturalism and the role of the Scottish Parliament. Revealed were mixed feelings about whether Scotland is or in the future could be multicultural, but the need for Parliament to act in combating racism and discrimination, also in its own ranks, and improving equal opportunities for minority groups in education was emphasised:

> Confidence in the Scottish Parliament will increase when there is action and not just words.

> Education at all levels of all sectors about awareness of different cultures that gives an understanding, which actually changes their feelings of superiority.

> See the Parliament as parents to the children. If MSPs are representative of different cultures and languages then automatically other organisations will follow (responses to question 4).

Responses to questions about belonging or lack of it do not match the advertising rhetoric above of a warm welcome for 'New Scots':

> They can't accept that we can be Scottish but that we wear Asian clothes because we are proud of our Asian identity.

> They like our food but they don't like us (responses to question 2).

The global context clearly is an important backdrop for the SE. The leaders of the two main parties in the executive have drawn up 'A Partnership for a better Scotland: Partnership Agreement', which 'sets out our vision for a Scotland where enterprise can flourish, where opportunity does exist for all and our people and our country have confidence to face the challenges of a global society' (under the link 'about SE'). Note, unlike Wallonia, this is not an agreement of joint responsibility between government and citizens, but between political parties. In the Scottish agreement, the 'people' are at times cast as rather passive consumers, not active stakeholders: 'The people of Scotland expect our Parliament and the Executive to listen to their concerns, respond to their wishes and make a positive difference to their daily lives. This Agreement sets out the policies and the direction for government to meet that expectation'.

Is there then a different understanding of citizenship in Wallonia and Scotland? Certainly, there is a strong theme of the 'civil' in the Wallonian discourse, where '*citoyenneté*' ('citizenship') is used in its behavioural sense of the civic and, for the region, there is a political and economic imperative in casting its 'citizens' as co-responsible stakeholders. In the Scottish discourse, neither the term 'citizenship' or 'citizen' is used; preferred referential and address terms are 'people of Scotland' or simply 'you'. This is perhaps not unexpected. McCrone (2001:103) argues that in the UK context, 'Britishness is a political identity, roughly equated with citizenship, but ...growing out of a pre-modern definition of people as 'subjects' of the Crown'. If citizenship and citizen are understood in the 'belonging to state x' sense and, in addition, connote Britishness, then they may be problematic terms, in the context of not only devolution in the UK, but the multicultural nature of present-day Scotland.

Like the SE, the SP website makes no reference to citizens. A rapid and rather superficial trawl through the websites of Glasgow and Edinburgh City Councils came up with one context for the use of the term 'citizen'; Edinburgh City Council has an online newspaper which is described as the 'online connection between council and citizens', and which refers to 'citizens' in its pages. That the terms are not used, of course, does not necessarily mean that the concepts are irrelevant or understood differently. There is perhaps less overt citizen-making in the SE website, but nonetheless it is there in that people are encouraged to be active, to give their views and to participate in the political process. Again we see the familiar characteristics of e-governance. The same applies to the SP website with its 'visit, learn and interact' link, which has, for instance, a sublink called 'Making your voice heard in the Scottish Parliament' and a further link 'How can I have my say in the running of Scotland', which suggests that one joins committees, stands for election, signs petitions or votes. There is, however, a tendency to cast 'the people' as consumers, receivers of governmental bounty, but with no joint, stake-holding responsibility: 'The Scottish Parliament is here to make a difference to your life, whatever you do and wherever you live in Scotland. These pages tell you about the Scottish Parliament, what it can do for you and how you can make your voice heard'. Shotter (1993:10) notes that the desire to be '*citizens* of one or another community, is to have a voice, and to be listened to seriously *as of right*'. As we see in Wallonia and Scotland, there are different institutional ways of constructing this voice.

Scotland: Devolving Identities?

Given its relatively recent status as a devolved entity, Scotland allows us to consider the possible effects of devolution on identity representation and perception. McCrone (2001: 107) states, giving no collaborating evidence, that '[T]o be Scottish is to define oneself as progressive and forward-looking'. Certainly this claim about Scottishness matches the image of Scotland that the SE and SP seem to be trying to present on their websites: a multicultural, dynamic Scotland ready to meet the demands of a global economy. In many ways, as in Wallonia, a more civic than ethnic conceptualisation of regional or national identity is in evidence with the emphasis on modernity, inclusiveness and innovation. But what about the past: the historical continuity, the myths and symbols that are seen, at least in some approaches to national identity, as vital (Smith, 1998)? Since nationalist politics have played a role in identity construction in Scotland (unlike Wallonia), we would not expect to find a devolved Scotland represented as a de-kilted, global player. From the perspective of tourism, there are certainly no surprises. The icons that were used in 'imagining' the nation (to borrow Anderson's [1983] notion) are still being used nowadays in branding it: highland rebels from William Wallace to Bonnie Prince Charlie, clans and their tartans, the swirl of the bagpipes, and those actively involved in the romantic mythologising of Scotland in the nineteenth century, such as Walter Scott and Robert Burns (Pittock, 1991), have become icons themselves (McCrone *et al.*, 1995). As noted by Berghoff and Korte (2002: 9), '[A]dvertising tourist products has always strongly relied on the creation and exploitation of national stereotypes'.

Worries about the traditional image of Scotland, and by extension the stereotypes, do seem to exist, however. In March 2004, at a meeting of the Scottish Parliament's European and External Relations Committee, concerns were expressed by one member about Scotland's image abroad. Referring to an international survey, he noted that:

> it would appear that when Scotland is mentioned to people in other countries, they immediately think of shortbread, tartan and castles. Some might argue that there is nothing wrong with that … However, I think that we have a problem in trying to project Scotland as a modern, successful knowledge economy.[12]

To some extent this committee member reflects the phenomenon known as the cultural cringe, defined by Wikipedia[13] as 'the sense of cultural inferiority felt by many Scots, particularly in relation to southern English culture', which may take the form of discomfort with national heritage, a servility in relation to English ways or a sense of victimisation by the English. However, Susan Stewart, the First Secretary of Scottish Affairs at the British Embassy in Washington, argued in 2003 that the cringe was no longer relevant:

> In the past we have been embarrassed by the shortbread-tin and Brigadoon associations, an age when these things were not considered cool. I think we have got over that. In tartan, we have an icon of international recognition.
>
> Modern Scotland is secure enough in its contemporary strengths, achievements and merits to assume icons of the past. If someone talks to me about penicillin, I talk to them about Dolly the sheep. If someone talks to me about Sir Walter Scott, I mention AL Kennedy or Ali Smith' (cited by MacMahon, 2004 [penultimate paragraph]).

In similar vein, the advantage of combining the traditional and the modern was also used by other committee members to counter the views expressed by their fellow committee member above: 'We can certainly build on the traditional values of Scotland's image and augment them with an image of a modern Scotland and

---

[12]   www.scottish.parliament.uk/business/committees/europe/or-04/eu04-0502.htm   (col. 445).

[13]   http://en.wikipedia.org/wiki/Scottis_Cringe.

a knowledge-intensive economy'.[14] One participant related the experiences of a Scottish business in the USA:

> They told me that Burns suppers, kilts and whisky give them openings, but they have to offer the expertise and financial services that they have. We should not worry about people's perceptions of our natural characteristics; we just have to be clever and use them to our advantage.[15]

The use of the adjective 'natural' here is interesting, suggesting that drinking whisky and wearing kilts is, in some sense, inherently, naturally Scottish (although possibly this is a misreporting and what is meant is 'national'). A good example perhaps of the business exploitation of national heritage and culture is that of national 'Tartan Day' in Canada and the USA, officially recognised as April 6th in both countries (from 1991 in Canada and 1998 in the USA), after lobbying by various North American Scottish and Caledonian groups, to celebrate the Scottish heritage of many North Americans and their contribution to that continent. April 6th was chosen as this was the date of the Arbroath Declaration in 1320, when Scottish barons, as part of a coordinated, diplomatic response to Pope John XXII, stated the independence of Scotland under Robert I and their resistance to Edward II. From the seventeenth century when the document became more widely known, it was to 'become a classic expression of Scottish national identity, much reprinted and quoted' (Webster, 1997: 88-89). Although 'Tartan Day' is a North American construction, its economic and cultural potential is recognised by the Scottish Parliament, who established a Tartan Day cross-party group to discuss appropriate celebrations in Scotland and beyond. This is an example of how transnational concerns and the impetus of a diaspora can nurture national myth-making.

Clearly devolution has not affected the importance of national images and heritage in marketing Scotland the brand. But what about the effects of devolution on Scottish identity itself? Generally this question is posed and answered in relation to an alternative identity, that of Britishness. Bond and Rosie (2002) note, on the basis of data from 1992–2002, that there has been a consistent trend of increasing identification with Scottishness and weakening identification with Britishness in Scotland. Devolution has not caused the trend, but neither has it changed it. Figures from 2001 found that 36 per cent see themselves as 'Scottish not British', 30 per cent see themselves as 'more Scottish than British' and 24 per cent as 'equally Scottish and British'; very few see themselves as 'more British than Scottish' or 'British' (Bond and Rosie, 2002 [table 3]). Generally national and political identity are not confounded; the majority of those claiming 'Scottish not British' or 'more Scottish than British' identities in 2001 supported neither independence nor the Scottish Nationalist Party; 51 per cent and 65 per cent, respectively, supported neither of these options. (Bond and Rosie, 2002 [tables 7 and 8]). Political identification for

---

[14]   www.scottish.parliament.uk/business/committees/europe/or-04/eu04-0502.htm (col. 446).

[15]   *Ibid.*

other national categorisations are not given, but questions relating to support for the Scottish Parliament and increased powers for that institution indicate that a majority of those with equally Scottish and British identity favour devolution (63 per cent) and greater devolved powers (54 per cent) (Bond and Rosie, 2002 [Tables 13 and 14]).

Although the trend towards prioritising Scottish national identity over British pre-dates devolution, Bond and Rosie (2002 [paragraph 8]) suggest that 'It could be that we have entered a post-devolution period in which a consistently high, and perhaps growing, number of Scots will allow no room for Britishness in their own national identity'. An interesting question here is to what extent any exclusion of Britishness relates to anti-Englishness, bearing in mind that since medieval times Scottish identity–making has always been done in the shadow of the threat of the English 'other' (Kidd, 1999, Webster, 1997). There is some survey evidence to suggest that 'Scottishness' might exclude English roots. Data from the Scottish Social Attitudes Survey 2003 found that 54 per cent would not allow an English-born, permanent resident in Scotland to claim Scottishness; compare this to the 23 per cent who would not allow a non-White, Scottish resident with a Scottish accent to claim Scottishness (Bond and Rosie, n.d. [bullet points 16 and 17]). The significance of accent in relation to skin colour is noted by Bond and Rosie, but the significance of accent in relation to the English should similarly be heeded; it could be that part of being Scottish is sounding it. The CHE interview data, referred to above, does indicate that for some minority groups, a Scottish accent gives a sense of belonging, but the barrier caused by skin colour is seen by many as preventing acceptance, e.g. 'Having Scottish accents, you can be ordering something on the phone and when you give your name you can hear it in their voice, you realise that they thought they were talking to a white person' (responses to question 2). It should also be noted that dual, even triple, identities are commonly expressed by these individuals:

I am a Malaysian Indian and I live in Scotland, so I carry 3 identities and they change depending on where I am and what I am doing.

My identity is definitely Scottish, Pakistani and Muslim as well. That part is stronger because that is what I do every day. Pakistan is where my parents were born, Scotland is where I was born, but the Muslim part is strongest.

From the multicultural perspective, the historically-based, Scottish-British dichotomy or continuum as a dimension of identity has limited relevance. Indeed, it may be that Scottish identity will slowly be redefined or re-oriented not because of devolution, but because of immigration.

Conclusion

The role of global corporate culture in identity-making by state institutions is beyond doubt, at least on the basis of the relevant websites. These have more than an informational function; they construct what the '*citoyen*', and the 'you' should be interested in and expect from government; they position the '*citoyen*', and the 'you' in terms of active citizenship, an interaction between state institution and citizen, but with a greater degree of co-responsibility for the outcome in Wallonia than in Scotland. This difference may be a consequence of Wallonia's years of decline as an autonomous unit; in 20 years' time a devolved Scotland might too be constructing stakeholder citizens. The websites also create an organisational identity, including characteristics such as inclusive, interactional, accessible to all, educational, informative, job-provider, tourist attraction. This corporate identity is perhaps stronger in Scotland. Finally, the websites project a regional or national identity, one which is unified so as to provide a common reference point for the insider as well as the outsider. In both Wallonia and Scotland, aspects of this common identity are similar – dynamic, innovative, progressive etc. – suggesting that globalisation is having an effect on the nature of the rhetoric itself.

Of course, regionalisation or devolution plays no direct role here, apart from the obvious fact that without these processes, there would be no de-centralised governments and Parliaments. What we are seeing are the operation of wider political, cultural and commercial trends: state institutions of all types as organisations, hence students, patients, citizens, residents as customers and consumers; the increasing prevalence of e-governance; place branding where cities, regions, and countries are products, be these tourist or investment products, and where coats of arms are increasingly accompanied by logos. Devolved and federal powers give local Parliaments a greater freedom to act within these trends, to go glocal in the exercise of paradiplomacy and in the pursuit of economic and political success.

Chapter 10

'Dire Deeds Awake, Dark is it Eastward': Citizenship and Devolution, and the British National Party

David Irwin

Introduction

The British National Party (BNP) is the latest lineal descendant of the British nationalist movement that has emerged since the British Union of Fascists in pre-World War II Britain was succeeded by the Union Movement, then by a British National Party in 1960, which later became part of the National Front, which in turn led to the formation in 1982 of the current BNP. among its policies is repatriation of all illegal immigrants; concomitant with this is the introduction of a system of voluntary, financially-aided repatriation for existing, legally-settled immigrants, the repeal of all equalities legislation, and the withdrawal of the United Kingdom from the European Union and the pursuit of protectionist economic measures. Its existence seeks 'to secure a future for the indigenous peoples of these islands in the North Atlantic which have been our homeland for millennia'.[1] Of particular note is its contention that non-whites cannot be British. Therefore by using the term 'indigenous' it seeks to perpetuate an ideology that is mutually supported by a cultural heritage that complements continuities with 'people whose ancestors were the earliest settlers here after the last great Ice Age and which have been complemented by the historic migrations from mainland Europe'. The purpose of this chapter accordingly is to examine how BNP ideology of devolution is putatively constructed as an euphemism for nationalism and as a consequence how BNP ideology is incapable of locating its devolution within the republican and liberal paradigms necessary for devolution to be realised in the first place.

The BNP and Nationalism

The inclusion of Anglo-Saxons, Celts, Danes, and Norse who have all been 'instrumental in defining the character of our family of nations' realises a totalising

---

[1]   All unattributed quotes in this paper have been taken from the BNP website http://www.bnp.org.uk/.

thematic which underwrites history such that present circumstances are retrofitted to create its 'approved' history even though the continuities of reality which are perceived through a retrospective prism reveal a flimsy pedigree. This type of historical orthodoxy is in fact a strategic deployment of 'an approved public history as substitute for antiquity' (Boyce & O'Day 1996: 2). This orthodoxy actually obfuscates antagonism of 'approved' ethnic, cultural, and religious groups within the British Isles as the *raison d'être* of BNP ideology as a convenient shield against the existence of contemporary political structures in Britain which it perceives to be simultaneously pro-Islamic, pro-Zionist, and pro-Communist and therefore politically and civically unacceptable. Part of the reason for such orthodoxy can be attributed to racist and Eurosceptic tensions that constrain the BNP's ultramontanist view of Britain as England while at the same time accepting as co-equal other 'approved' races that inhabit these north western islands off the European 'mainland' only because of their capability to preserve Britain's Tolkienesque pastoralism from non-white interference.

No clearer picture of such irredentism can be presented as the BNP view of cultural education:

> We will introduce the requirement that all children will be taught English as their first language in Britain, but also learn about their local ancestral language as well. This will apply to Welsh, Cornish, Manx, Scots Gallic, Doric or Lallans in Great Britain, and Ulster Lallans and Gaelic in Northern Ireland. English children will also be given an appreciation of the language of the Anglo-Saxon folk and to appreciate the beauty of Anglo-Saxon culture, such as its poetry, art and the meaning of citizenship.

Such latent tensions particular to the BNP are in fact typical of 'right-wing' parties where there is no standard definition of nationalism. In terms of the BNP nationalism can be an ideology that makes reference to a 'nation', and not merely to a socio-religious type of group. Nationalism can also be considered as a system of ideas, values and norms, which enables a group to construct a worldview that has a particular currency and sense of 'domestic' identification that homogenises a group spatially. These nuances mean that nationalism for the BNP activates social cohesion and social solidarity by setting and arguably achieving and focusing on specific goals. Thus the characteristics of nationalism in general and with the BNP 'spin' in particular come to represent communal language, origins, character and culture that demand subordination either to a communal belief or to a particular type of state power. Thus devolution is merely a euphemism for monocultural state control in the name of the nation.

In its publications about cultural diversity, the BNP is against 'the arrival of huge numbers of outsiders in their territory – whether loggers in the Amazon jungle or Third World settlers in Europe'. Yet its apparent accommodation of approved races within the British Isles presents similar challenges because its conditional equality is cultural appreciation and based on the *seigneural* model of feudalism which privileges Anglo-Saxon culture and in particular the English language. That the Anglo-Saxons did not speak English is a point lost on the BNP!

Associated with this rationale which privileges as central Anglo-Saxon culture in general and English in particular is a belief that the natural resistance of all native peoples must cease to be demonised as 'racism' and understood as a natural and laudable survival mechanism. Ultimately, this means that 'we, as the sole political representatives of the Silent Majority of the English, Scots, Irish and Welsh who formed and were formed by our island home, have one overriding demand: We want our country back!'. Interestingly Scandinavian, Norman, Gallic and Hispanic influences are tolerated in so far as they are historical inevitabilities within the acceptable cartography of BNP *lebensraum*.

Alter (1985: 4–5) professes a definition of nationalism as neither a status group, 'nor religious conviction, nor a dynasty or a particularistic state, nor a physical landscape, nor genealogical roots, not even social class which determine the supra-individual frame of reference'. This dismissal is based on the assumed fact that there is a corollary between historical and cultural heritage and particular forms of political life. Weber (1978), on the other hand, suggests that nationalism constitutes itself as language, culture, historical consciousness, mores, social communication, religion and political goals which endow an individual's historical, cultural heritage, and political forms with meaning. In effect, nationalism can be defined as operating between the interstice of loyalty and attachment to a supra-individual sense of belonging to a nation, and of identification based on a temporal association of common culture and consciousness. In reality, such a definition in the context of the British National Party is problematic because nationalism is used interchangeably with irredentist neo-republicanism. In other words, the BNP's worldview signifies a state in which sovereignty resides in the people first and then in the administration by elected officers representing the people. This means that government is a necessary centralising and normalising force from which assent is given by the periphery of approved nations (i.e. Scots, Welsh, English, and Irish). Under such a Weberian model neither regionalism nor devolution can occur.

According to the BNP worldview, the state is a historically evolved territory and approved nationality is the fundamental basis of citizenship such that the political nation is composed of 'politically aware citizens equal before the law irrespective of their social and economic status, ethnic origin and religious beliefs' (Alter, 1985: 9). Such a distinction in the current dominant context of civil society means that nationality is a counter-paradigm where nationality is a 'social group which regards itself as an ethnic minority within a given state and desires no more than respect as a separate community' (*ibid.* 11). This means that although citizens seek to exercise cultural and political autonomy within the state, they do so not on 'their' terms but simply because this is the manner in which civil society engages with political power. Justification for this argument is based on the simple assumption that nationality can be equated with citizenship on the grounds that it demands an engagement with theories of the state; in particular, the state's prerogative to form structures of governance. From its perspective the BNP views the restoration of democracy to support 'the right of all free-born Britons to debate in public the facts as they see them by restoring true freedom of speech to Britain'. Such democracy has as its foundation the ethnic and civic undertone that those who inhabit the British Isles are 'genetically pre-determined ... [*sic.* to] shape our culture around such institutions, and in turn tend to be reinforced by that culture'.

The BNP and the Concept of Civil Society

Of particular concern for the BNP are the rules of civil society which underpin 'the space of un-coerced human association' which exist through such relational networks as family, ideology, gender and ethnicity in order to support the validity of economic relations as the nexus of a discourse of civic pluralism (Walzer 1992: 89). In its view 'we are all the same under the skin' is an unsustainable myth as is the equally refutable 'egalitarian claim that everyone within a given population is born as a blank slate with the same innate potential'. In addition, the constraint imposed by international agreements and the consequences of the universalistic discourses of political space require consideration as they subordinate conventional notions of ethnicity and kinship. Turner's (1992) critique of Michael Mann's (1987) 'ruling-class strategy' is important in this regard because it argues against the idea that rights are commodities that are handed down in such a manner as to bring about 'some degree of amelioration of social conflict and which is therefore a major contribution to social integration' (Turner, 1992: 44). Mann's view of citizenship does not actually engage in such an analysis of citizenship as a site of contestation over resources. Nonetheless, the contention of 'ruling-class strategy' as far as notions of citizenship are concerned is between Mann's thesis of the award of rights in exchange for pragmatic co-operation, and Turner's valorisation of Frederick Engels' view of rights as 'the outcome of radical struggle by subordinate groups for benefits' (*ibid.* 45). By conflating the top-down hierarchy of Mann with the bottom-up paradigm proposed by Engels it is clear that citizenship can be deemed to operate in both public and private spheres with radical implications for each sphere.

For instance, the revolutionary context of citizenship in the public sphere in the bottom-up paradigm invariably collapses into a form of totalitarianism in the name of the people. Similarly in the context of liberal pluralism, bottom-up hierarchies promote the right to privatised dissent on the grounds that social participation is registered against, and on the basis of, particular interests of particular socio-political groupings. By contrast, the top-down paradigm places the citizen as a subject 'rather than an active bearer of effective claims against society via the state' (*ibid.* 46). This means that the citizen passively accepts as legitimate the operation of state institutions without establishing reasons to continue the struggle against the state for further as yet unarticulated rights. The extent of societal regulation that is promulgated by such passive assent leads to 'plebiscitary authoritarianism' with the consequence that the citizen elects representatives who are effectively shielded from the electorate by the bureaucracy of representative institutions (*ibid.* 45).

From the BNP perspective Mann's 'ruling class strategy' recognises pragmatic co-operation as acceptance that 'unapproved' minorities must be law-abiding in order 'to remain here and to enjoy the full protection of the law against any form of harassment or hostility' and secondary to 'the importance of the prior status of the aboriginal people'. Furthermore, the BNP recognises as intellectual fantasy that there is any 'deeply ingrained human need to belong and to identify with people with whom one shares special things in common' while consequently holding to the view that the only genuine nation-state is one that is racially pure. This translates as the endorsement of a racially aware political establishment that inculcates among its citizens the realisation that a genuine nation-state is one where it is the duty of the elite 'to mind their own nation's business and look after their own people'. Since such centralisation cannot permit nor legislate for decentralisation (*sic*. devolution) the only locus of control that is rational for the BNP is one located at the centre. To explain this contradiction it is important to differentiate between competing forms of citizenship, the requirements of such citizenship, and the relationship between citizen and state.

Turner proposes a model that addresses this contestation through an analysis of citizen, state and government that is less obviously influenced by Marxist concerns over strategies of domination and subordination. In their place he promotes a comparison between the passive-active forms of citizenship and the concept of public-private space. The passive-active forms are broadly similar to the domination and subordination paradigm of class as they rely on opposing positions of regent-vassal and of the aggregate of citizenry to apportion passive and active roles based on their momentum within top-down and bottom-up paradigms. Alternatively, the concept of public and private space deals with tensions between constitutionalism and absolutism. The achievement of constitutionalism, for instance, signifies a degree of active citizenship resting on an agreement of what constitutes a national entity that is based upon two opposing forms. One form is based on the Rousseauian contention that institutions exist by selective de-centralisation so as to promote the integration of citizen with the state. The other form is based on the Burkean essence of citizenship as the continuity of centralising hierarchical groups. This form is absolutist in so far as the groups are spatially and functionally associated on the basis of local through regional and finally national orders. Neither the Rousseauian nor Burkean views are mutually exclusive when registered against BNP ideology as both contentions find complementary expression in its Euroscepticism. The BNP regards the European Union as an anachronism, rejecting the union as facile and as an unnecessary encroachment on the superior hierarchy of British traditions and institutions.

By recasting the Rousseauian and Burkean contentions as signifying technologies of governance, paying excessive homage to the past can now be recast in terms of a communitarian understanding of citizenship as moral agency. In the contemporary sense of history, Walzer argues that Rousseauian idealism presumes that citizenship legitimises itself with reference to the historical rubrics of the historical past. According to this understanding, BNP style nationalism or neo-republicanism is little more than a simplistic world-view that is presented as a counter-measure to the perceived levels of dissonance and fragmentation in modern society. Such a view means that the exercise of power is designed to produce an understanding of the world by constituting both knowledge and discourse as objects for socio-political and scientific study. The effect of this process explicitly removes the necessary subversive space of political awareness and agency from the people and renders civil society as a programmable object of government by Government. Towards this goal is BNP ideology propelled.

This interpretation is certainly consistent with a reductionist view of BNP ideology as incapable of accommodating the citizen as a member of a wider political community even though it demands of its supporters an articulation of what constitutes the common good for the politicised community. Thus the promotion of communitarianism as a central feature of a BNP neo-republican discourse of civil society is chimerical because it misleads the citizen to mis-articulate the nature and extent of what constitutes the public sphere of political action in the first place. In this context, devolution and centralisation are floating signifiers that can only be relied upon to mean what each does according to what the BNP wants it to mean. This process of mis-articulation by the BNP as to what constitutes the common good necessarily reveals competing hierarchies between various socio-economic and ethno-cultural, and politically aware and able groups within society, which can only be accommodated within a homogenised nation – itself a floating signifier. As a result the parameters of the common good within civil society can only be resolved through the challenge and arbitration presented by the technologies of state power.

Walzer suggests that civil society is capable of challenging state power. However, it can be argued that society's status as a site of contestation is unsustainable because the site of struggle is not concerned with the plurality of sectional groups but with the localisation of the private sphere occupied by these groups. In other words, the issue becomes one of state incorporation of the public sphere as a form of corporate citizenship from the periphery (*sic.* devolution or any other form of decentralisation) to the centre. For the BNP this means returning 'power to the men and women of Britain, the taxpayers, pensioners, mums and dads and workers, and [removing] it from the unelected commissioners in Europe'. It means providing 'a safe environment for all, where there is freedom from fear of crime, freedom from repression of the State, freedom of association and freedom of speech'. Typically this means that localisation is merely a standard that restores 'honesty, integrity and transparency … to civic and public institutions'.

Ironically, the BNP's perpetuation of floating signifiers to fix its ideology itself becomes a challenge to civil society to challenge the hegemony of state power by deploying, in name but not in fact, socio-economic, ethno-political and cultural-historical alliances to refute the nihilism of state power. For the BNP to avoid nihilistic inertia associated with such a reading of state power it contends that civil society's only response to the singularity of state power is the decentralisation of the state, the socialisation of the economy, and the localisation of nationalism as a centre it defines. Thus BNP power needs to work with political power in order 'to underwrite and subsidize the most desirable associational activities' (Walzer, 1992:106).

Preferring to privilege ideas about micro-dependencies as transformations of political mobilisation – in its broadest sense – Walzer endeavours to give back to associated networks of groups a degree of political agency that superscribes the organising strategies and historical guarantees provided by state action. Thus the devolution or decentralisation of the state is proffered as a representation of micro dependency 'so that there are more opportunities for citizens to take responsibility for (some of) its activities' (*ibid.* 106). His socialisation of the economy is designed to promote 'greater diversity of market agents' (*ibid.* 106). And his strategy to pluralise nationalism centres on ways to realise and accommodate contrasting historical identities simultaneously. This is more especially so where BNP support seeks to harness antithetical sentiment among privileged network-associations of citizens to the expulsion and exclusion of others as far as dominant modes of civic responsibility are imposed because of the degree to which their reluctance and/or unwillingness to reconfigure their codes, status and identities is based on the problematic of the diminution and perceived loss of their power.

The BNP Relationship with Republicanism and Liberalism

In his text *The Wretched of the Earth* (1990), Frantz Fanon calls for the history of decolonisation to replace the history of colonisation. The linear progression Fanon sees taking place situates the nation at the apex of struggle, and as something superseding processes of colonisation and nationalism. Colin Graham (1994) also endorses such an evolution, and in order to justify this he suggests that the Gramscian idea of subaltern groups align with minorities and marginalised groups to provide an epistemic historiography wherein the minority group is cast in a predetermined manner in time to play a central role in the 'ethically-embedded nation-narrative' (Graham, 1994: 31). It can be argued that the broad socio-economic ultramontanist consensus that the BNP endorses merely reflects a hegemonised nationalism that is conceptually conditioned to imitate the coloniser the more anti-imperial it becomes. This idea partially explains the BNP's 'ethical idolatry' of segregation, insularity and self-containment as fixed points to maintain the moral and political triumph of BNP 'nationalism' in the face of colonial and post-colonial realities.

Ironically, Graham suggests that subalternism supplants ideological nationalism and replaces it with neo-Marxist commitments 'to groups oppressed by the workings of nationalism' (*ibid.* 36). In this regard he endorses a sentiment articulated by Professor Seamus Deane though paraphrased in this current paper to the effect 'that … [*sic.*] British … nationalism, without the pernicious influence of Britain, would have been liberating' (*ibid.* 3637)! Therefore, the removal of nationalism replaces the methodological assumption of historical continuity and the binary effect of blame-innocence as the motivational force behind the need to differentiate difference. With the removal of nationalism, the concept of 'the nation' loses its effectiveness as a force for constraint and embraces a plurality of historiography: not simply as histories but as unmasked cross-colonial phenomena of nationalities and nations. To this conclusion the BNP has no alternative.

An idea of citizenship based on the idea of public good as the superordinating principle over individual and sectional interest has provided a working model for republican and liberal social critiques. The qualified use by the BNP of republicanism to the exclusion of other communities reveals what Mouffe (1992) argues as the substantial difference between civic republicanism and liberal democracy where the latter is representative of a view that 'a modern democratic political community cannot be organized around a single substantive idea of the common good' (Mouffe, 1992: 227). This clearly presents interpretative difficulties because republicanism is coercive and totalitarian in its utilisation of a substantive idea of the common good. According to Berlin (1969:122), 'coercion implies the deliberate interference of other human beings within the area in which I could otherwise act'. By analogy critics of civic republicanism's valorisation of the common good stress that participatory citizenship should not be at the expense of sublimating individual liberty.

Skinner (1990), alternatively, sees no difficulty in conflating political participation along liberal lines of individual liberty with civic republicanism. According to Skinner 'the attainment of our fullest liberty, in short, presupposes our recognition of the fact that only certain determinate ends are rational for us to pursue' (Skinner, 1992: 295). To this end, the BNP would take Britain out of the North Atlantic Treaty Organisation (NATO), increase national defence spending, increase reliance on 'home-grown' organic produce, repatriate 'foreigners', discontinue relief to the Third World, and reduce unemployment and disability benefits. This means that coercion and constraint would be inherently necessary to force the ideas of individual and societal liberty as essentially similar and dependent on the forum of public service so that the rights of the individual citizen can be achieved through political participation as a citizen.

Participation as a citizen in the republican sense presupposes an engagement in the public space of political action. The public sphere signifies a context wherein political action occurs and actualises the principles of political inquiry based on formalised political rights of freedom and exchange. However, while the extent of active participation presupposes a willing degree of agency on the part of the citizen, it is by no manner certain that citizens willingly engage in the public sphere of political action. Therefore, the presence of political parties is indicative of the manner in which citizens order the public sphere first and foremost through network associations. These associations in turn create 'a linkage among the participants in the association, allowing us to speak of a political "community"' (Mouffe, 1992:231). In republican terms, this community then establishes the link between active citizenship and effective political agency and articulates the sublimation of individual liberty within the paradigm of the common good.

If liberalism is particularly preoccupied with the state's requirement to provide the liberating space for the pacified individual to enjoy private state-sponsored rights, then the articulating principle of republicanism is necessarily universal since it articulates a public conception of citizenship. Republicanism as a public space therefore establishes a form of collective identity, which can then engage and interpret the degrees of struggle and social solidarity among network associations. Clearly, the formulation of norms and values permits the conception of participatory citizenship that circumvents the *sine qua non* of liberal values accorded to homogeneity of political representation.

Taylor (1989:170) argues that such action in the context of a republican regime demands a differentiation between 'common as against convergent goods' in order to situate the ordering objectivity of discourse to locate the 'we-identities as against convergent I-identities'. In other words, citizenship is not considered as simply reducible to either territorial identification or the individual liberty of the citizen – where individual agency is presumed to affect the consequences of participatory self-government. Rather the emphasis is now on the extent to which patriotism can be redefined to provide the necessary space for citizens to register their status as citizens through participatory and common action. Such a thesis does not acknowledge as valid a potential liberal riposte of republicanism in favour of a thesis of citizenship as grounded in self-enlightened motivation. A fundamental criticism of this liberal conception of citizenship is the fact that it promotes the idea of electoral democracy which then creates agencies of governance so as to frame rights for citizens who can themselves withdraw as active citizens because the state now regulates their civic identities.

Conclusion

The type of devolution enunciated by the BNP is as a system of formation not primarily concerned with the status of devolution as a means of either political autonomy or regional and cultural identity. Instead its focus is on the extent to which a society can attain a degree of devolved social freedom conditional upon the allegiance of the individual as citizen to the centralised idea of homogeneous nation. That the BNP is neither liberal nor republican can be demonstrated in two ways. First any attempt to re-align this status of the individual within a paradigm of common good tends to fracture on the degree of participation of the citizen as a citizen in government. This fracturing occurs because of liberalism's advocacy of the participatory status of the individual citizen without such participation being interpreted as personalism and party-political clientelism. In the BNP world-view notions of common good merely signify what is good for England first and what is good for the regions is secondary. From the republican perspective the extent of personalism and clientelism as inherent features of network associations are selectively evident in the BNP link with the self-styled paramilitary grouping Combat 18.

The extent of BNP commitment to devolution is an empty rallying cry for those disaffected with central government and those excluded from social advantage. This is clearly demonstrable in its political *credo* to:

give the British people, that choice, and thus to restore and defend the basic democratic rights we have all been denied. We favour more democracy, not less, not just at national but at regional and local level. Power should be devolved to the lowest level possible so that local communities can make decisions which affect them. We will remove legal curbs on freedom of speech imposed by successive Governments over the last 40 years. We will implement a Bill of Rights guaranteeing fundamental freedoms to the British people. We will ensure that ordinary British people have real democratic power over their own lives and that Government, local and national, is truly accountable to the people who elect it.

From such ideology the BNP has spawned a worldview that empowers through disenfranchisement and is not without allegorical significance with the result that its policies read as if from the self-comforting reassurance of J.R.R. Tolkien's *The Lord of the Rings* in so far as the BNP is the hero of its own fiction and its self-sufficient pastoralism is a literal transposition from Tolkien's epic text. However, unlike Tolkien's text, the BNP's political ideology has halted at Tolkien's penultimate chapter, 'The Scouring of the Shire'. Republicans can only hope that Tolkien's last chapter, 'The Grey Havens', will be in time a fitting epitaph for the BNP because it has scoured and misused republicanism to legitimise its failed irredentist policies of racial, cultural and political exclusivity through a discourse of meaningless devolution.

Epilogue

In the Context of Devolution

Gerry Philipsen

In the winter of 1966, I made my first and longest (ten weeks) visit to England, Scotland, Wales, Northern Ireland, and the Republic of Ireland. The circumstance was a tour of twenty-six universities to participate in debates in students' unions, as a member of the two-person *US International Debate Team*. Among the many remarkable experiences of that tour was the debate in the superb debating chamber at Glasgow University, where the main speakers were seated facing each other on two sides of the hall, assigned to sit with the political parties with which they affiliated – Conservative, Labour, Liberal, and so forth. It was the 'so forth' that continues to come back to me, vividly, after all these years: My preparatory study of Politics in Britain, prior to embarking on the tour, had not prepared me to anticipate or appreciate the Scottish National Party, but there it was, with its place at the table and its turn to speak, and speak its members did.

Of course, I had read about Scottish nationalism, its history and contemporaneous presence, but to meet and hear real live proponents of it, and quite serious they were, was something that even then, after a month of debating in England, surprised me. As an American, whose view of his own country was that it had settled the matter of union and disunion a hundred years before (a very long time, as an American would reckon it), it struck me as remarkable that here in this united kingdom were people who could and did take the floor right there in something modelled after the kingdom's House of Commons, and speak in the name of disunion. I will never forget the Scottish National Party's main speaker for his passion and his eloquence in the service of what I assumed to be a lost cause.

The memory of that speaker was in my mind as I read through this volume of essays about devolution in the contemporary United Kingdom. Specifically, my memory of him was refreshed as I read such expressions, as are found in this volume, as 'under devolution' and 'in the context of devolution'. The last of those expressions is taken from Sharon Millar's chapter and I have taken it as the title of this epilogue. The principal theme that I will address in the epilogue concerns that expression, what it stands for, and how what it stands for has and has not been addressed in the parts and the whole of this volume of highly informative studies. What does it mean to say 'in the context of devolution'? What counts as something that is what it is, at least in part, by virtue of some one or more acts of devolution that precede, accompany, enable, or help to explain it? Was the SNP speaker in the Glasgow debate not speaking 'in the context of devolution', that is, was his act of speaking not part of a movement that could be described as devolutionary, and could we not go back many more than forty years ago to find other examples with which to put the question?

The editors have set forth a clear idea as to what they mean by devolution and as to what they intend in assembling a collection of essays on its present significance, and in so doing they provide one way of saying what the context of devolution is. They mean by devolution the program set out in 1997 by the Labour Government in terms of laws and policies. Specifically, they mention as acts of devolution (1) the transfer of power to a subordinate elected body, (2) the transfer of power on a geographical basis, and (3) the transfer of functions that at present are exercised by a central legislative body, in this case the British Parliament. Such transfers are manifested in specific laws and policies that can be named and dated, and in the deletion of certain functions at the level of the central authority and the establishment of those functions at a newly created regional assembly or parliament. It is such laws, policies, and concrete transfers of function that establish, for the editors, a context of devolution. It is thus explicit, public, materialised, and dated, as of 1997 or later. Presumably, these acts of devolution constitute a context or background against which to set events that followed.

The question the editors ask about devolution, as they have defined it, is what consequences devolution has had and will have for the construction and reconstruction of national forms of identity in the UK countries. The editors are concerned with what they refer to as the 'impact' of constitutional transformations on issues of personal and group identity in and across the respective regions concerned. Where others have examined devolution in terms of law, politics, and economics, looking at its effects from a macro perspective, the editors have explicitly encouraged attention to meanings, expressed in everyday personal interactions, with attention given to the views and opinions of the individuals who are presumably experiencing the effects of devolution in their everyday social life. And the editors express a special concern with how, in this post-devolution era, Britishness fares in everyday interaction among persons. This sets out a clear mission for the volume: To look into everyday social life, and the interactions that comprise it, for evidence of effects of nameable, datable acts of a national government, on identity constructions by particular people, and with special reference to the place of Britishness in those constructions. To put it simply, if too crudely, now that several devolutionary acts have been passed and implemented, how do people in the devolved, or devolving, countries think differently about themselves, or express themselves differently, in terms of their identification with Britishness?

The editors present ten studies here that, taken together, provide insight into a great variety of topics, and that spread across all of the four regions or countries and, indeed, beyond, to the Republic of Ireland and to Wallonia. There was no apparent template or common methodology guiding the production or selection of these studies, except perhaps a combination of the availability of useful work and a commitment to variety in regional emphasis and domains of everyday life. In any case, there is regional balance in the inclusion of cases and there is a varied approach across the cases, although there is a definite advantage given to observations of and statements made by people who are experiencing the world of post-devolution and there is some privileging of those peoples' own words, freely spoken or written, as an object of analysis.

Given that the particular question the editors asked about devolution (its impacts on identity construction and meaning, in the everyday lives of people, and in relation to the identity category of Britishness), I think the regional, topical, and methodological variety is fortunate; the subject is too complex, and too understudied, to try to accommodate it with even a very sophisticated format that is highly pre-determined. A closed-question survey that drew out information, across the regions, pre- and post-devolution, and that deals with a variety of social, economic, and political topics might yield something of value, but my hunch is that most of the knowledge that would be needed even to construct such surveys would have to be found through such rich, qualitatively-focused cases as we have here. And to my tastes, I appreciate the fact that these essays were written by scholars who are, so to speak, on the ground, writing from the countries of interest here. Nonetheless, this nuanced, open, and varied approach, yielding as it has such a variety of types of results, suggests three issues that bear discussion, and in this essay I hope to suggest some bases for such a discussion that are suggested by these ten studies. It is their variety, in large part, that has evoked in me the question that I address here of how the various studies, singly and taken together, address the context of devolution, in terms of the construction of identities in everyday life.

The editors have set up this volume with an eye to a particular set of constitutional transformations that occurred very recently, that is, the constitutional transformations that were implemented ca 1997. As with any study of change, it is important to pay attention to temporal markers, and therefore I ask about the precision with which the present studies locate and observe change. That is, *how, if at all, do these studies show a clear linkage between the constitutional transformations in question and everyday life, with particular reference to the time-ordering of devolutionary acts and identity expressions that presumably follow (from) them?*

The ten studies in this volume vary as to whether, and if so to what degree, they ask a question grounded in a clear linkage between concrete, recent devolutionary activity and changes in identity construction in everyday life. Some acknowledge explicitly the recent, formalised acts of devolution and then observe putative impacts of them. For example, John Wilson and Karyn Stapleton suggest that recent legislation provides official recognition and financial support to activities associated with the Ulster Scots movement, although they do not specify which pieces of legislation to which they refer or just how the legislation does what they claim it does.

Nikolas Coupland and Hywel Bishop examine critically some discourse about language policy that was issued from the newly established National Assembly for Wales (and they examine some other discourse as well that seems to originate from a source that was not created through the auspices of formal devolutionary acts). The writers of letters to the editor whom Richard Fitzgerald and William Housley quote in their essay make reference to the creation of the National Assembly for Wales.

Dominic Bryan starts with specific governmental decisions by the Northern Ireland Assembly, with special reference to the display of national flags and emblems, and then he describes and assesses the vagaries of implementing those decisions. Carol Ann Barnes and Arthur Aughey examine the efforts to commemorate, or not, in Northern Ireland, the bicentennial of the Act of Union of Great Britain and Ireland, with special reference to how the Belfast Agreement of 1998 influenced those efforts. Carmel Roulston concerns herself with the creation in three countries – Northern Ireland, Scotland, and Wales – of processes for establishing devolved institutions and what follows from those processes, with special reference to campaigns for affecting the gender distribution of participation in these processes.

Thus, with the studies mentioned in the preceding paragraph there is a relatively straightforward design: the author or authors locate some concrete aspect of devolution per se and then examine how it was responded to or taken up by one or more people or groups. The logic of inference is not so simple as to say, this is what happened after 1997, therefore we can observe an 'impact' of devolution; rather in most cases the authors point to some specific structural change that provided some particular moment or space in which to respond, and/or some changed circumstance to which to respond. For example, in 'Engendering Devolution' Carol Roulston shows that the establishment of new governmental bodies and functions at the regional level, in Northern Ireland, Scotland, and Wales – that is, devolution as the editors define it – provided a moment in which (1) regional preparation for deliberation about the process of devolution was begun and then there was (2) regional voting as to policies and of elected officials for newly created governmental bodies. These moments provided opportunities, in each of the three countries, to create new institutions based on 'a fairer distribution of political power and influence between men and women' than had been achieved in pre-devolution regional politics, and this created what Roulston refers to as 'new "discursive spaces"' in which to campaign for, negotiate, and, in some cases establish, such a new distribution of power and influence between men and women.

To have specific, datable actions, such as referred to in the previous two paragraphs, that people then use as a resource for participating in subsequent activities, provides an opportunity to search for what the editors refer to as the impact of such actions and to link those impacts to the actions themselves. That many of the studies in this volume do not make reference to a concrete, observable change in structural conditions as a precursor to changes in identity construction does not, however, mean they are not pertinent to the aims of the volume. All of the impacts of devolution, whether traceable to specific devolutionary actions or not, take place in a larger social and historical context. And this wider and longer set of influences surely animates the uptake of specific devolutionary actions in any given case.

Studies not tied directly to a specific devolutionary action presumably can have their own rationale in the larger project of understanding devolution. For example, Susan Condor and Jackie Abell provide highly nuanced, data-based examinations of how some Scottish and English people conceptualise their sense of their own and others' national identities; the constructions that Condor and Abell's study report suggest what differences in self-construal in relation to national identity might look like across two different countries; and if there is to be an eventual systematic body of knowledge about the impact of devolution on national identities and their meanings to those who experience them, it will of necessity be built with the type of data that Condor and Abell provide. Presumably, the complex identity constructions that Condor and Abell have been able to tease out of respondent discourse have their source in something that pre-dates devolution *per se*, something that is attested to by the words of their respondents, such as when they speak about people of generations past.

William Housley's study of Welsh artists and artists in Wales, and the discourse about art in Welsh cultural life that some artists in Wales expressed to Housley, provide important clues to a source of identity that might inform and reflect devolutionary processes even if all such activity is not directly traceable, or immediately traceable, to legislative changes. Certainly Housley has put his finger on a phenomenon that is of potential importance to the identity of Welsh people. The image that one of his respondents paints, as it were, of busloads of Welsh schoolchildren being brought to Cardiff to visit the National Museum to see a permanent collection of Welsh artists, suggests a possibility for identity construction among Welsh schoolchildren, who would, presumably, through the creation of such a venue, experience themselves experiencing Welsh art in a way that they otherwise might not do. If the specific activities of governmental devolution in Wales to date have not evoked the sort of campaigns that women's organisations have organised in Northern Ireland, Scotland, and Wales to achieve more inclusive representation in the political process, nonetheless devolution provides the possibility of seeing windows of opportunity that were not previously present or present in the same way. Housley's study identifies possibilities, even if possibilities unrealised, for opening such windows.

Sharon Millar's study of regional government web-pages in Scotland and Wallonia does not mention devolution per se, but by going outside the devolutionary frame it introduces a dimension, global-local, that might be just as important as, or more-so than, the dimension regional-national, in understanding the forces at work in a particular society as they impact on identity, particularly national identity. And David Irwin's study examines a campaign that, if successful, would have an enormous devolutionary effect on England; this campaign and the possibilities it evokes are an important data point in the larger conversation about devolution and identity in England – and elsewhere. And it is an important resource in case some of the people Irwin quotes turn out to be right, in their warnings that the movement could catch fire; if those warnings are right, the movement should be watched carefully.

What is at stake here? The authors themselves, each in their own way, invoke some sort of explanatory mechanism – some loose connection between, say, the acts of devolution commended in 1997, mediated, to be sure, by the uptake made of them by people with agency. But in addition to devolution as an explanatory mechanism, some authors invoke history and yet others the determination and pluck of individuals. Carmel Roulston illustrates nicely what I mean here. She shows how efforts to effect participation by women in the deliberative processes of setting up and realising devolution varied across three countries, with Northern Ireland showing less success than either Scotland or Wales, and she explains this difference in the concluding words of her essay: 'In the final analysis, it was women's willingness to take the chance, to demand fair and equal participation in determining the future of their countries that made the difference'. Her explanation is plausible enough, given the account she gives of the process in the three countries, and as an American I have a soft spot for explanations that emphasise the importance of individual initiative. But if we juxtapose Roulston's carefully grounded empirical account to, say, Dominic Bryan's equally nuanced and well-grounded account of how decisions about the flying of flags and the display of emblems can be fraught with difficulties owing to the multiplicity of historical meanings of symbols and the weight of history in affecting how people negotiate the display of symbols, we find a case where historical forces might explain, at least in part, why it was so difficult, in the situations that Bryan describes, to implement the ideals of new policies designed to help work through historical differences, regardless of how much pluck and persistence there might be. The point is that it might not always be individual effort, or the effort to communicate, that explains matters, and it might not always be the structural tools that devolution provides that explains matters. There are other factors at work and to understand any particular local situation requires sorting out the force of these various factors.

Given the orientation to everyday constructions of identity that is the special concern of this volume, it should be no surprise to find that the words of individual people, as they have spoken and written them, have been quoted here extensively and have been taken seriously by the authors who have quoted them. It is in such words that people are likely to express the sense they have of their lives in terms of national, group, and personal identities, and the volume is, in this regard, a rich resource. For someone who reads these words at far remove, there is the sense of overhearing a conversation that is laced with identity expression and construction that could not have been imagined, only experienced. These are indelible discursive fragments that give one powerful word pictures of some of the fine details of identity construction in the context of a devolved United Kingdom.

Having read each chapter, and paid special attention to the words recorded, transcribed, and quoted, I became curious as to whether and how these words provided evidence that the speakers or writers of them were in some way orienting to devolution. That is, *did these speakers and writers, whom the chapter authors have quoted, manifest in some way, in their situated talk and text, that they were orienting to the devolutionary process that was initiated ca 1997?* Some individual speakers and writers who are quoted in this volume do use the word 'devolution' or the words 'Assembly' (as in 'Northern Ireland Assembly' or 'National Assembly for Wales') or 'Parliament' (as in 'Scottish Parliament'). But these words appear very rarely, indeed hardly at all, in the quoted passages. Furthermore, they appear, where they do, chiefly in quotations drawn from government, official, or collective sources (e.g., in an anonymous newspaper editorial or an Assembly or Council pronouncement). Perhaps even more noteworthy, they appear rarely even in the words of the authors of the volume's chapters, although less rarely there than in the words of others that the authors quote or re-present.

If the people whose words have been quoted as evidence of how devolution has had an impact on their daily lives, and in particular on their sense of identity in relation to 'Britishness', themselves had used such words as 'devolution', 'assembly' or 'parliament', that would provide, prima facie, a discursive place to look for evidence that these speakers or writers were orienting to devolution as the editors have defined it here. This would be one concrete way to suggest that a particular utterance is in some way responsive to the events from 1997 forward, as opposed to being only, or primarily, part of the long-standing conversation of which the student speaker from the SNP in the Glasgow Debates Union in 1966 was one participant. Having found such discursive places, places that in some way could be tied to 1997 onward, one could then look there to find evidence that the speaker or writer was also commenting on their personal, social, or collective identity in relation to some aspect of the recent devolution activities. Collocations and the like would provide such fortunate data points, from which arguments and interpretations could be made about the 'impact' of 'devolution' in terms of its meaning to those who have commented about it.

In the absence of quotations of research participants themselves using such words as 'devolution' and 'assembly', we do have in this volume a nonetheless rich array of discursive material. For example, there is the Ulster Scots man who, reflecting on the decisions he had to make about how to state his national identity, while filling out a British passport, complained that there was a tick box for British-Irish, but that that configuration was unacceptable to him, because he considers himself to be of a particular strain of British and expresses opposition to the Irish. He does not want to choose from among the available options: British-English, British-Welsh, British-Scottish, or British-Welsh. He wants, rather, a tick box for Ulster Scots.

Fitzgerald and Housley make a similar comment about the elision of Welsh identity within the census form as one that is grounded within a systematic historical process characterised by the relentless subjugation of Welsh to British identity. There is the Scottish woman quoted in Condor and Abell's chapter who sharply defines her own people in highly appreciative terms, identifies herself with those of her own Scottish nationality, characterises the English as having no culture, and constructs very nuanced accounts of the essences and differences she observes, formulating them in terms of psychological and not only social difference. In the same chapter there is the English woman who expresses a strong sense of Englishness as opposed to Britishness and who, moments after making that distinction, expresses disavowal at any pride in being English, although the disavowal might be part of the rhetoric of Englishness and not something to be taken at face value.

The artist in Wales, whose words Housley reports and examines, and who declares that he is perhaps the only artist he knows of who paints 'in Welsh' provides yet another unforgettable example of identity construction linked to a devolved country. And there is the Northern Ireland man or woman who, Barnes and Aughey report, upon leaving the exhibition commemorating the bicentenary of the Act of Union of Great Britain and Ireland, leaves behind a comment card with the words on it, 'Crap, this is Free Ireland'. These utterances and snippets of conversation speak volumes about the ways in which contemporary respondents do and do not express their identification with Britishness and, taken together, they suggest the regional differences in just how these matters of identification get taken up.

Nonetheless, we are left with the contextual question again, are the various identity expressions such as are to be found reproduced in this volume, even with all their subtlety and power to evoke allegiance to one or another region as opposed to an encompassing 'Britain' or 'Britishness' (a word used by the English respondent quoted above), expressions that owe something, as it were, to concrete acts of devolution or are these simply part of the ongoing lives of the people who produced them, lives affected by history so much that the actions taking place at the level of government play little role in contemporary expressions of identity? How far back can one go to hear these expressions as echoes, fantastic or otherwise? I found it difficult to tease out the influence of recent devolutionary actions, as opposed to the hands of history, in the identity constructions so made and expressed in the respondent talk and text. These words that were quoted in the chapters of this volume, and then displayed again in the preceding paragraph, might not all be directly traceable to specific acts of devolution. However, they do seem to me themselves to constitute what may be thought of as the context of devolution, that is, poignant indicators of a present reality, a context that itself is constituted discursively.

How has Britishness fared in the context of devolution? One way to answer this question is through a small exercise in the analysis of the appearance of the word 'Britishness' in the quoted speech, reproduced in this volume, of speakers who identify themselves in terms of, or who distance themselves from, the term 'Britishness'. If, as an exercise in how one might go about answering the question in this way, we take all such instances as can be found in the present volume, we find there are three. One is taken from the transcribed speech of a man from Northern Ireland who identifies himself as 'British' and 'Ulster Scots', the second is taken from the speech of a woman who identifies herself as 'Scottish' and the third is from the speech of a woman who identifies herself as 'English'.

The first of the three uses of 'Britishness' that appears in quoted speech in this volume is found in the speech of M, a man from Northern Ireland, whose statement as transcribed in *Extract 4* from the chapter by Wilson and Stapleton appears below. He says about his sense of the words 'British' and 'Britishness':

> ... someone who feels British, for example, well what does that <u>mean</u>? (.) And it means, essentially, an amalgam (.) of different <u>regionalisations</u>. (.) So to <u>me</u>, 'British' (.) does, does not really have a <u>meaning</u> as such (...) A lot of the sense of Britishness is (.) well I suppose it's been (.) really <u>dissipated</u>, over the years. You know, and when we talk about the future, and regionalisation, and where we go with <u>Europe</u>, and all the rest (.) y'know nation states have less and less relevance. (.) But the <u>bedrock</u> of it all lies in your own culture, and your own <u>identity</u>.

A second use of 'Britishness' is taken from the interview of the Scotswoman Mary in the Chapter by Condor and Abell. The authors of the chapter provide a heading for what they label as *Extract 2* with a quotation of Mary's statement 'I've never been challenged on my Britishness'. That utterance is followed by Mary's 'I've been challenged on my Scottishness'. Mary says that her Britishness is not a matter of pride, not something she has thought much about or something she has had to think about, while her presentation of herself in terms of Scottishness is something that she has felt she has had to, and has wanted to, that she has wanted to attend to in her self presentations and management of her interactions with others.

The third of the three uses of 'Britishness' in respondent talk quoted in the volume is also from the chapter by Condor and Abell; here they quote Karen, an Englishwoman, in an interview with Jackie. Karen is the woman who says she feels more 'English' than 'British':

Karen:	I do, I think have a very strong sense of my Englishness, as opposed to Britishness, I would say, now, don't ask me why, cos I, I,
Jackie:	You do, or you don't?
Karen:	I do.
Jackie:	You do.
Karen:	I do think I do have, yeah, I mean, if you ask me 'How do you think of yourself?' I will say 'English'.
Jackie:	Really?
Karen:	Yes, I would. I know that's terrible and it's not PC, but it's true.
Jackie:	Why is that terrible?
Karen:	I've not been actually brought up to think like that, either, my parents are very, like, you know, we live in Great Britain, and, that sort of thing.

In the three segments quoted or displayed immediately above, the only three in which respondent speech quoted in the book contains the word 'Britishness', the importance of Britishness to the speaker is in some way minimised, diminished, or made to seem irrelevant by the person who speaks it. The man from Northern Ireland asserts that the 'sense' of Britishness has been 'dissipated'; and he provides a temporal marker, 'over the years'. Furthermore, he links the dissipation of meaning of Britishness to the diminution of the importance of nation states, the rising importance of regionalisation, and an orientation to Europe. That is, he refers to the dissipation of Britishness in terms of the (increasingly important) contexts in which it has lost its ability to hold together. The Scotswoman plainly makes her Britishness a matter of little concern relative to her Scottishness. The Englishwoman seems to apologise for her professed distance from Britishness relative to her 'sense', as she put it, of Englishness, and appears to treat the former as a category in need of protection or special treatment (that is, guarded by political correctness). The Englishwoman, like the man from Northern Ireland, also temporalises Britishness, as something that was made important to her as she grew up but as important in the context of an earlier generation.

The preceding is an exercise, inspired by the materials, and readings of them, provided by authors of two of the chapters in this volume, those chapters in which the word 'Britishness' was quoted in everyday talk. Although it is an exercise using very little in the way of data, it is a strikingly suggestive pattern of results, in the ways in which each speaker, each in his or her way, positions 'Britishness' as in some way a quality that is of secondary importance or has been diminished in its meaning or force. Other exercises would be possible, for example, expanding the data set to all uses, in respondent talk or text, of the word 'British'. This yields 21 uses of the word 'British' across nine different extracts, segments, or passages. They appear in five of the ten chapters. I will mention just a few of these to suggest the flavour of them and to illustrate the idea that 'British', like 'Britishness', does not fare very well in the talk and text reported here. In their *Extract 3*, Wilson and Stapleton present the words of M3, a man in Northern Ireland, who says 'young Protestants now, coming on…are keen to forge a, an identity…'. They 'do see', he says:

> Ulster Scots as a viable identity. A few years ago, you didn't know whether you were Northern Irish (.) or British, or whatever. But Ulster Scots is a viable, it is a place where they can (.) they can hang their, their coat on that there, and say 'I'm an Ulster-Scot (.) I'm not Irish (.) Um, I am British, but I'm an Ulster-Scot first'. And, uh, it is, it's a place (.) there's a, you know it's a home for these people. Or a home for a lot of people.

This passage shows two things: (1) the respondent's assertion of a temporal change, in 'A few years ago, you didn't know' whether, as an Ulster Scot, you were Northern Irish, British, or 'whatever'. But, he says, 'Ulster Scots' is now a viable means by which one can say that 'I am British, but I'm an Ulster-Scot first', and (2) the respondent's assertion that it is, now, at least for those who have embraced it, the case that 'Ulster-Scots' as an identity expression trumps either 'British' or 'Irish'.

A passage from another of Wilson and Stapleton's respondents suggests a different if related point to those made by the previous speaker. M2 says:

> I'm not just British. I'm British, but (.) I come from this part of (.) Northern Ireland. That there's Ulster Scots connections, and that you identify with Scottish people more.

Following his statement that he is 'not just British', M2 makes it a matter of regional identity, specifically Ulster Scots, over the more general identity of being British. Wilson and Stapleton's respondent quoted in *Extract 10* provides a further elaboration of the identity work expressed by 'British':

> Well, I think (.) it's got to the stage (.) I think amongst, I'll use the term Protestants (.) Ulster Scots (.) that whenever you refer to being British, you're really thinking about (.) y'know, the Royal Family, and the sense of value associated (.) um, around democracy. The principle of democracy, and the Parliament. (.) But I think, um (.) what has been said before (.) and we may not like it, but it's true, that um (.) as far as day-to-day life goes, we would probably have more in common with our Irish counterparts than we do with the average person in Britain. Like there are differences between us and the, the personalities and the way of life in Britain (.) So I think personally, yes, we have moved away a bit from Britain.

The respondent elaborates a sense of the identity expressed with the word 'British', associating it with the Royal Family, 'democracy' and 'Parliament, then asserts that for him and his Irish counterparts in Northern Ireland, 'we have moved away a bit from Britain', suggesting a temporally marked shift in attitudinal space. Condor and Abell's informant Peter reduces it all to a social construction produced linguistically when he says, about 'a place called Britain', that 'if we say there is, then there is, if we accept it socially, then there is …. [There's some]thing inside me that makes me stick at saying British, and makes me prefer to say English'.

Finally, I turn to the use of 'British' in the British National Party's statement of purpose, as quoted in David Irving's chapter: 'This is the British National Party. The British People …'. Here 'British' appears in a manifesto obviously presented to reclaim some existential, moral, and political ground for things British. As with the uses, in the talk and text quoted in this volume, of 'Britishness', so with 'British' – the word does not fare well as a valorised resource for the expression of identity. Where it is used, it is used as something in decline, out of favour, or of secondary importance, or as something that, if used affirmatively, is used in response to a perceived assault. Of course, the corpus is not systematic and I do not for a moment suggest that the snippets made available here provide a basis for generalisation. But the pattern that can be discerned in these materials, some of which were uttered or written by speakers or writers who are avowedly pro 'British', is striking in the ways it reveals these two words as words that do not enjoy the pride of expression they once might have had. Furthermore, in some instances, there are traces of expression in the talk and text that reveal the speakers or writers linking their attitudes to changes that have occurred over time.

The speaker quoted above from *Extract 10* of Wilson and Stapleton's chapter uses 'British' in a way that is obviously quite common, certainly the way it is predominantly used by the authors themselves of the chapters in this volume and by the scholars they quote when these writers are writing as scholars. Here I refer to the use of 'British' in such contexts as 'British history', 'British and Irish history', the 'British Embassy', and so forth, to use examples that appear in this volume. These are the uses of 'British' as a term that enters into the expression of a civic dimension, something that the respondent in *Extract 10* glosses as the Royal Family and democracy/Parliament. This raises the question of how Britishness, as an abstract quality fares in the context of devolution or, alternatively, how such a notion is itself a context which people post-devolution orient to and use as a resource.

To use 'Britishness' in such a way that foregrounds what it stands for requires the specification of such content or meaning. Here I conduct another exercise by taking as a heuristic resource one particular formulation of Britishness against which to juxtapose some of the developments reported in this volume, in the interest of answering in a different way how Britishness fares in the context of devolution. One obvious way is to treat Britishness in terms of such conventional symbols as the Royal Family, democracy, and Parliament, to borrow the list provided by Wilson and Stapleton's respondent in *Extract 10*. This is a perfectly serviceable way to formulate the notion, it seems to me, and it is consistent with the way the authors in this volume treat it. However, as a heuristic exercise, I shall take a different approach.

One of the central concerns of this volume, and indeed of the issues surrounding devolution, is whether there is a core of Britishness that is worth preserving as a feature of a common culture that might cut across the contemporary United Kingdom. Given that, I think it would be useful to ask, not only about 'Britishness' or 'British' as terms of political identification and not only about British practices and customs, but also whether there is a cultural ideal that can be associated with Britishness. If there is such a thing, this could provide a resource for asking in a different way how Britishness is faring under devolution. As a resource for this exercise, I turn to a formulation provided by Richard Hoggart in a collection of essays some of which he wrote while serving at the Paris headquarters of UNESCO in the 1960s and that were published in 1972 as the *B.B.C. Reith Lectures* of 1971. In the concluding chapter of the book, *A Common Ground,* Hoggart (1972: 110) distills what he takes to be the distinctive assumptions and value commitments of British culture, and in the end boils it down to two 'main groups of assumptions, that it matters to communicate and that one can communicate'.

That it matters to communicate and that one can communicate are the sorts of expressions that can send one screaming for a bit of text to examine, but I would suggest neither of these groups of assumptions is everywhere a given or an imperative and that, once we get over the seeming triteness of them, there is something there worth considering. If a people or a political unit have in common such a pair of assumptions, and at least acknowledge the importance of such practices as those assumptions and value commitments would seem to imply, that is a powerful resource. It would be worth thinking long and hard before throwing out such a resource, and, indeed, it is something one might be willing to fight for against efforts to deplete it or give it away. And so it seems worth asking whether devolutionary efforts threaten or enhance the existence and realisation of such an ideal. In any case, the probative use of the ideal can be a worthy exercise.

One of the more specific assumptions that can be subsumed under the first group of assumptions, 'that it matters to communicate', is that it is valuable in a society to 'have many voices arguing in different ways, especially voices arguing against the prevailing outlook' (Hoggart, 1972:107). If we ask, how is such a value faring in the context of devolution, we can then look to some of the specific cases presented in this volume. Right away it seems that most of the chapters provide a record of efforts that realise in practice such a value: chiefly, diverse ways of expressing one's social identity and the creation of new spaces for artistic and political expression.

There is as well a sharply contrasting juxtaposition that can be made of two of the present cases, those of Coupland and Bishop's chapter on post-devolution ideologies of language and community in Wales set against David Irwin's chapter on citizenship, devolution, and the British National Party. Coupland and Bishop quite cogently and rightly point out the essentialising fallacies in the treatment by Iaith Pawb of a language (Welsh) and of communities (Welsh communities in particular) as unitary, fixed, and unchanging. It is harder for an outsider to judge the fairness of their critique of the discourse that employs the words 'language' and 'community(ies)' in Iaith Pawb and by Cymuned. Coupland and Bishop take to task the words written on behalf of the Welsh language and Welsh communities in part because of the seeming way they construct language and community as more unitary than they really are and in part because of the political program that seemingly articulates with such usage, specifically, as manifested in such a statement as Iaith Pawb's endorsement of increasing:

> the opportunities for newcomers and non-Welsh speaking adults in Welsh-speaking areas to learn the language, so they can fully participate in all aspects of life in their new community and contribute to supporting and sustaining one of the most distinctive features of that community.

However misguided the sociolinguistic theory underlying such a statement might be, it strikes me that it endorses something that is fundamentally different from what, say, the British Nationalist Party endorses: segregation, insularity, and self-containment, indeed the wholesale sending away of people not considered to be English. If the followers of Iaith Pawb and of Cymuned turn out to have their way, that conceivably could turn out to be a realisation of Hoggart's ideal of a diversity of voices; but if the followers of the British National Party have their way, the ideal Hoggart proposes as quintessentially British would almost certainly be undermined.

As to Hoggart's second group of assumptions, that 'one can communicate', there is a mixed report, given the news of the present set of ten chapters. As Irwin describes it, the case of the British Nationalist Party is not germane because the party does not want to try to communicate. It simply wants to segregate people, to send them away, although this in itself is saying something, but not, I think, saying the sort of thing that Hoggart had in mind with 'communication'. Some of the chapters show how devolutionary acts have created new opportunities to communicate across barriers that previously had seemed rather steep and that indeed there has been a considerable meeting of the minds. Carmel Roulston's stories of the success of women's groups in Scotland and Wales provide perhaps the sharpest examples of success at creating new ways of communicating and connecting. The stories from Northern Ireland, specifically, those told by Dominic Bryan, Carol Anne Barnes and Arthur Aughey, and by Carmel Roulston (regarding the Northern Ireland case as contrasted with the Scottish and Welsh cases) provide a less favorable record in terms of this second group of assumptions; in these cases the effort to communicate was strong, but the positive results less impressive.

To conclude, I refer back to the SNP speaker in the Glasgow Debates Union in the winter of 1966. What sort of world does he now inhabit? Has his sort of rhetoric, and the impulses behind such, played a role in the establishment of devolutionary acts and, then, have those devolutionary acts themselves had an impact on the lived experience of those who have been exposed to them? Or have whatever changes to be observed in the construction of identities in a post-devolution United Kingdom come about because of the very forces to which his rhetoric, forty years, served to give voice? Have the acts initiated in 1997 played a role in providing for, or shaping, new rhetorics of identity, or are those acts merely an accompaniment to social processes already underway? Have the surface features of Britishness been undermined in the context of devolution, or is Britishness a more robust and durable code that has itself been reproduced in some, but not all, of post-devolutionary identity discourse? The chapters of this volume provide a remarkable resource for posing such questions and for sketching some possible lines along which answers can be anticipated.

Bibliography

Abell, J., Condor, S. and Stevenson, C. (2006), '"We are an island": Geographical imagery and dilemmas of British identity in Scotland and in England', *Political Psychology* 27: 191–217.

Adamson, I., (1991), *The Ulster People: Ancient, Medieval and Modern*, Bangor, Northern Ireland: Pretani.

Aitchison, J. and Carter, H. (2004), *Spreading the Word: The Welsh Language 2001*, Talybont, Wales: Y Lolfa.

Alter, P. (1985), *Nationalism*, London: Edward Arnold.

Anderson, B., (1983), *Imagined Communities: Reflections on the Origin and Spread of Nationalism*, London: Verso.

Antaki, C., Billig, M., Edwards, D. and Potter, J., (2003), 'Discourse analysis means doing analysis: A critique of six analytic shortcomings', *Discourse Analysis Online* 1, http://extra.shu.ac.uk/daol/previous/v1_n1.html.

Antaki, C. Condor, S. and Levine, M., (1996), 'Social identities in talk: Speakers' own orientations', *British Journal of Social Psychology* 35: 473–492.

Antaki, C. and Widdicombe, S., (1998) (eds), *Identities in Talk*, London: Sage.

Atkinson, P. and Housley, W., (2003), *Interactionism*, London: Sage.

Aughey, A., (1989), *Under Siege: Ulster Unionism and the Anglo-Irish Agreement*, Belfast: Blackstaff.

Aughey, A., (1995), 'The idea of the union', in J.W. Foster (ed.), *The Idea of the Union*, Vancouver: Belcouver Press.

Aughey, A., (2001), *Nationalism, Devolution and the Challenge to the United Kingdom State*, London: Pluto Press.

Aughey, A., (2003), '"As others see us": Reflections on contemporary Scotland', *Scottish Affairs* 42 (Winter): 1–12.

Barker, C. and Galasinski, D., (2001), *Cultural Studies and Discourse Analysis: A Dialogue on Language and Identity*, London: Sage.

Barnes, C-A., (2004), *Whose History is it Anyway?*, Undergraduate dissertation submitted for BA (Hons) Humanities, University of Ulster at Jordanstown.

Bauman, Z., (1987), *Legislators and Interpreters: On Modernity, Postmodernity and the Intellectuals*, Cambridge: Polity Press.

Bauman, Z., (1990), *Thinking Sociologically*, Oxford: Blackwell.

Bauman, Z., (1992), *Intimations of Postmdernity*, London: Routledge.

Bauman, Z., (1998), *Globalization: The Human Consequences*, Cambridge: Polity Press.

Bauman, Z., (2001a), *Community: Seeking Safety in an Insecure World*, Cambridge: Polity Press.

Bauman, Z., (2001b), *The Individualised Society*, Cambridge: Polity Press.

Bauman, Z., (2002), *Society Under Siege*, Cambridge: Blackwell.

Bauman, Z., (2003), *Liquid Love*, Cambridge: Polity Press.

Bechhofer, F., McCrone, D., Kiely, R. and Stewart, R., (1999), 'Constructing national identity: Arts and landed elites in Scotland', *Sociology* 33: 515–534.

Beckerson, J., (2002), 'Marketing British tourism: Government approaches to the stimulation of a service sector, 1880–1950', in H. Berghoff, B. Korte, R. Schneider and C. Harvie (eds), *The Making of Modern Tourism*, Basingstoke: Palgrave Macmillan.

Benhabib, S., (2002), *The Claims of Culture: Equality and Diversity in the Global Era*, NJ: Princeton University Press.

Benwell, B. and Stoke, E., (2006), *Discourse and Identity*, Edinburgh: Edinburgh University Press.

Berghoff, H. and Korte, B., (2002), 'Britain and the making of modern tourism: An interdisciplinary approach', in H. Berghoff, B. Korte, R. Schneider and C. Harvie (eds), *The Making of Modern Tourism*, Basingstoke: Palgrave.

Berlin, I., (1969), *Four Essays on Liberty*, Oxford: Oxford University Press.

Bew, P., (2001), 'Why is the government so ashamed of our birthday?', *The Daily Telegraph*, 2 January.

Bew, P., Gibbon, P. and Patterson, H., (2002), *Northern Ireland 1921/2001: Political Forces and Social Classes*, London: Verso.

Billig, M. (1995), *Banal Nationalism*, London: Sage.

Billig, M. (1996), 'Remembering the particular background of social identity theory', in W.P. Robinson (ed.), *Social Groups and Identities: Developing the Legacy of Henri Tajfel*, (pp. 337–358), Oxford: Butterworth-Heinemann.

Billig, M., Condor, S., Edwards, D., Gane, M. Middleton, D. and Radley, A., (1988), *Ideological Dilemmas*, London: Sage.

Bloor, D., (1976), *Knowledge and Social Imagery*, London: Routledge.

Blum, A. and McHugh, P., (1971), 'The social ascription of motives', *American Sociological Review* 36: 98–109.

Bogdanor, V., (1999), *Devolution in the United Kingdom*, Oxford: Oxford University Press.

Bond, R. and Rosie, M., (2002), 'National identities in post-devolution Scotland', www.institute-ofgovernance.org/onlinepub/bondrosie.html.

Bond, R. and Rosie, M., (n.d.), *Summary of Project Findings*, www.institute-of-governance.org/forum/Leverhulme/summaries/public_opinion_summary.html.

Bourdieu, P., (1977), *Outline of a Theory of Practice*, Cambridge: Cambridge University Press.

Bourdieu, P., (1991), *Language and Symbolic Power*, Cambridge, MA: Harvard University Press.

Boyce, D.G. and O'Day, A., (1996), 'Introduction: "Revisionism" and the "revisionist controversy"', in D.G. Boyce and A. O'Day (eds), *The Making of Modern Irish History: Revisionism and the Revisionist Controversy*, London: Routledge.

Brown, A., (1998), 'Deepening democracy: Women and the Scottish Parliament', *Regional and Federal Studies* 6: 103–119.

Brown, A., Donaghy, T.B., Mackay, F. and Meehan, E., (2002), 'Women and constitutional change in Scotland and Northern Ireland', *Parliamentary Affairs* 55: 71–84.

Brown, K. and MacGinty, R., (2003), 'Public attitudes towards partisan and neutral symbols in post-Agreement Northern Ireland', *Identities: Global Structures in Culture and Power* 10: 83–108.

Brubaker, R., (1992), *Citizenship and Nationhood in France and Germany*, Cambridge, MA: Harvard University Press.

Bryan, D., (2000), *Orange Parades: The Politics of Ritual Tradition and Control*, London: Pluto Press.

Bryan, D. and Gillespie, G., (2005), *Transforming Conflict: Flags and Emblems*, Report to the Office of the First Minister and Deputy First Minister. Funded by the ESRC, Belfast: Institute of Irish Studies.

Bryson, L. and McCartney, C., (1994), *Clashing Symbols: A Report on the Use of Flags, Anthems and Other National Symbols in Northern Ireland*, Belfast: Institute of Irish Studies.

Buckley, A., (1985), 'The Chosen Few: Biblical texts in the regalia of an Ulster secret society', *Folk Life* 24: 5–24.

Buell, E.H. Jr., (1975), 'Eccentrics or gladiators? People who write about politics in letters-to-the-editor', *Social Science Quarterly* 56: 440–449.

Cable, V., (1994), *The World's New Fissure: Identities in Crisis*, London: Demos.

Calder, G., (2004), 'Communitarianism and New Labour', *Social Issues* 2, http://www.whb.co.uk/socialissues/index.htm.

Carmichael, P., (1999), 'Territorial management in the "New Britain": Towards devolution-plus in Northern Ireland?', *Regional and Federal Studies* 9: 130–156.

Centre for Human Ecology (CHE) (n.d.), *Embracing Multicultural Scotland: The People Speak*, www.che.ac.uk/publications/EMSReport/thepeoplespeak.htm.

Chambers, I., (1989), 'Narratives of nationalism: Being British', *New Formations* 7: 83–103.

Chaney, P., (2003), *Women and Constitutional Change in Wales*, Occasional Paper 7, Belfast: Centre for the Advancement of Women in Politics, Queen's University, Belfast.

Chaney, P. and Fevre, R., (2001), 'Welsh nationalism and the challenge of "inclusive" politics', *Research in Social Movements Conflict and Change* 23: 227–254.

Chaney, P. and Fevre, R., (2002), 'Is there a demand for descriptive representation? Evidence from the UK's devolution programme', *Political Studies* 50: 897–915.

Chilton, P., (2004), *Analysing Political Discourse: Theory and Practice*, London: Routledge.

Clark, H.H. and Gerrig, R., (1990), 'Quotations as demonstrations', *Language* 66: 764–805.

Clark, J.C.D., (1990), 'J.C.D. Clark', in J. Gardiner (ed.), *The History Debate*, London: Collins and Brown.

Clark, J.C.D, (2003), *Our Shadowed Present: Modernism, Postmodernism and History*, London: Atlantic Books.

Clayman, S. and Heritage, J., (2002), *The News Interview: Journalists and Public Figures on the Air*, Cambridge: Cambridge University Press.

Cochrane, F., (2001), 'Unsung heroes? The role of peace and conflict resolution organisations in the Northern Ireland conflict', in J. McGarry (ed.), *Northern Ireland and the Divided World: Post-Agreement Northern Ireland in Comparative Perspective*, Oxford: Oxford University Press.

Cockburn, C., (1998), *The Space Between Us: Negotiating Gender and National Identities in Conflict*, London: Zed Books.

Cohen, A.P., (1985), *The Symbolic Construction of Community*, Tavistock: Ellis Horwood.

Cohen, A.P., (1996), 'Personal nationalism: A Scottish view of some rites, rights, and wrongs', *American Ethnologist*, 23: 802–815.

Cohen, R., (1994), *Frontiers of Identity: The British and the Others*, London: Longman.

Collingwood, R.G., (1961), *The Idea of History*, Oxford: Oxford University Press.

Collins, H.M. and Evans, R.J., (2002), 'The third wave of science studies: Studies of expertise and experience', *Social Studies of Science* 32: 235–296.

Condor, S. (1996), 'Unimagined community? Some social psychological aspects of English national identity', in G. Breakwell and E. Lyons (eds), *Changing European Identities*, Oxford: Butterworth Heinemann.

Condor, S., (2000), 'Pride and prejudice: Identity management in English people's talk about "this country"', *Discourse and Society* 11: 163–193.

Condor, S., (2001), 'Nations and nationalisms: Particular cases and impossible myths', *British Journal of Social Psychology* 40: 177–181.

Condor, S. and Abell, J., (2006), 'Romantic Scotland, tragic England, ambiguous Britain: Uses of 'the Empire' in post-devolution national accounting', *Nations and Nationalism* 12: 451–470.

Condor, S., Gibson, S. and Abell, J., (2006), 'English identity and ethnic diversity in the context of UK constitutional change', *Ethnicities* 6: 123–158.

Conover, P.J., Crewe, I.M. and Searing, D.D., (1991), 'The nature of citizenship in the United States and Great Britain', *Journal of Politics* 53: 800–832

Creeber, G., (2004), '"Hideously white": British television, glocalization, and national identity', *Television and New Media* 5: 27–39.

Coupland, N., (2003), 'Sociolinguistic authenticities', *Journal of Sociolinguisitcs* 7: 417–431.

Coupland, N., Bishop, H., Evans, B. and Garrett, P., (under review), 'Imagining Wales and the Welsh language: Ethnolinguistic subjectivities and demographic flow', *Journal of Language and Social Psychology*.

Coupland, N., Bishop, H. and Garrett, P., (in press), 'How many Wales? Reassessing diversity in Welsh ethnolinguistic identification', *Contemporary Wales*.

Cowell–Meyers, K., (2003), *Women Legislators in Northern Ireland: Gender and Politics in the New Legislative Assembly*, Occasional Paper 3, Belfast: Centre for the Advancement of Women in Politics, Queen's University, Belfast.

Crooke, E., (2001), 'Confronting a troubled history: Which past in Northern Ireland's museums?', *International Journal of Heritage Studies* 7: 119–136.

Curtice, J. and Heath, A., (2000), 'Is the English lion about to roar? National identity after devolution', in R. Jowell, J. Curtice, A. Park, K. Thomson, L. Jarvis, C. Bromley and N. Stratford (eds), *British Social Attitudes: The 17th Report*, London: Sage.

Curtice, J. and Seyd, B., (2001), 'Is devolution strengthening or weakening the UK?', in A. Park, J. Curtice, K. Thomson., L. Jarvis, and C. Bromley (eds), *British Social Attitudes: The 18th Report*, London, Sage.

Curtis, T., (2000), *Welsh Artists Talking*, Bridgend: Seren Books.

Davies, N., (1999), *The Isles: A History*, London: Macmillan.

De Cillia, R., Reisigl, M. and Wodak, R., (1999), 'The discursive construction of national identities', *Discourse and Society* 10: 149–175.

Denney D., Borland J. and Fevre R., (1991), 'The social construction of nationalism: Racism and conflict in Wales', *Contemporary Wales* 4: 49–165.

Destatte, P., (1998), 'Present-day Wallonia: The search for an identity without nationalist mania', in K. Deprez and L. Vos (eds), *Nationalism in Belgium: Shifting Identities 1780–1995*, Basingstoke: Palgrave.

Dicks, B., (1996), 'Regeneration versus representation in the Rhondda: The story of the Rhondda Heritage Park', *Contemporary Wales* 9: 56–73.

Dicks, B., (1997), 'The life and times of community: Spectacles of collective identity at the Rhondda Heritage Park', PhD thesis, University of Wales.

Dicks, B., (1999), 'The view from our hill: Communities on display as local heritage', *International Journal of Cultural Studies* 2: 349–368.

Dicks, B., (2000), *Heritage, Place and Community*, Cardiff: University of Wales Press.

Dixon, J.A. and Durrheim, K., (2000), 'Displacing place identity: A discursive approach to locating self and other', *British Journal of Social Psychology* 39: 27–44.

Driver, S. and Martell, L., (1997), 'New Labour's communitarianisms', *Critical Social Policy* 52: 27–46.

Driver, S. and Martell, L., (1998), *New Labour: Politics after Thatcherism*, Cambridge: Polity.

Drükne, H., (2005), 'Introduction', in H. Drükne (ed), *Local Electronic Government: A Comparative Study*, London: Routledge.

Dunn, S. and Morgan, V., (1994), *Protestant Alienation in Northern Ireland*, Coleraine, Northern Ireland: Centre for the Study of Conflict.

EOCNI (1995), *Men and Women in Northern Ireland*, Belfast: EOCNI.

Edensor, T., (2002), *National Identity, Popular Culture and Everyday Life*, Oxford: Berg.

Edwards, D., (1997), *Discourse and Cognition*, London: Sage.

Edwards, D., (1999), 'Emotion discourse', *Culture and Psychology*, 5: 271–291.

Edwards, D. and Potter, J., (1992), *Discursive Psychology* London: Sage.

Edwards, D. and Potter, J., (2005), 'Discursive psychology, mental states and descriptions', in H. te Molder and J. Potter (eds), *Conversation and Cognition*, Cambridge: Cambridge University Press.

Evason, E., (1991), *Against the Grain: the Contemporary Women's Movement in Northern Ireland*, Dublin: Attic Press.

Fairclough, N., (2000), *New Labour, New Language?*, London: Routledge.

Fanon, F., (1990), *The Wretched of the Earth*, Harmondsworth: Penguin.

Farrell, M., (1980), *Northern Ireland: The Orange State*, London: Pluto Press.

Faulkner, M., Condor, S. and Abell, J., (2002), 'Discourses of national identity and integration in England and in Scotland', Paper presented at the *International Society for the Study of European Ideas ISSEI 8th International Conference*, July, Aberystwyth, Wales.

Favell, A., (1998), *Philosophies of Integration: Immigration and the Idea of Citizenship in France and Britain*, Basingstoke: Palgrave.

Fearon, K., (1999), *Women's Work: The Story of the Northern Ireland Women's Coalition*, Belfast: Blackstaff Press.

Fearon, K. and McWilliams M., (2000), 'Swimming against the mainstream: The Northern Ireland Women's Coalition', in C. Roulston and C. Davies (eds), *Gender, Democracy and Inclusion in Northern Ireland*, Basingstoke: Palgrave Macmillan.

Feldman, A., (1991), *Formations of Violence: The Narrative of the Body and Political Terror in Northern Ireland*, Chicago: University of Chicago Press.

Fevre, R., (2000), *The Demoralization of Western Culture*, London: Continuum.

Fevre R., Borland J. and Denney D., (1997), 'Class, status and party in the analysis of nationalism: Lessons from Max Weber', *Nations and Nationalism* 3: 559–577.

Fevre R., Borland J. and Denney D., (1999), 'Nation, community and conflict: Housing policy and immigration in North Wales', in R. Fevre and A. Thompson (eds), *Nation, Identity and Social Theory: Perspectives from Wales*, Cardiff, Wales: University of Wales Press.

Fevre, R. and Thompson, T., (1999) (eds), *Nation, Identity and Social Theory: Perspectives from Wales*, Cardiff, Wales: University of Wales Press.

Finlayson, A., (1996), 'Nationalism as ideological interpellation: The case of Ulster Loyalism', *Ethnic and Racial Studies* 19: 88–112.

Finlayson, A., (1999), 'Loyalist political identity after the peace', *Capital and Class* 69: 47–76.

Fitzgerald, R., (2004), 'Reflections from Scotland', in E. Breitenbach (ed.), *Engendering Democracy: Women's Organisations and their Influence on Policy-Making within the Devolved Administrations in Northern Ireland, Scotland and Wales*, Report of a seminar held in December 2003, University of Edinburgh and Queen's University, Belfast.

Fitzgerald, R. and Housley, W., (2002), 'Identity, categorization and sequential organization: The sequential and categorical flow of identity in a radio phone-in', *Discourse and Society* 13: 579–602.

Fitzmaurice, J., (1996), *The Politics of Belgium: A Unique Federalism*, London: Hurst & Company.

Foster, R.F., (2001), *The Irish Story: Telling Tales and Making It Up in Ireland*, London: Penguin.

Furedi, F., (1992), *Mythical Past, Elusive Future*, London: Pluto Press.

Galligan, Y. and Wilford, R., (1999), 'Women's political representation in Ireland', in Y. Galligan, E. Ward and R. Wilford (eds), *Contesting Politics: Women in Ireland, North and South*, Boulder, CO: Westview Press.

Gardiner, J., (1990), 'Introduction', in J. Gardiner (ed.), *The History Debate*, London: Collins and Brown.

Garfinkel, H., (1967), *Studies in Ethnomethodology*, Oxford: Polity.

Garfinkel, H. and Sacks, H., (1970), 'On formal structures of practical action', in John C. McKinney and Edward A. Tiryakian (eds), *Theoretical Sociology: Perspectives and Developments*, New York: Appleton-Century-Crofts.

Garrett, P., Coupland, N. and Bishop H., (2005), 'Globalisation and the visualisation of Wales and Welsh America: *Y Drych*, 1948–2001', *Ethnicities* 5: 530–564.

Giddens, A., (1991), *Modernity and Self-Identity: Self and Society in the Late Modern Age*, Stanford, CA: Stanford University Press.

Giles, J. and Middleton, T., (1995), *Writing Englishness 1900–1950: An Introductory Sourcebook on National Identity*, London: Routledge.

Gillis, J.R., (1994), 'Memory and identity: The history of a relationship', in J.R. Gillis (ed.), *Commemorations: The Politics of National Identity*, Princeton: Princeton University Press.

Goffman, E., (1974/1986), *Frame Analysis*, New York: Harper and Row

Goffman, E., (1981), 'Footing', in E. Goffman (ed.), *Forms of Talk*, Oxford: Blackwell.

Goldstein, R.G., (1995), *Saving 'Old Glory': The History of the American Flag Desecration Controversy*, Boulder, CO: Westview Press.

Gould, P., (1998), *The Unfinished Revolution: How the Modernisers Saved the Labour Party*, London: Little, Brown & Co.

Graham, B., (1998), 'Contested images of place among Protestants in Northern Ireland', *Political Geography* 17: 129–144.

Graham, C., (1994), 'Liminal spaces: Post-colonial theories and Irish culture', *The Irish Review* 16 (Autumn-Winter): 29–43.

Gruffudd, P., (1999), 'Prospects of Wales: Contested geographical imaginations', in R. Fever and A. Thompson (eds), *Nation, Identity and Social Theory*, Cardiff: University of Wales Press.

Habermas, J., (1987), *The Theory of Communicative Action, Vol. Two*, Cambridge: Polity Press.

Habermas, J., (1989), *The Structural Transformation of the Public Sphere: An Inquiry into a Category of Bourgeois Society*, Cambridge MA: MIT Press.

Habermas, J., (2001), *The Inclusion of the Other: Studies in Political Theory*, (3rd print), Cambridge, MA: MIT Press.

Harbinson, J. and Manwah Lo, A., (2004), 'The impact of devolution on community relations', in K. Lloyd, P. Devine, A.M. Gray and D. Heenan (eds), *Social Attitudes in Northern Ireland: The Ninth Report*, London: Pluto Press.

Hardman, R., (2000), 'No celebrations for the UK's 200th birthday', *The Daily Telegraph*, 11 February.

Harrison, S., (1995), 'Four types of symbolic conflict', *Journal of the Royal Anthropological Institute (NS)* 1: 255–272.

Harvey, C., (2003), 'Stick to the terms of the Agreement', *Fortnight*, 416: 9, (July/ August).

Haseler, S., (1996), *The English Tribe: Identity, Nation and Europe*, London: Macmillan.

Hazell, R., (2003) (ed.), *The State of the Nation 2003: The Third Year of Devolution in the United Kingdom*, Exeter: Academic Imprint.

Heaney, S., (1993), 'The sense of the past', *History Ireland* 1: 33–37.

Heenan, D., (2004), 'Culture in Northern Ireland', in K. Lloyd, P. Devine, A.M. Gray and D. Heenan (eds), *Social Attitudes in Northern Ireland: The Ninth Report*, London: Pluto Press.

Herrero, M., (2000), 'Towards a sociology of art collections', *International Sociology* 17: 57– 72.

Hester, S. and Eglin, P., (1997), 'The reflexive constitution of category, predicate and task', in S. Hester and P. Eglin (eds), *Culture in Action*, Lanham, MD: University Press of America.

Hester, S. and Francis, D., (1994), 'Doing data: The local organization of a sociological interview', *British Journal of Sociology* 45: 675–695.

Hester, S. and Housley, W., (2002) (eds), *Language, Interaction and National Identity*, Aldershot: Ashgate.

Hobbs, J., (1990), 'Topic drift', in B. Dorval (ed.), *Conversational Organization and its Development*, Norwood, NJ: Ablex.

Hoggart, R., (1972), *On Culture and Communication: The B.B.C. Reith Lectures 1971*, New York: Oxford University Press.

Horowitz, D.L., (2002), 'Explaining the Northern Irish Agreement: The sources of an unlikely constitutional consensus', *British Journal of Political Science* 32: 193–220.

Housley, W., (2000), 'Story, narrative and team work', *The Sociological Review* 48: 425–443.

Housley, W., (2002), 'Moral discrepancy and "fudging the issue" in a radio news interview', *Sociology* 36: 5–21.

Housley, W., (in press), 'Visions of Wales: Visual artists and cultural futures', *Contemporary Wales*.

Housley, W. and Fitzgerald, R., (2001), 'Categorisation, narrative and devolution in Wales', *Sociological Research Online* 6, http://www.socresonline.org.uk/6/2/housley.html.

Housley, W. and Fitzgerald, R., (2002a), 'National identity, categorisation and debate', pp. 38–59, in S. Hester and W. Housley (eds), *Language, Interaction and National Identity*, Aldershot: Ashgate.

Housley, W. and Fitzgerald, R., (2002b), 'The reconsidered model of Membership Categorisation', *Qualitative Research* 2: 59–74.

Housley, W. and Fitzgerald, R., (in press), 'Categorisation, interaction, policy and debate', *Journal of Critical Discourse Studies*.

Hurting, R., (1977), 'Towards a functional theory of discourse', in R.O. Freedle (ed.), *Discourse Production and Comprehension*, Norwoord, NJ: Ablex.

Hynds, E.C., (1994), 'Editors at most U.S. dailies see vital role for editorial page', *Journalism Quarterly* 71: 573–582.

Ignatieff, Michael (1994), *Blood and Belonging*, London: Vintage Press.

Jacobson, J., (2002), 'When is a nation not a nation? The case of Anglo-British nationhood', *Geopolitics* 7: 173–192.

Jarman, N., (1997), *Material Conflicts: Parades and Visual Displays in Northern Ireland*, Oxford: Berg.

Jarman, N., (2003), 'Intersecting Belfast', in B. Bender (ed.), *Landscape: Politics and Perspectives*, Oxford: Berg.

Jarman, N. and Bryan, D., (1998), *From Riots to Rights: Nationalist Parades in the North of Ireland*, Coleraine, Northern Ireland: Centre for the Study of Conflict.

Jayyusi, L., (1984), *Categorisation and the Moral Order*, London: Routledge and Kegan Paul.

Jeffery, C., (2004), (collated), *Devolution: What Difference has it Made?*, Interim Findings from the ESRC Research Programme on Devolution and Constitutional Change, http://www.devolution.ac.uk/pdfdata/Interim_Findings_04.pdf.

Jenkins, B. and Sofos, S., (1996) (eds), *Nation and Identity in Contemporary Europe*, London: Routledge.

Keating, M., (1999), 'Regions and international affairs: Motives, opportunities and strategies', in F. Aldecoa and M. Keating (eds), *Paradiplomacy in Action: The Foreign Relations of Subnational Governments*, London: Frank Cass.

Keating, M., (2001), *Plurinational Democracy: Stateless Nations in a Post-Sovereignty Era*, Oxford: Oxford University Press.

Kelly, J., (2003), 'Historiography of the Act of Union', in M. Brown, P.M. Geoghegan and J. Kelly (eds), *The Irish Act of Union 1800: Bicentennial Essays*, Dublin: Irish Academic Press.

Kenny, M., (2004), *The Politics of Identity*, Cambridge: Polity.

Kidd, C., (1999), *British Identities Before Nationalism: Ethnicities and Nationhood in the Atlantic World 1600–1800*, Cambridge: Cambridge University Press.

Kiely, R., Bechhofer, F., Stewart, R. and McCrone, D., (2001), 'The markers and rules of Scottish national identity', *The Sociological Review* 49: 33–55.

Kiely, R., McCrone, D. and Bechhofer, F., (2005), 'Whither Britishness? English and Scottish people in Scotland', *Nations and Nationalism* 11: 65–82.

Kumar, K., (2003), 'Britain, England and Europe: Cultures in contraflow', *European Journal of Social Theory* 6: 5–23.

Kuusisto Arponen, A.K., (2001), 'The end of violence and introduction of "real" politics: Tensions in peaceful Northern Ireland', *Geografiska Annaler* 83(B): 121–130.

Kymlicka, W., (1995), *Multicultural Citizenship*, Oxford: Clarendon Press.

Leonard, J., (1996), *The Culture of War Commemoration*, Dublin: Cultures of Ireland.

Leonard, M., (1997), *Britain™: Renewing our Identity*, London: Demos.

Lister, R., (1997), *Citizenship: Feminist Perspectives*, London: Macmillan.

Livingstone, S. and Lunt, P., (1994), *Talk on Television: Audience Participation and Public Debate*, London: Routledge.

Llewellyn, N., (2004), 'In search of modernization: The negotiation of social identity in organizational reform', *Organzisation Studies* 25: 947–968.

Loftus, B., (1990), *Mirrors: William III and Mother Ireland*, Dundrum, Northern Ireland: Picture Press.

Loftus, B., (1994), *Mirrors: Orange and Green*, Dundrum, Northern Ireland: Picture Press.

Longley, E., (2001), 'Northern Ireland: Commemoration, elegy, forgetting', in I. McBride (ed.), *History and Memory in Modern Ireland*, Cambridge: Cambridge University Press.

Lord, P., (2000), *Imaging the Nation*, Cardiff, Wales: University of Wales Press.

Loughlin, J. and Williams, C.H., (in press), 'Language and governance: The intellectual inheritance', in C.H. Williams (ed.), *Language and Governance*, Cardiff: University of Wales Press.

Lunt, P. and Stenner, P., (2005), 'The Jerry Springer Show as an emotional public sphere', *Media, Culture & Society* 27: 59–81.

Lynch, M. and Bogen, D., (1996), *The Spectacle of History*, Durham: Duke University Press.

Mackay, F., (2001), *Love and Politics: Women Politicians and the Ethic of Care*, London: Pinter.

Mackay, F., (2004), 'Access, voice and influence? Women's organisations in post-devolution Scotland, in E. Breitenbach (ed.), *Engendering Democracy: Women's Organisations and their Influence on Policy-Making within the Devolved Administrations in Northern Ireland, Scotland and Wales*, Report of a seminar held in December 2003, University of Edinburgh and Queen's University, Belfast.

MacMahon, D., (2004), 'Scotland at the Smithsonian: Beyond the cultural cringe?', *Scottish Affairs* 47, www.scottishaffairs.org/onlinepub/sa/macmahon_sa47_spr04.html.

Maines, D.R., (2001), *The Faultline of Consciousness: A View of Interactionism in Sociology*, New York: Aldine de Gruyter.

Mann, M., (1987), 'Ruling class strategies and citizenship', *Sociology* 21: 339–354.

Mason, R., (2004), 'Changing representations of national identity in Scottish and Welsh museums', in H. Brocklehurst and R. Phillips (eds), *History, Nationhood and the Question of Britain*, Basingstoke: Palgrave Macmillan.

May, S., (2001), *Language and Minority Rights: Ethnicity, Nationalism and the Politics of Language*, Harlow: Longman.

May, S., (2005) (ed.), *Sociolinguistics and Minority Rights*, Thematic issue of *Journal of Sociolinguistics* 9 (2).

McBride, I., (1997), *The Siege of Derry in Ulster Protestant Mythology*, Dublin: Four Courts Press.

McBride, I., (2001), 'Memory and national identity in modern Ireland', in I. McBride (ed.), *History and Memory in Modern Ireland*, Cambridge: Cambridge University Press.

McCall, C., (2002a), 'The protean British identity in Britain and Northern Ireland', *Soundings: A Journal of Politics and Culture* 18: 154–68.

McCall, C., (2002b), 'Political transformation and the reinvention of the Ulster-Scots identity and culture', *Identities: Global Studies in Culture and Power* 9: 197–218.

McCartan, D., (2001), 'Bicentenary of UK may still be marked', *The Belfast Telegraph*, 2 January.

McCausland, N., (n.d.), *The Greening of the Museum*, (No publication details).

McCormick, J. and Jarman, N., (2005), 'Death of a mural', *Journal of Material Culture* 10: 49–71.

McCrone, D., (1998), *The Sociology of Nationalism*, London: Routledge.

McCrone, D., (2001), 'Scotland and the union: Changing identities in the British state', in D. Morley and K. Robins (eds), *British Cultural Studies: Geography, Nationality and Identity*, Oxford: Oxford University Press.

McCrone, D., (2002), 'Who do you say you are? Making sense of national identities in modern Britain', *Ethnicities* 2: 301–20.

McCrone, D., Morris, A. and Kiely, R., (1995), *Scotland the Brand: The Making of Scottish Heritage*, Edinburgh: Polygon.

McCrone, D., Stewart, R., Kiely, R. and Bechhofer, F., (1998), 'Who are we? Problematising national identity', *The Sociological Review* 46: 631–652.

McHoul, A. and Watson, D.R., (1984), 'Two axes for the analysis of "commonsense" and "formal" geographical knowledge in classroom talk', *British Journal of Sociology of Education* 5: 281–302.

McIntosh, G., (1999), *The Force of Culture: Unionist Identities in Twentieth-Century Ireland*, Cork: Cork University Press.

McKeown, C., (2001), 'What kind of Union will it be in 200 years?', *News Letter* (Belfast), 22 January.

Meinhof, U.H., (2002) (ed.), *Living (with) Borders: Identity discourses on East-West Borders in Europe*, Aldershot: Ashgate.

Miller, D., (1978), *Queen's Rebels: Ulster Loyalism in Historical Perspective*, Dublin: Gill and Macmillan.

Miller, D., (1995), *On Nationality*, Oxford: Clarendon Press.

Miller, R., (1998), 'Conclusion', in R. Miller and R. Wilford (eds), *Women, Ethnicity and Nationalism*, London: Routledge.

Miller, R. and Wilford, R., (1998) (eds), *Women, Ethnicity and Nationalism*, London: Routledge.

Miller, R., Wilford, R. and Donoghue, F., (1996), *Women and Political Participation in Northern Ireland*, Aldershot: Avebury.

Mills, C.W., (1978), *The Sociological Imagination*, Harmondsworth: Penguin.

Mitchell, C., (2003), 'Protestant identification and political change in Northern Ireland', *Ethnic and Racial Studies* 26: 612–631.

Mitchell, J., (2000), 'Devolution and the end of Britain?', *Contemporary British History* 14: 61–82.

Morley, D. and Robins, K., (2001), 'Introduction: The national culture in its new global context', in D. Morley and K. Robins (eds), *British Cultural Studies: Geography, Nationality and Identity*, Oxford: Oxford University Press.

Mouffe, C., (1992), 'Democratic citizenship and the political community', in C. Mouffe (ed.), *Dimensions of Radical Democracy: Pluralism, Citizenship, Community*, London: Verso.

Murray, D., (2000), *Protestant Perceptions of the Peace Process in Northern Ireland*, Limerick: Centre for Peace and Development Studies.

Narayan, U., (1997), 'Towards a feminist vision of citizenship: Rethinking the implications of dignity, political participation and nationality', in M.L. Shanley and U. Narayan (eds), *Reconstructing Political Theory*. Cambridge: Polity Press.

Nic Craith, M. (2001). 'Politicized linguistic consciousness: The case of Ulster-Scots', *Nations and Nationalism* 7: 21–37.

Nic Craith, M., (2002), *Plural Identities, Singular Narratives: The Case of Northern Ireland*, Oxford: Berghahn Books.

Nekvapil, J. and Leudar, I., (2002), 'On dialogical networks: Arguments about the migration law in Czech mass media in 1993', in S. Hester and W. Housley (eds), *Language, Interaction and National Identity*, Aldershot: Ashgate.

Northern Ireland Life and Times Survey, (2002), http://www.ark.ac.uk/nilt/.

OECD, (2003), *The E-government Imperative*, Paris: OECD.

Ohmae, K., (1995), *The End of the Nation-State: The Rise of Regional Economies*, New York: The Free Press.

Parkhill, T., (2002–2003), 'That's their history: Can a museum's historical programme inform the reconciliation process in a divided society?', *Folk Life: The Journal of Ethnological Studies*, 42: 37–38.

Pateman, C., (1989), *The Disorder of Women: Democracy, Feminism and Political Theory*, Cambridge: Polity Press.

Paterson, L., (2002), 'Is Britain disintegrating? Changing views of "Britain" after devolution', *Regional and Federal Studies* 12: 21–42.

Patrick, P.L., (2004), 'The speech community', in J. Chambers, P. Trudgill and N. Schilling-Estes (eds), *Handbook of Language Variation and Change*, Oxford: Blackwell.

Patterson, H., (1999), 'Party versus Order: Ulster Unionism and the Flags and Emblems Act', *Contemporary British History* 13:105–129.

Pearce, L., (2000) (ed.), *Devolving Identities: Feminist Readings in Home and Belonging*, Aldershot: Ashgate.

Pennycook, A., (1998), 'The right to language: Towards a situated ethics of language possibilities', *Language Sciences* 20: 73–87.

Pennycook, A., (2004), 'Language policy and the ecological turn', *Language Policy* 3: 213–239.

Pilkington, C., (2002), *Devolution in Britain Today*, Manchester: Manchester University Press.

Pittock, M., (1991), *The Invention of Scotland: The Stuart Myth and the Scottish Identity, 1638 to the Present*, London: Routledge.

Plummer, K., (1995), *Telling Sexual Stories: Change, Power, and Social Worlds*, London: Routledge.

Pomerantz, A.M., (1986), 'Extreme case formulations: A new way of legitimating claims', *Human Studies* 9: 219–230.

Porter, E., (1998), 'Identity, location, plurality: Women, nationalism and Northern Ireland', in R. Wilford and R. Miller (eds), *Women, Ethnicity and Nationalism: The Politics of Transition*, London and New York: Routledge.

Potter, J., (2003), 'Discursive Psychology: Between method and paradigm', *Discourse and Psychology* 14: 783–794.

Potter, J. and Edwards, D., (1999), 'Social representations and discursive psychology: From cognition to action', *Culture and Psychology* 5: 447–458.

Potter, J. and Wetherell, M., (1987), *Discourse and Social Psychology: Beyond Attitudes and Behaviour*, London: Sage.

Racioppi, L. and O'Sullivan See, K., (2001), '"This we will maintain": Gender, ethno-nationalism and the politics of unionism in Northern Ireland', *Nations and Nationalism* 7: 93–112.

Radford, K., (2001), 'Creating an Ulster Scots revival', *Peace Review*, 13: 51–57.

Rampton, B., (1998), 'Speech community', in J. Verschueren, J.-O. Östman, J. Blommaert and C. Bulcaen (eds), *Handbook of Pragmatics*, Amsterdam/Philapdelphia: John Benjamins.

Rampton, B., (2006), *Language in Late Modernity: Interaction in an Urban School*, Cambridge: Cambridge University Press.

Reicher, S. and Hopkins, N., (2001), *Self and Nation*, London: Sage.

Robbins K., (2001), 'Devolution in Britain: Will the UK survive?', *European Studies: A Journal of European Culture, History and Politics* 16: 53–65.

Rolston, B., (1991), *Politics and Painting: Murals and Conflict in Northern Ireland*, London and Toronto: Associated Universities Press.

Rolston, B., (1992), *Drawing Support 1: Murals in the North of Ireland*, Belfast: Beyond the Pale Publications.

Rolston, B., (1995), *Drawing Support 2: Murals of War and Peace*, Belfast: Beyond the Pale Publications.

Rolston, B., (1998), 'Culture as battlefield: Political identity and the state in the North of Ireland', *Race and Class* 39: 23–35.

Rolston, B., (2003), *Drawing Support 3: Murals and Transition in the North of Ireland*, Belfast: Beyond the Pale Publications.

Rosie, M., MacInnes, J., Petersoo, P., Condor, S. and Kennedy, J., (2004), 'Nation speaking unto nation? National identity and the Press in the devolved UK', *Sociological Review* 52: 437–458.

Ross, K., (2004), 'Political talk radio and democratic participation: Caller perspectives on election call', *Media, Culture & Society* 26: 785–801.

Roulston, C., (1997), 'Women on the margin: The Women's Movement in Northern Ireland', in L. West (ed.), *Feminist Nationalisms*, New York: Routledge.

Roulston, C. and Davies, C., (2000) (eds), *Gender, Democracy and Inclusion in Northern Ireland*, Basingstoke: Palgrave Macmillan.

Sacks, H., (1974), 'On the analysability of stories by children', in R. Turner (ed.), *Ethnomethodology*, Harmondsworth: Penguin.

Sacks, H., (1992), *Lectures on Conversation*, (ed. G. Jefferson), Oxford: Blackwell.

Sales, R., (1997), *Women Divided: Gender, Religion and Politics in Northern Ireland*, London: Routledge.

Samuel, R., (1990), 'Raphael Samuel', in J. Gardiner (ed.), *The History Debate*, London: Collins and Brown.

Samuel, R., (1998), *Island Stories: Unravelling Britain*, London: Verso.

Sandford, M., (2002), 'What place for England in an asymmetrically devolved UK?', *Regional Studies* 36: 789–796.

Santino, J., (2001), *Signs of War and Peace: Social Conflict and the Use of Public Symbols in Northern Ireland*, Basingstoke: Palgrave.

Scott, J.W., (2001), 'Fantasy echo: History and the construction of identity', *Critical Inquiry* 27: 284–304.

Scott, M.B. and Lyman, S.M., (1968), 'Accounts', *American Sociological Review* 33: 46–62.

Scourfield, J., Davies, A. and Holland, S., (2003), 'Wales and Welshness in middle childhood', *Contemporary Wales* 16: 83–100.

Seale, C., (1999), *The Quality of Qualitative Research*, London: Sage.

Shields, S.A., (2005), 'The politics of emotion in everyday life: "Appropriate" emotion and claims on identity', *Review of General Psychology* 9: 3–15.

Shirlow, P., (2001), 'Devolution in Northern Ireland/Ulster/the North/six counties: Delete as appropriate', *Regional Studies* 35: 743–752.

Shirlow, P., (2005), 'Segregation, ethno-sectarianism and the "new" Belfast', in M. Cox, A. Guelke and F. Stephen (eds), *A Farewell to Arms? Beyond the Good Friday Agreement*, Manchester: Manchester University Press.

Shirlow, P. and McGovern, M., (1997) (eds), *Who are the People? Unionism, Protestantism and Loyalism in Northern Ireland*, London: Pluto Press.

Shotter, J., (1993), 'Becoming someone: Identity and belonging', in N. Coupland and J. Nussbaum (eds), *Discourse and Lifespan Identity*, London: Sage.

Sigelman, L. and Walkosz, B., (1992), 'Letters to the editor as a public opinion thermometer: The Martin Luther King holiday vote in Arizona', *Social Science Quarterly* 73: 938–946.

Silverman, D., (1998), *Harvey Sacks: Social Science and Conversation Analysis*, Cambridge: Polity Press.

Silverman, D., (2000), *Doing Qualitative Research*, London: Sage.

Skinner, Q., (1990), 'The republican ideal of political liberty', in G. Block, Q. Skinner and M. Viroli (eds), *Machiavelli and Republicanism*, Cambridge: Cambridge University Press.

Skinner, Q., (1992), 'On justice, the common good, and the priority of liberty', in C. Mouffe (ed.), *Dimensions of Radical Democracy: Pluralism, Citizenship, Community*, London: Verso.

Skutnabb-Kangas, T., (1998), 'Human rights and language wrongs – a future for diversity?', *Language Sciences* 20: 5–28.

Skutnabb-Kangas, T. and Phillipson, R., (1994) (eds), *Linguistic Human Rights: Overcoming Linguistic Discrimination*, Berlin: Mouton de Gruyter.

Smith, A., (1999), *Myths and Memories of the Nation*, Oxford: Oxford University Press.

Sparrow, A., (2001), 'Government hints at U-turn over Act of Union celebrations', *The Daily Telegraph*, 2 January.

Squires, J., (2004), 'Representation, quotas and mainstreaming in the context of constitutional change', Paper presented to the *Political Studies Association UK Annual Conference*, University of Lincoln.

Stapleton, J., (2005), 'Citizenship versus patriotism in twentieth-century England', *The Historical Journal* 48: 151–178.

Stapleton, K. and Wilson, J., (2003). 'A discursive approach to cultural identity: The case of Ulster Scots', *Belfast Working Papers in Language and Linguistics* 16: 86–99.

Stapleton, K. and Wilson, J., (2004a), 'Ulster Scots identity and culture: The missing voice(s)', *Identities: Global Studies in Culture and Power* 11: 563–591.

Stapleton, K. and Wilson, J., (2004b), 'Gender, nationality and identity: A discursive study', *European Journal of Women's Studies* 11: 45–60.

Stevenson, C., Condor, S. and Abell, J., (2004), '"As others see us": Asymmetries in lay theories of intergroup relations in Anglo-Scottish stereotypes', Paper presented at the *British Psychology Society Social Psychology Section Annual Conference*, September, Liverpool, England.

Stewart, A.T.Q., (1977), *The Narrow Ground: Aspects of Ulster, 1909–1969*, Belfast: Blackstaff Press.

Stewart, A.T.Q., (2001), *The Shape of Irish History*, Belfast: Blackstaff Press.

Tajfel, H. (1978) (ed), *Differentiation Between Social Groups: Studies in the Social Psychology of Intergroup Relations*, London: Academic Press.

Taylor, C., (1989), 'Cross-purposes: The Liberal-Communitarian Debate', in N.L. Rosenblum (ed.), *Liberalism and the Moral Life*, Cambridge, MA: Harvard University Press.

Taylor, S. and Wetherell, M., (1999), 'A suitable time and place: Speakers' use of "time" to do discursive work in narratives of nation and personal life', *Time and Society* 8: 39–58.

Thomas, W.I., (1937), *Primitive Behavior: An Introduction to the Social Sciences*, New York: McGraw-Hill.

Thornton, C., (2001), 'Act of Union events start storm', *Belfast Telegraph*, 23 January.

Tollefson, J., (1991), *Planning Language, Planning Inequality: Language Planning in the Community*, London: Longman.

Tosh, J., (2002), *The Pursuit of History: Aims, Methods and New Directions in the Study of Modern History*, (revised 3rd edition), London: Longman.

Turner, B. (1992), 'Outline of a theory of citizenship', in C. Mouffe (ed.), *Dimensions of Radical Democracy: Pluralism, Citizenship, Community*, London: Verso.

Turner, J.C., (1987), 'A self-categorization theory', in J.C. Turner, M.A. Hogg, P.J. Oakes, S.D. Reicher and M.S. Wetherell (eds), *Rediscovering the Social Group*, Oxford: Blackwell.

Van Dam, D., (1997), *Flandre, Wallonie: Le Rêve Brisé*, Ottignies: Editions Quorum.

Van Dijk, T.A., (1984), *Prejudice and Discourse: An Analysis of Ethnic Prejudice in Cognition and Conversation*, Amsterdam: Benjamins.

Wahl-Jorgensen, K., (2002), 'Understanding the conditions for public discourse: Four rules for selecting letters to the editor', *Journalism Studies* 3: 69–81.

Walker, B., (1996), *Dancing to History's Tune: History, Myth and Politics in Ireland*, Belfast: Institute of Irish Studies.

Walker, B., (2000), *Past and Present: History, Identity and Politics in Ireland*, Belfast: Institute of Irish Studies.

Walker, G., (2000), 'PR peer takes the spin of history', *The Belfast Telegraph*, 25 March.

Walzer, M., (1992), 'The civil society argument', in C. Mouffe (ed.), *Dimensions of Radical Democracy: Pluralism, Citizenship, Community*, London: Verso.

Watson, R., (1997), 'Some general reflections on "categorization" and "sequence" in the analysis of conversation', in S. Hester and P. Eglin (eds), *Culture in Action*, Lanham, MD: University Press of America.

Weber, M., (1978), *Economy and Society: An Outline of Interpretive Sociology*, Berkeley, CA: University of California Press.

Webster, B., (1997), *Medieval Scotland: The Making of an Identity*, Basingstoke: Palgrave Macmillan.

Weight, R., (2003), *Patriots: National Identity in Britain 1940–2000*, London: Macmillan.

Wetherell, M., (1998), 'Positioning and interpretative repertoires: Conversation Analysis and post-structuralism in dialogue', *Discourse and Society* 9: 387–416.

Wetherell, M. and Potter, J., (1992), *Mapping the Language of Racism*, London: Harvester Wheatsheaf.

Williams, Charlotte, Evans, N. and O'Leary, P., (2003) (eds), *A Tolerant Nation? Exploring Ethnic Diversity in Wales*, Cardiff: University of Wales Press.

Williams, C., (2005), '*Iaith Pawb*: The doctrine of plenary inclusion', *Contemporary Wales* 17: 1–27.

Williams, R., (2003), *Who Speaks for Wales? Nation, Culture, Identity*, (ed. D. Williams), Cardiff: University of Wales Press.

Wilson, J. and Stapleton, K., (2003), 'Nation state, devolution and the parliamentary discourse of minority languages', *Journal of Language and Politics* 2: 5–30.

Wilson, J. and Stapleton, K., (2005), 'Voices of commemoration: The discourse of celebration and confrontation in Northern Ireland', *Text: An Interdisciplinary Journal for the Study of Discourse* 25: 633–664.

Wilson, J. and Stapleton, K., (2006), 'New politics, new identities? The case of Northern Ireland', *The International Journal of the Humanities.*

Wilson, J. and Stapleton, K. (forthcoming, 2007), 'The discource of resistance: Social change and policing in Northern Ireland', *Language in Society.*

Wilson, J. and Stapleton, K., (under review), 'Narratives of lesser-used languages in Europe: The case of Ulster Scots'.

Wilson, R., (2003), 'Less moaning, more policy', *Fortnight* 416: 2 (July/Aug).

Windisch, U., (1990), *Speech and Reasoning in Everyday Life*, Cambridge: Cambridge University Press.

Wittgenstein, L., (1958), *Philosophical Investigations*, Oxford: Blackwell.

Wodak, R., de Cillia, R., Reisigl, M., Liebhart, K., (1999), *The Discursive Construction of National Identity*, Edinburgh: Edinburgh University Press.

Young, I.M., (1990), *'Throwing Like a Girl' and Other Essays in Feminist Philosophy and Social Theory*, Bloomington: Indiana University Press.

Index